Long Day's Journey Into Night

LONG DAY'S
JOURNEY
INTO
NIGHT

EUGENE O'NEILL

CRITICAL EDITION

Edited by William Davies King
Foreword by Jessica Lange

Yale UNIVERSITY PRESS/NEW HAVEN & LONDON

Printed in the United States of America.

Library of Congress Control Number: 2013956573
ISBN: 978-0-300-18641-3 (pbk.)
10 9 8 7 6 5 4 3 2 1

Contents

Foreword

Jessica Lange

I had the opportunity of doing a production of *Long Day's Journey Into Night* in London some years ago. There are roles that arrive like gifts. Given and received. Mary Tyrone was that. No part I have played on stage or in film has ever captured me more. Actors can fall in love with characters they play, obsess over them, cling to them . . . sometimes we're haunted by them.

I loved Mary Tyrone. I longed to get to the theater each evening so I could experience her. So I could lose myself in her. The part of Mary Tyrone is a bottomless well. Impossible to exhaust.

We went into rehearsals in late fall and played through the long winter of 2000–2001. London is the perfect setting to experience this masterful play. The gloom and dampness, the fog and the grayness mirror the atmosphere of the play.

Our set was more dreamlike than what O'Neill describes in the stage directions. It had a ghostly feel, more memory than reality. As the light moved east to west across the stage during the course of the long day, the fog seemed to seep through the walls. The foghorn a constant reminder of old sorrows . . . a plaintive, haunting refrain.

"Why is it fog makes everything sound so sad and lost, I wonder?"

Memorizing lines proved difficult at first. I found I would often lose track of where I was in the play. I came to understand it was due to the circular nature of the play, which is structured like a piece of music where the composer creates a melody and then repeats it again and again in altered forms. Theme and variations. The cycles of punishment and forgiveness, recriminations and excuses. A tragic score of love and hate.

It is linear only in the passage of time, morning to night, and the effects of the morphine increasing steadily as the day wears on.

Mary's addiction has been singled out in the family as the greatest transgression. But there are four addicts living in that house. The men are alcoholics. Morphine is less acceptable, less social, more mysterious, and therefore more isolating. It sets Mary apart, separating her even more from the rest of them.

One heroin addict I talked to when I was preparing to do the play described how it felt like being wrapped in a warm blanket. I imagine that's what Mary is looking for.

But like many addicts, she is a master of deceit, a champion liar.

"How could you believe me—when I can't believe myself? I've become such a liar."

Mary is also a master of manipulation. She controls every moment she is on stage, and at the same time she is barely in control of herself. Her innocence and helplessness and, in the next moment, her capacity for cruelty, to wound those she loves the dearest. Her shifting alliances, her need to lay blame, to accuse and then excuse. To punish and then forgive. She is the most complex and fully realized character I have ever played.

Mary is torn between her love and her need for her husband and sons and her desire to lose herself in the morphine: to disappear.

"You're lying to yourself again. You wanted to get rid of them. Their contempt and disgust aren't pleasant company. You're glad they're gone. Then Mother of God, why do I feel so lonely?"

It is these contradictions and the layering of emotions—woven into a patchwork pattern of sorrow, grief, guilt, anger, blame, love, desire, hate—that make Mary a profound and fascinating character. Playing multiple emotions in the same moment is exciting. Her elusiveness and quicksilver shifts are thrilling. The fluidity and velocity are staggering but feel inevitable. In a single page of dialogue with James, O'Neill describes some of these shifts: *"forcing a laugh . . . sharply . . . then pleadingly . . . with dull anger . . . in stubborn defiance . . . then accusingly . . . bitterly . . . pleadingly . . . strickenly . . . slipping away into her strange detachment—quite casually . . . piteously . . . into that stubborn denial again."*

I have always considered this play a great love story. Mary and James share a deep and abiding devotion to each other. The memory of their passion and romance is so close to the surface. Those memories are in their fingertips when they touch.

When she tells Cathleen of their first meeting, you hear the girl—her sensuality, her sexual discovery. She loves this story. How, in her innocence and beauty, she won the most handsome, famous man of the day. How they fell deeply in love and couldn't bear to be separated. The evocation of that moment transports her out of this place she despises. It is a classic sense-memory exercise for an actor.

But it is a story of a great love damaged by loneliness and despair, by disappointment. Those romantic stories exist hand in hand with the most grievous memories.

"James! We've loved each other! We always will! Let's remember only that, and not try to understand what we cannot understand, or help things that cannot be helped."

Mary speaks of that night on her honeymoon—an innocent young bride waiting in an ugly hotel room, hour after hour, terrified that something has happened to James. How his barroom friends brought him home and deposited him drunk outside the hotel room door. She goes on to say that many more of those nights were to come.

James, overwhelmed by shame, asks her, "Mary! Can't you forget—?" And she answers: "No, dear. But I forgive. I always forgive you."

No one in this play is ever allowed to forget.

The end of act 4, midnight of this long and harrowing day, brings Mary back onstage. In our production she seemed to appear out of nowhere—a spectral presence trailing her wedding dress behind her. "The Mad Scene, Enter Ophelia!" Jamie says.

The Chopin waltz and the wedding dress illuminate how far back in time she has retreated. How far out of their reach. More past than present. "The past is the present, isn't it?"

It is the most beautiful scene to play. The image is heartbreaking and the language, so simple, yet so powerful. She speaks of looking for something she lost. The word *lost* is repeated many times, her sad refrain in the closing moments. At the final curtain, we have the tableau of a family trapped by one another and their shared history. Doomed to repeat their chorus of love, pity, hate, blame, guilt. Forgiving but never forgetting.

Mary's curtain speech is one the great moments in the theater for an actress. The simple truth that speaks to the quiet tragedy of her life.

"Then in the spring something happened to me. Yes, I remember. I fell in love with James Tyrone and was so happy for a time."

The four actors onstage, absolutely still, all lost in Mary's sad dream. You could hear a pin drop in the audience. It is a sublime moment to play. Unforgettable.

Long Day's Journey Into Night

LONG DAY'S
JOURNEY
INTO
NIGHT

EUGENE O'NEILL

Publisher's Note, 1989

Since its first publication in February 1956, *Long Day's Journey Into Night* has gone through numerous reprintings. With this printing, the sixty-first, we have taken the opportunity to correct several errors recently reported by scholars who have made careful examinations of final typescripts of the play. It has been discovered that Carlotta O'Neill, retyping from a previous version heavily edited by O'Neill, accidentally dropped lines in several places.

We wish to take note first of a correction that was silently made in the fifth printing after Donald Gallup called our attention to missing lines on page 170. The dialogue and stage directions restored were those beginning with "Kid" in line 22 and ending with "old" in line 24.

For the corrections made in this printing, we thank the following: Michael Hinden (for pointing out missing lines on pages 97, 106, and 167 and errors on page 158), Judith E. Barlow (for missing lines on page 97), and Stephen Black (for an error on page 111). On page 97 a sentence ("Anyway, by tonight, what will you care?") has been added to Edmund's dialogue at lines 18–19. On page 97 lines 29–33 are printed for the first time. On page 106 a sentence ("It's a special kind of medicine.") has been restored at line 1. The errors corrected on pages 111 and 158 were minor, although puzzling, misprints (e.g., "fron" for "front," "sibject" for "subject"). On page 167 a sentence ("No one hopes more than I do you'll knock 'em all dead.") has been restored in line 20.

For Carlotta, on our 12th Wedding Anniversary

*Dearest: I give you the original script of this play of old sorrow,
written in tears and blood. A sadly inappropriate gift, it would
seem, for a day celebrating happiness. But you will understand.
I mean it as a tribute to your love and tenderness which gave me
the faith in love that enabled me to face my dead at last and write
this play—write it with deep pity and understanding and forgiveness for all the four haunted Tyrones.*

*These twelve years, Beloved One, have been a Journey into Light—
into love. You know my gratitude. And my love!*

*Gene
Tao House
July 22, 1941.*

Characters

JAMES TYRONE

MARY CAVAN TYRONE, *his wife*

JAMES TYRONE, JR., *their elder son*

EDMUND TYRONE, *their younger son*

CATHLEEN, *second girl*

Scenes

Act One

Living room of James Tyrone's summer home on a morning in August, 1912.

At rear are two double doorways with portieres. The one at right leads into a front parlor with the formally arranged, set appearance of a room rarely occupied. The other opens on a dark, windowless back parlor, never used except as a passage from living room to dining room. Against the wall between the doorways is a small bookcase, with a picture of Shakespeare above it, containing novels by Balzac, Zola, Stendhal, philosophical and sociological works by Schopenhauer, Nietzsche, Marx, Engels, Kropotkin, Max Stirner, plays by Ibsen, Shaw, Strindberg, poetry by Swinburne, Rossetti, Wilde, Ernest Dowson, Kipling, etc.

In the right wall, rear, is a screen door leading out on the porch which extends halfway around the house. Farther forward, a series of three windows looks over the front lawn to the harbor and the avenue that runs along the water front. A small wicker table and an ordinary oak desk are against the wall, flanking the windows.

In the left wall, a similar series of windows looks out on the grounds in back of the house. Beneath them is a wicker couch with cushions, its head toward rear. Farther back is a large, glassed-in bookcase with sets of Dumas, Victor Hugo, Charles Lever, three sets of Shakespeare, The World's Best Literature in fifty large volumes, Hume's History of England, Thiers' History of the Consulate and Empire, Smollett's History of England, Gibbon's Roman Empire and miscellaneous volumes of old plays, poetry, and several histories of Ireland. The astonishing thing about these sets is that all the volumes have the look of having been read and reread.

The hardwood floor is nearly covered by a rug, inoffensive in design and color. At center is a round table with a green shaded reading lamp, the cord plugged in one of the four sockets in the chandelier above. Around the table within reading-light range are four chairs, three of them wicker armchairs, the fourth (at right front of table) a varnished oak rocker with leather bottom.

It is around 8.30. Sunshine comes through the windows at right.

As the curtain rises, the family have just finished breakfast. MARY TYRONE *and her husband enter together from the back parlor, coming from the dining room.*

Mary is fifty-four, about medium height. She still has a young, graceful figure, a trifle plump, but showing little evidence of middle-aged waist and hips, although she is not tightly corseted. Her face is distinctly Irish in type. It must once have been extremely pretty, and is still striking. It does not match her healthy figure but is thin and pale with the bone structure prominent. Her nose is long and straight, her mouth wide with full, sensitive lips. She uses no rouge or any sort of make-up. Her high forehead is framed by thick, pure white hair. Accentuated by her pallor and white hair, her dark brown eyes appear black. They are unusually large and beautiful, with black brows and long curling lashes.

What strikes one immediately is her extreme nervousness. Her hands are never still. They were once beautiful hands, with long, tapering fingers, but rheumatism has knotted the joints and warped the fingers, so that now they have an ugly crippled look. One avoids looking at them, the more so because one is conscious she is sensitive about their appearance and humiliated by her inability to control the nervousness which draws attention to them.

She is dressed simply but with a sure sense of what becomes her. Her hair is arranged with fastidious care. Her voice is soft and attractive. When she is merry, there is a touch of Irish lilt in it.

Her most appealing quality is the simple, unaffected charm of a shy convent-girl youthfulness she has never lost—an innate unworldly innocence.

JAMES TYRONE *is sixty-five but looks ten years younger. About five feet eight, broad-shouldered and deep-chested, he seems taller and slenderer because of his bearing, which has a soldierly quality of head up, chest out, stomach in, shoulders squared. His face has begun to break down but he is still remarkably good looking—a big, finely shaped head, a handsome profile, deep-set light-brown eyes. His grey hair is thin with a bald spot like a monk's tonsure.*

The stamp of his profession is unmistakably on him. Not that he indulges in any of the deliberate temperamental posturings of the stage star. He is by nature and preference a simple, unpretentious man, whose inclinations are still close to his humble beginnings and his Irish farmer forebears. But the actor shows in all his unconscious habits of speech, movement and gesture. These have the quality of belonging to a studied technique. His voice is remarkably fine, resonant and flexible, and he takes great pride in it.

His clothes, assuredly, do not costume any romantic part. He wears a threadbare, ready-made, grey sack suit and shineless black shoes, a collar-less shirt with a thick white handkerchief knotted loosely around his throat. There is nothing picturesquely careless about this get-up. It is commonplace shabby. He believes in wearing his clothes to the limit of usefulness, is dressed now for gardening, and doesn't give a damn how he looks.

He has never been really sick a day in his life. He has no nerves. There is a lot of stolid, earthy peasant in him, mixed with streaks of sentimental melancholy and rare flashes of intuitive sensibility.

Tyrone's arm is around his wife's waist as they appear from the back parlor. Entering the living room he gives her a playful hug.

TYRONE

You're a fine armful now, Mary, with those twenty pounds you've gained.

MARY

Smiles affectionately.
I've gotten too fat, you mean, dear. I really ought to reduce.

TYRONE

None of that, my lady! You're just right. We'll have no talk of reducing. Is that why you ate so little breakfast?

MARY

So little? I thought I ate a lot.

TYRONE

You didn't. Not as much as I'd like to see, anyway.

MARY

Teasingly.
Oh you! You expect everyone to eat the enormous breakfast you do. No one else in the world could without dying of indigestion.
She comes forward to stand by the right of table.

TYRONE

Following her.
I hope I'm not as big a glutton as that sounds.
With hearty satisfaction.
But thank God, I've kept my appetite and I've the digestion of a young man of twenty, if I am sixty-five.

MARY

You surely have, James. No one could deny that.
She laughs and sits in the wicker armchair at right rear of table. He comes around in back of her and selects a cigar from a box on the table and cuts off the end with a little clipper. From the dining room Jamie's and Edmund's voices are heard. Mary turns her head that way.

Why did the boys stay in the dining room, I wonder? Cathleen must be waiting to clear the table.

TYRONE

Jokingly but with an undercurrent of resentment.

It's a secret confab they don't want me to hear, I suppose. I'll bet they're cooking up some new scheme to touch the Old Man.

She is silent on this, keeping her head turned toward their voices. Her hands appear on the table top, moving restlessly. He lights his cigar and sits down in the rocker at right of table, which is his chair, and puffs contentedly.

There's nothing like the first after-breakfast cigar, if it's a good one, and this new lot have the right mellow flavor. They're a great bargain, too. I got them dead cheap. It was McGuire put me on to them.

MARY

A trifle acidly.

I hope he didn't put you on to any new piece of property at the same time. His real estate bargains don't work out so well.

TYRONE

Defensively.

I wouldn't say that, Mary. After all, he was the one who advised me to buy that place on Chestnut Street and I made a quick turnover on it for a fine profit.

MARY

Smiles now with teasing affection.

I know. The famous one stroke of good luck. I'm sure McGuire never dreamed—

Then she pats his hand.

Never mind, James. I know it's a waste of breath trying to convince you you're not a cunning real estate speculator.

TYRONE

Huffily.

I've no such idea. But land is land, and it's safer than the stocks and bonds of Wall Street swindlers.

Then placatingly.
But let's not argue about business this early in the morning.
A pause. The boys' voices are again heard and one of them has a fit of coughing. Mary listens worriedly. Her fingers play nervously on the table top.

MARY

James, it's Edmund you ought to scold for not eating enough. He hardly touched anything except coffee. He needs to eat to keep up his strength. I keep telling him that but he says he simply has no appetite. Of course, there's nothing takes away your appetite like a bad summer cold.

TYRONE

Yes, it's only natural. So don't let yourself get worried—

MARY

Quickly.
Oh, I'm not. I know he'll be all right in a few days if he takes care of himself.
As if she wanted to dismiss the subject but can't.
But it does seem a shame he should have to be sick right now.

TYRONE

Yes, it is bad luck.
He gives her a quick, worried look.
But you musn't let it upset you, Mary. Remember, you've got to take care of yourself, too.

MARY

Quickly.
I'm not upset. There's nothing to be upset about. What makes you think I'm upset?

TYRONE

Why, nothing, except you've seemed a bit high-strung the past few days.

MARY

Forcing a smile.
I have? Nonsense, dear. It's your imagination.

With sudden tenseness.

You really must not watch me all the time, James. I mean, it makes me self-conscious.

TYRONE

Putting a hand over one of her nervously playing ones.

Now, now, Mary. That's your imagination. If I've watched you it was to admire how fat and beautiful you looked.

His voice is suddenly moved by deep feeling.

I can't tell you the deep happiness it gives me, darling, to see you as you've been since you came back to us, your dear old self again.

He leans over and kisses her cheek impulsively—then turning back adds with a constrained air.

So keep up the good work, Mary.

MARY

Has turned her head away.

I will, dear.

She gets up restlessly and goes to the windows at right.

Thank heavens, the fog is gone.

She turns back.

I do feel out of sorts this morning. I wasn't able to get much sleep with that awful foghorn going all night long.

TYRONE

Yes, it's like having a sick whale in the back yard. It kept me awake, too.

MARY

Affectionately amused.

Did it? You had a strange way of showing your restlessness. You were snoring so hard I couldn't tell which was the foghorn!

She comes to him, laughing, and pats his cheek playfully.

Ten foghorns couldn't disturb you. You haven't a nerve in you. You've never had.

TYRONE

His vanity piqued—testily.

Nonsense. You always exaggerate about my snoring.

MARY

I couldn't. If you could only hear yourself once—
A burst of laughter comes from the dining room. She turns her head, smiling.
What's the joke, I wonder?

TYRONE

Grumpily.
It's on me. I'll bet that much. It's always on the Old Man.

MARY

Teasingly.
Yes, it's terrible the way we all pick on you, isn't it? You're so abused!
She laughs—then with a pleased, relieved air.
Well, no matter what the joke is about, it's a relief to hear Edmund laugh. He's been so down in the mouth lately.

TYRONE

Ignoring this—resentfully.
Some joke of Jamie's, I'll wager. He's forever making sneering fun of somebody, that one.

MARY

Now don't start in on poor Jamie, dear.
Without conviction.
He'll turn out all right in the end, you wait and see.

TYRONE

He'd better start soon, then. He's nearly thirty-four.

MARY

Ignoring this.
Good heavens, are they going to stay in the dining room all day?
She goes to the back parlor doorway and calls.
Jamie! Edmund! Come in the living room and give Cathleen a chance to clear the table.
Edmund calls back, "We're coming, Mama." She goes back to the table.

TYRONE
Grumbling.
You'd find excuses for him no matter what he did.

MARY
Sitting down beside him, pats his hand.
Shush.
Their sons JAMES, JR., *and* EDMUND *enter together from the back parlor. They are both grinning, still chuckling over what had caused their laughter, and as they come forward they glance at their father and their grins grow broader.*

Jamie, the elder, is thirty-three. He has his father's broad-shouldered, deep-chested physique, is an inch taller and weighs less, but appears shorter and stouter because he lacks Tyrone's bearing and graceful carriage. He also lacks his father's vitality. The signs of premature disintegration are on him. His face is still good looking, despite marks of dissipation, but it has never been handsome like Tyrone's, although Jamie resembles him rather than his mother. He has fine brown eyes, their color midway between his father's lighter and his mother's darker ones. His hair is thinning and already there is indication of a bald spot like Tyrone's. His nose is unlike that of any other member of the family, pronouncedly aquiline. Combined with his habitual expression of cynicism it gives his countenance a Mephistophelian cast. But on the rare occasions when he smiles without sneering, his personality possesses the remnant of a humorous, romantic, irresponsible Irish charm — that of the beguiling ne'er-do-well, with a strain of the sentimentally poetic, attractive to women and popular with men.

He is dressed in an old sack suit, not as shabby as Tyrone's, and wears a collar and tie. His fair skin is sunburned a reddish, freckled tan.

Edmund is ten years younger than his brother, a couple of inches taller, thin and wiry. Where Jamie takes after his father, with little resemblance to his mother, Edmund looks like both his parents, but is more like his mother. Her big, dark eyes are the dominant feature in his long, narrow Irish face. His mouth has the same quality of hypersensitiveness hers possesses. His high forehead is hers accentuated, with dark brown hair, sunbleached to red at the ends, brushed straight back from it. But his nose is his father's and his face in profile recalls Tyrone's. Edmund's hands are noticeably like his mother's, with the same exceptionally long fingers. They even have to a minor degree the same nervousness. It is in the quality of extreme nervous sensibility that the likeness of Edmund to his mother is most marked.

He is plainly in bad health. Much thinner than he should be, his eyes appear feverish and his cheeks are sunken. His skin, in spite of being sunburned a deep brown, has a parched sallowness. He wears a shirt, collar and tie, no coat, old flannel trousers, brown sneakers.

MARY
Turns smilingly to them, in a merry tone that is a bit forced.
I've been teasing your father about his snoring.
To Tyrone.
I'll leave it to the boys, James. They must have heard you. No, not you, Jamie. I could hear you down the hall almost as bad as your father. You're like him. As soon as your head touches the pillow you're off and ten foghorns couldn't wake you.
She stops abruptly, catching Jamie's eyes regarding her with an uneasy, probing look. Her smile vanishes and her manner becomes self-conscious.
Why are you staring, Jamie?
Her hands flutter up to her hair.
Is my hair coming down? It's hard for me to do it up properly now. My eyes are getting so bad and I never can find my glasses.

JAMIE
Looks away guiltily.
Your hair's all right, Mama. I was only thinking how well you look.

TYRONE
Heartily.
Just what I've been telling her, Jamie. She's so fat and sassy, there'll soon be no holding her.

EDMUND
Yes, you certainly look grand, Mama.

She is reassured and smiles at him lovingly. He winks with a kidding grin.
I'll back you up about Papa's snoring. Gosh, what a racket!

JAMIE
I heard him, too.
He quotes, putting on a ham-actor manner.
"The Moor, I know his trumpet."
His mother and brother laugh.

TYRONE
Scathingly.
If it takes my snoring to make you remember Shakespeare instead of the dope sheet on the ponies, I hope I'll keep on with it.

MARY
Now, James! You mustn't be so touchy.
Jamie shrugs his shoulders and sits down in the chair on her right.

EDMUND
Irritably.
Yes, for Pete's sake, Papa! The first thing after breakfast! Give it a rest, can't you?
He slumps down in the chair at left of table next to his brother. His father ignores him.

MARY
Reprovingly.
Your father wasn't finding fault with you. You don't have to always take Jamie's part. You'd think you were the one ten years older.

JAMIE
Boredly.
What's all the fuss about? Let's forget it.

TYRONE
Contemptuously.
Yes, forget! Forget everything and face nothing! It's a convenient philosophy if you've no ambition in life except to—

MARY

James, do be quiet.

She puts an arm around his shoulder — coaxingly.

You must have gotten out of the wrong side of the bed this morning.

To the boys, changing the subject.

What were you two grinning about like Cheshire cats when you came in? What was the joke?

TYRONE

With a painful effort to be a good sport.

Yes, let us in on it, lads. I told your mother I knew damned well it would be one on me, but never mind that, I'm used to it.

JAMIE

Dryly.

Don't look at me. This is the Kid's story.

EDMUND

Grins.

I meant to tell you last night, Papa, and forgot it. Yesterday when I went for a walk I dropped in at the Inn —

MARY

Worriedly.

You shouldn't drink now, Edmund.

EDMUND

Ignoring this.

And who do you think I met there, with a beautiful bun on, but Shaughnessy, the tenant on that farm of yours.

MARY

Smiling.

That dreadful man! But he is funny.

TYRONE

Scowling.

He's not so funny when you're his landlord. He's a wily Shanty Mick, that one. He could hide behind a corkscrew. What's he complaining about now, Edmund — for I'm damned sure he's complaining. I suppose he wants his rent lowered. I let him have the place for almost nothing, just to keep someone on it, and he never pays that till I threaten to evict him.

EDMUND
No, he didn't beef about anything. He was so pleased with life he even bought a drink, and that's practically unheard of. He was delighted because he'd had a fight with your friend, Harker, the Standard Oil millionaire, and won a glorious victory.

MARY
With amused dismay.
Oh, Lord! James, you'll really have to do something—

TYRONE
Bad luck to Shaughnessy, anyway!

JAMIE
Maliciously.
I'll bet the next time you see Harker at the Club and give him the old respectful bow, he won't see you.

EDMUND
Yes. Harker will think you're no gentleman for harboring a tenant who isn't humble in the presence of a king of America.

TYRONE
Never mind the Socialist gabble. I don't care to listen—

MARY
Tactfully.
Go on with your story, Edmund.

EDMUND
Grins at his father provocatively.
Well, you remember, Papa, the ice pond on Harker's estate is right next to the farm, and you remember Shaughnessy keeps pigs. Well, it seems there's a break in the fence and the pigs have been bathing in the millionaire's ice pond, and Harker's foreman told him he was sure Shaughnessy had broken the fence on purpose to give his pigs a free wallow.

MARY
Shocked and amused.
Good heavens!

TYRONE
Sourly, but with a trace of admiration.
I'm sure he did, too, the dirty scallywag. It's like him.

EDMUND
So Harker came in person to rebuke Shaughnessy.
He chuckles.
A very bonehead play! If I needed any further proof that our ruling
plutocrats, especially the ones who inherited their boodle, are not
mental giants, that would clinch it.

TYRONE
With appreciation, before he thinks.
Yes, he'd be no match for Shaughnessy.
Then he growls.
Keep your damned anarchist remarks to yourself. I won't have them
in my house.
But he is full of eager anticipation.
What happened?

EDMUND
Harker had as much chance as I would with Jack Johnson. Shaughnessy got a few drinks under his belt and was waiting at the gate to
welcome him. He told me he never gave Harker a chance to open
his mouth. He began by shouting that he was no slave Standard Oil
could trample on. He was a King of Ireland, if he had his rights,
and scum was scum to him, no matter how much money it had
stolen from the poor.

MARY
Oh, Lord!
But she can't help laughing.

EDMUND
Then he accused Harker of making his foreman break down the
fence to entice the pigs into the ice pond in order to destroy them.

The poor pigs, Shaughnessy yelled, had caught their death of cold. Many of them were dying of pneumonia, and several others had been taken down with cholera from drinking the poisoned water. He told Harker he was hiring a lawyer to sue him for damages. And he wound up by saying that he had to put up with poison ivy, ticks, potato bugs, snakes and skunks on his farm, but he was an honest man who drew the line somewhere, and he'd be damned if he'd stand for a Standard Oil thief trespassing. So would Harker kindly remove his dirty feet from the premises before he sicked the dog on him. And Harker did!

He and Jamie laugh.

MARY
Shocked but giggling.
Heavens, what a terrible tongue that man has!

TYRONE
Admiringly before he thinks.
The damned old scoundrel! By God, you can't beat him!
He laughs — then stops abruptly and scowls.
The dirty blackguard! He'll get me in serious trouble yet. I hope you told him I'd be mad as hell—

EDMUND
I told him you'd be tickled to death over the great Irish victory, and so you are. Stop faking, Papa.

TYRONE
Well, I'm not tickled to death.

MARY
Teasingly.
You are, too, James. You're simply delighted!

TYRONE
No, Mary, a joke is a joke, but—

EDMUND
I told Shaughnessy he should have reminded Harker that a Standard Oil millionaire ought to welcome the flavor of hog in his ice water as an appropriate touch.

TYRONE

The devil you did!

Frowning.

Keep your damned Socialist anarchist sentiments out of my affairs!

EDMUND

Shaughnessy almost wept because he hadn't thought of that one, but he said he'd include it in a letter he's writing to Harker, along with a few other insults he'd overlooked.

He and Jamie laugh.

TYRONE

What are you laughing at? There's nothing funny—A fine son you are to help that blackguard get me into a lawsuit!

MARY

Now, James, don't lose your temper.

TYRONE

Turns on Jamie.

And you're worse than he is, encouraging him. I suppose you're regretting you weren't there to prompt Shaughnessy with a few nastier insults. You've a fine talent for that, if for nothing else.

MARY

James! There's no reason to scold Jamie.

Jamie is about to make some sneering remark to his father, but he shrugs his shoulders.

EDMUND

With sudden nervous exasperation.

Oh, for God's sake, Papa! If you're starting that stuff again, I'll beat it.

He jumps up.

I left my book upstairs, anyway.

He goes to the front parlor, saying disgustedly,

God, Papa, I should think you'd get sick of hearing yourself—

He disappears. Tyrone looks after him angrily.

MARY

You mustn't mind Edmund, James. Remember he isn't well.

Edmund can be heard coughing as he goes upstairs. She adds nervously.
A summer cold makes anyone irritable.

JAMIE
Genuinely concerned.
It's not just a cold he's got. The Kid is damned sick.
His father gives him a sharp warning look but he doesn't see it.

MARY
Turns on him resentfully.
Why do you say that? It *is* just a cold! Anyone can tell that! You
always imagine things!

TYRONE
With another warning glance at Jamie — easily.
All Jamie meant was Edmund might have a touch of something
else, too, which makes his cold worse.

JAMIE
Sure, Mama. That's all I meant.

TYRONE
Doctor Hardy thinks it might be a bit of malarial fever he caught
when he was in the tropics. If it is, quinine will soon cure it.

MARY
A look of contemptuous hostility flashes across her face.
Doctor Hardy! I wouldn't believe a thing he said, if he swore on
a stack of Bibles! I know what doctors are. They're all alike. Anything, they don't care what, to keep you coming to them.
*She stops short, overcome by a fit of acute self-consciousness as she catches
their eyes fixed on her. Her hands jerk nervously to her hair. She forces
a smile.*
What is it? What are you looking at? Is my hair — ?

TYRONE
*Puts his arm around her — with guilty heartiness, giving her a playful
hug.*
There's nothing wrong with your hair. The healthier and fatter you

get, the vainer you become. You'll soon spend half the day primping before the mirror.

MARY
Half reassured.
I really should have new glasses. My eyes are so bad now.

TYRONE
With Irish blarney.
Your eyes are beautiful, and well you know it.
He gives her a kiss. Her face lights up with a charming, shy embarrassment. Suddenly and startlingly one sees in her face the girl she had once been, not a ghost of the dead, but still a living part of her.

MARY
You musn't be so silly, James. Right in front of Jamie!

TYRONE
Oh, he's on to you, too. He knows this fuss about eyes and hair is only fishing for compliments. Eh, Jamie?

JAMIE
His face has cleared, too, and there is an old boyish charm in his loving smile at his mother.
Yes. You can't kid us, Mama.

MARY
Laughs and an Irish lilt comes into her voice.
Go along with both of you!
Then she speaks with a girlish gravity.
But I did truly have beautiful hair once, didn't I, James?

TYRONE
The most beautiful in the world!

MARY
It was a rare shade of reddish brown and so long it came down below my knees. You ought to remember it, too, Jamie. It wasn't until after Edmund was born that I had a single grey hair. Then it began to turn white.
The girlishness fades from her face.

TYRONE
Quickly.
And that made it prettier than ever.

MARY
Again embarrassed and pleased.
Will you listen to your father, Jamie—after thirty-five years of marriage! He isn't a great actor for nothing, is he? What's come over you, James? Are you pouring coals of fire on my head for teasing you about snoring? Well then, I take it all back. It must have been only the foghorn I heard.
She laughs, and they laugh with her. Then she changes to a brisk businesslike air.
But I can't stay with you any longer, even to hear compliments. I must see the cook about dinner and the day's marketing.
She gets up and sighs with humorous exaggeration.
Bridget is so lazy. And so sly. She begins telling me about her relatives so I can't get a word in edgeways and scold her. Well, I might as well get it over.
She goes to the back-parlor doorway, then turns, her face worried again.
You musn't make Edmund work on the grounds with you, James, remember.
Again with the strange obstinate set to her face.
Not that he isn't strong enough, but he'd perspire and he might catch more cold.
She disappears through the back parlor. Tyrone turns on Jamie condemningly.

TYRONE
You're a fine lunkhead! Haven't you any sense? The one thing to avoid is saying anything that would get her more upset over Edmund.

JAMIE
Shrugging his shoulders.
All right. Have it your way. I think it's the wrong idea to let Mama go on kidding herself. It will only make the shock worse when she

has to face it. Anyway, you can see she's deliberately fooling herself with that summer cold talk. She knows better.

TYRONE

Knows? Nobody knows yet.

JAMIE

Well, I do. I was with Edmund when he went to Doc Hardy on Monday. I heard him pull that touch of malaria stuff. He was stalling. That isn't what he thinks any more. You know it as well as I do. You talked to him when you went uptown yesterday, didn't you?

TYRONE

He couldn't say anything for sure yet. He's to phone me today before Edmund goes to him.

JAMIE

Slowly.
He thinks it's consumption, doesn't he, Papa?

TYRONE

Reluctantly.
He said it might be.

JAMIE

Moved, his love for his brother coming out.
Poor kid! God damn it!
He turns on his father accusingly.
It might never have happened if you'd sent him to a real doctor when he first got sick.

TYRONE

What's the matter with Hardy? He's always been our doctor up here.

JAMIE

Everything's the matter with him! Even in this hick burg he's rated third class! He's a cheap old quack!

TYRONE

That's right! Run him down! Run down everybody! Everyone is a fake to you!

JAMIE

Contemptuously.

Hardy only charges a dollar. That's what makes you think he's a fine doctor!

TYRONE

Stung.

That's enough! You're not drunk now! There's no excuse—

He controls himself—a bit defensively.

If you mean I can't afford one of the fine society doctors who prey on the rich summer people—

JAMIE

Can't afford? You're one of the biggest property owners around here.

TYRONE

That doesn't mean I'm rich. It's all mortgaged—

JAMIE

Because you always buy more instead of paying off mortgages. If Edmund was a lousy acre of land you wanted, the sky would be the limit!

TYRONE

That's a lie! And your sneers against Doctor Hardy are lies! He doesn't put on frills, or have an office in a fashionable location, or drive around in an expensive automobile. That's what you pay for with those other five-dollars-to-look-at-your-tongue fellows, not their skill.

JAMIE

With a scornful shrug of his shoulders.

Oh, all right. I'm a fool to argue. You can't change the leopard's spots.

TYRONE

With rising anger.

No, you can't. You've taught me that lesson only too well. I've lost all hope you will ever change yours. You dare tell me what I can afford? You've never known the value of a dollar and never will! You've never saved a dollar in your life! At the end of each season you're penniless! You've thrown your salary away every week on whores and whiskey!

JAMIE

My salary! Christ!

TYRONE

It's more than you're worth, and you couldn't get that if it wasn't for me. If you weren't my son, there isn't a manager in the business who would give you a part, your reputation stinks so. As it is, I have to humble my pride and beg for you, saying you've turned over a new leaf, although I know it's a lie!

JAMIE

I never wanted to be an actor. You forced me on the stage.

TYRONE

That's a lie! You made no effort to find anything else to do. You left it to me to get you a job and I have no influence except in the theater. Forced you! You never wanted to do anything except loaf in barrooms! You'd have been content to sit back like a lazy lunk and sponge on me for the rest of your life! After all the money I'd wasted on your education, and all you did was get fired in disgrace from every college you went to!

JAMIE

Oh, for God's sake, don't drag up that ancient history!

TYRONE

It's not ancient history that you have to come home every summer to live on me.

JAMIE

I earn my board and lodging working on the grounds. It saves you hiring a man.

TYRONE

Bah! You have to be driven to do even that much!
His anger ebbs into a weary complaint.
I wouldn't give a damn if you ever displayed the slightest sign of gratitude. The only thanks is to have you sneer at me for a dirty miser, sneer at my profession, sneer at every damned thing in the world—except yourself.

JAMIE

Wryly.
That's not true, Papa. You can't hear me talking to myself, that's all.

TYRONE

Stares at him puzzledly, then quotes mechanically.
"Ingratitude, the vilest weed that grows"!

JAMIE

I could see that line coming! God, how many thousand times—!
He stops, bored with their quarrel, and shrugs his shoulders.
All right, Papa. I'm a bum. Anything you like, so long as it stops the argument.

TYRONE

With indignant appeal now.
If you'd get ambition in your head instead of folly! You're young yet. You could still make your mark. You had the talent to become a fine actor! You have it still. You're my son—!

JAMIE

Boredly.
Let's forget me. I'm not interested in the subject. Neither are you.
Tyrone gives up. Jamie goes on casually.
What started us on this? Oh, Doc Hardy. When is he going to call you up about Edmund?

TYRONE

Around lunch time.

He pauses—then defensively.

I couldn't have sent Edmund to a better doctor. Hardy's treated him whenever he was sick up here, since he was knee high. He knows his constitution as no other doctor could. It's not a question of my being miserly, as you'd like to make out.

Bitterly.

And what could the finest specialist in America do for Edmund, after he's deliberately ruined his health by the mad life he's led ever since he was fired from college? Even before that when he was in prep school, he began dissipating and playing the Broadway sport to imitate you, when he's never had your constitution to stand it. You're a healthy hulk like me—or you were at his age—but he's always been a bundle of nerves like his mother. I've warned him for years his body couldn't stand it, but he wouldn't heed me, and now it's too late.

JAMIE

Sharply.

What do you mean, too late? You talk as if you thought—

TYRONE

Guiltily explosive.

Don't be a damned fool! I meant nothing but what's plain to any-one! His health has broken down and he may be an invalid for a long time.

JAMIE

Stares at his father, ignoring his explanation.

I know it's an Irish peasant idea consumption is fatal. It probably is when you live in a hovel on a bog, but over here, with modern treatment—

TYRONE

Don't I know that! What are you gabbing about, anyway? And keep your dirty tongue off Ireland, with your sneers about peasants and bogs and hovels!

Accusingly.

The less you say about Edmund's sickness, the better for your conscience! You're more responsible than anyone!

JAMIE
Stung.
That's a lie! I won't stand for that, Papa!

TYRONE
It's the truth! You've been the worst influence for him. He grew up admiring you as a hero! A fine example you set him! If you ever gave him advice except in the ways of rottenness, I've never heard of it! You made him old before his time, pumping him full of what you consider worldly wisdom, when he was too young to see that your mind was so poisoned by your own failure in life, you wanted to believe every man was a knave with his soul for sale, and every woman who wasn't a whore was a fool!

JAMIE
With a defensive air of weary indifference again.
All right. I did put Edmund wise to things, but not until I saw he'd started to raise hell, and knew he'd laugh at me if I tried the good advice, older brother stuff. All I did was make a pal of him and be absolutely frank so he'd learn from my mistakes that—
He shrugs his shoulders—cynically.
Well, that if you can't be good you can at least be careful.
His father snorts contemptuously. Suddenly Jamie becomes really moved.
That's a rotten accusation, Papa. You know how much the Kid means to me, and how close we've always been—not like the usual brothers! I'd do anything for him.

TYRONE
Impressed—mollifyingly.
I know you may have thought it was for the best, Jamie. I didn't say you did it deliberately to harm him.

JAMIE
Besides it's damned rot! I'd like to see anyone influence Edmund more than he wants to be. His quietness fools people into thinking they can do what they like with him. But he's stubborn as hell

35

inside and what he does is what he wants to do, and to hell with anyone else! What had I to do with all the crazy stunts he's pulled in the last few years — working his way all over the map as a sailor and all that stuff. I thought that was a damned fool idea, and I told him so. You can't imagine me getting fun out of being on the beach in South America, or living in filthy dives, drinking rotgut, can you? No, thanks! I'll stick to Broadway, and a room with a bath, and bars that serve bonded Bourbon.

TYRONE

You and Broadway! It's made you what you are!
With a touch of pride.
Whatever Edmund's done, he's had the guts to go off on his own, where he couldn't come whining to me the minute he was broke.

JAMIE

Stung into sneering jealousy.
He's always come home broke finally, hasn't he? And what did his going away get him? Look at him now!
He is suddenly shamefaced.
Christ! That's a lousy thing to say. I don't mean that.

TYRONE

Decides to ignore this.
He's been doing well on the paper. I was hoping he'd found the work he wants to do at last.

JAMIE

Sneering jealously again.
A hick town rag! Whatever bull they hand you, they tell me he's a pretty bum reporter. If he weren't your son —
Ashamed again.
No, that's not true! They're glad to have him, but it's the special stuff that gets him by. Some of the poems and parodies he's written are damned good.
Grudgingly again.
Not that they'd ever get him anywhere on the big time.
Hastily.
But he's certainly made a damned good start.

TYRONE

Yes. He's made a start. You used to talk about wanting to become a newspaper man but you were never willing to start at the bottom. You expected—

JAMIE

Oh, for Christ's sake, Papa! Can't you lay off me!

TYRONE

Stares at him—then looks away—after a pause.
It's damnable luck Edmund should be sick right now. It couldn't have come at a worse time for him.
He adds, unable to conceal an almost furtive uneasiness.
Or for your mother. It's damnable she should have this to upset her, just when she needs peace and freedom from worry. She's been so well in the two months since she came home.
His voice grows husky and trembles a little.
It's been heaven to me. This home has been a home again. But I needn't tell you, Jamie.
His son looks at him, for the first time with an understanding sympathy. It is as if suddenly a deep bond of common feeling existed between them in which their antagonisms could be forgotten.

JAMIE

Almost gently.
I've felt the same way, Papa.

TYRONE

Yes, this time you can see how strong and sure of herself she is. She's a different woman entirely from the other times. She has control of her nerves—or she had until Edmund got sick. Now you can feel her growing tense and frightened underneath. I wish to God we could keep the truth from her, but we can't if he has to be sent to a sanatorium. What makes it worse is her father died of consumption. She worshiped him and she's never forgotten. Yes, it will be hard for her. But she can do it! She has the will power now! We must help her, Jamie, in every way we can!

JAMIE
Moved.
Of course, Papa.
Hesitantly.
Outside of nerves, she seems perfectly all right this morning.

TYRONE
With hearty confidence now.
Never better. She's full of fun and mischief.
Suddenly he frowns at Jamie suspiciously.
Why do you say, seems? Why shouldn't she be all right? What the hell do you mean?

JAMIE
Don't start jumping down my throat! God, Papa, this ought to be one thing we can talk over frankly without a battle.

TYRONE
I'm sorry, Jamie.
Tensely.
But go on and tell me—

JAMIE
There's nothing to tell. I was all wrong. It's just that last night—Well, you know how it is, I can't forget the past. I can't help being suspicious. Any more than you can.
Bitterly.
That's the hell of it. And it makes it hell for Mama! She watches us watching her—

TYRONE
Sadly.
I know.
Tensely.
Well, what was it? Can't you speak out?

JAMIE
Nothing, I tell you. Just my damned foolishness. Around three o'clock this morning, I woke up and heard her moving around in the spare room. Then she went to the bathroom. I pretended to be

asleep. She stopped in the hall to listen, as if she wanted to make sure I was.

TYRONE
With forced scorn.
For God's sake, is that all? She told me herself the foghorn kept her awake all night, and every night since Edmund's been sick she's been up and down, going to his room to see how he was.

JAMIE
Eagerly.
Yes, that's right, she did stop to listen outside his room.
Hesitantly again.
It was her being in the spare room that scared me. I couldn't help remembering that when she starts sleeping alone in there, it has always been a sign—

TYRONE
It isn't this time! It's easily explained. Where else could she go last night to get away from my snoring?
He gives way to a burst of resentful anger.
By God, how you can live with a mind that sees nothing but the worst motives behind everything is beyond me!

JAMIE
Stung.
Don't pull that! I've just said I was all wrong. Don't you suppose I'm as glad of that as you are!

TYRONE
Mollifyingly.
I'm sure you are, Jamie.
A pause. His expression becomes somber. He speaks slowly with a superstitious dread.
It would be like a curse she can't escape if worry over Edmund—It was in her long sickness after bringing him into the world that she first—

JAMIE
She didn't have anything to do with it!

39

TYRONE

I'm not blaming her.

JAMIE

Bitingly.

Then who are you blaming? Edmund, for being born?

TYRONE

You damned fool! No one was to blame.

JAMIE

The bastard of a doctor was! From what Mama's said, he was another cheap quack like Hardy! You wouldn't pay for a first-rate—

TYRONE

That's a lie!

Furiously.

So I'm to blame! That's what you're driving at, is it? You evil-minded loafer!

JAMIE

Warningly as he hears his mother in the dining room.

Ssh!

Tyrone gets hastily to his feet and goes to look out the windows at right. Jamie speaks with a complete change of tone.

Well, if we're going to cut the front hedge today, we'd better go to work.

Mary comes in from the back parlor. She gives a quick, suspicious glance from one to the other, her manner nervously self-conscious.

TYRONE

Turns from the window—with an actor's heartiness.

Yes, it's too fine a morning to waste indoors arguing. Take a look out the window, Mary. There's no fog in the harbor. I'm sure the spell of it we've had is over now.

MARY

Going to him.

I hope so, dear.

To Jamie, forcing a smile.

Did I actually hear you suggesting work on the front hedge, Jamie?
Wonders will never cease! You must want pocket money badly.

JAMIE
Kiddingly.
When don't I?
He winks at her, with a derisive glance at his father.
I expect a salary of at least one large iron man at the end of the
week—to carouse on!

MARY
*Does not respond to his humor—her hands fluttering over the front of
her dress.*
What were you two arguing about?

JAMIE
Shrugs his shoulders.
The same old stuff.

MARY
I heard you say something about a doctor, and your father accusing
you of being evil-minded.

JAMIE
Quickly.
Oh, that. I was saying again Doc Hardy isn't my idea of the world's
greatest physician.

MARY
Knows he is lying—vaguely.
Oh. No, I wouldn't say he was, either.
Changing the subject—forcing a smile.
That Bridget! I thought I'd never get away. She told me all about
her second cousin on the police force in St. Louis.
Then with nervous irritation.
Well, if you're going to work on the hedge why don't you go?
Hastily.
I mean, take advantage of the sunshine before the fog comes back.
Strangely, as if talking aloud to herself.
Because I know it will.

Suddenly she is self-consciously aware that they are both staring fixedly at her—flurriedly, raising her hands.

Or I should say, the rheumatism in my hands knows. It's a better weather prophet than you are, James.

She stares at her hands with fascinated repulsion.

Ugh! How ugly they are! Who'd ever believe they were once beautiful?

They stare at her with a growing dread.

TYRONE

Takes her hands and gently pushes them down.

Now, now, Mary. None of that foolishness. They're the sweetest hands in the world.

She smiles, her face lighting up, and kisses him gratefully. He turns to his son.

Come on Jamie. Your mother's right to scold us. The way to start work is to start work. The hot sun will sweat some of that booze fat off your middle.

He opens the screen door and goes out on the porch and disappears down a flight of steps leading to the ground. Jamie rises from his chair and, taking off his coat, goes to the door. At the door he turns back but avoids looking at her, and she does not look at him.

JAMIE

With an awkward, uneasy tenderness.

We're all so proud of you, Mama, so darned happy.

She stiffens and stares at him with a frightened defiance. He flounders on.

But you've still got to be careful. You mustn't worry so much about Edmund. He'll be all right.

MARY

With a stubborn, bitterly resentful look.

Of course, he'll be all right. And I don't know what you mean, warning me to be careful.

JAMIE

Rebuffed and hurt, shrugs his shoulders.

All right, Mama. I'm sorry I spoke.

He goes out on the porch. She waits rigidly until he disappears down the steps. Then she sinks down in the chair he had occupied, her face betraying a frightened, furtive desperation, her hands roving over the table top, aimlessly moving objects around. She hears Edmund descending the stairs in the front hall. As he nears the bottom he has a fit of coughing. She springs to her feet, as if she wanted to run away from the sound, and goes quickly to the windows at right. She is looking out, apparently calm, as he enters from the front parlor, a book in one hand. She turns to him, her lips set in a welcoming, motherly smile.

MARY

Here you are. I was just going upstairs to look for you.

EDMUND

I waited until they went out. I don't want to mix up in any arguments. I feel too rotten.

MARY

Almost resentfully.
Oh, I'm sure you don't feel half as badly as you make out. You're such a baby. You like to get us worried so we'll make a fuss over you.
Hastily.
I'm only teasing, dear. I know how miserably uncomfortable you must be. But you feel better today, don't you?
Worriedly, taking his arm.
All the same, you've grown much too thin. You need to rest all you can. Sit down and I'll make you comfortable.
He sits down in the rocking chair and she puts a pillow behind his back.
There. How's that?

EDMUND

Grand. Thanks, Mama.

MARY

Kisses him—tenderly.
All you need is your mother to nurse you. Big as you are, you're still the baby of the family to me, you know.

EDMUND

Takes her hand—with deep seriousness.

Never mind me. You take care of yourself. That's all that counts.

MARY

Evading his eyes.

But I am, dear.

Forcing a laugh.

Heavens, don't you see how fat I've grown! I'll have to have all my dresses let out.

She turns away and goes to the windows at right. She attempts a light, amused tone.

They've started clipping the hedge. Poor Jamie! How he hates working in front where everyone passing can see him. There go the Chatfields in their new Mercedes. It's a beautiful car, isn't it? Not like our secondhand Packard. Poor Jamie! He bent almost under the hedge so they wouldn't notice him. They bowed to your father and he bowed back as if he were taking a curtain call. In that filthy old suit I've tried to make him throw away.

Her voice has grown bitter.

Really, he ought to have more pride than to make such a show of himself.

EDMUND

He's right not to give a damn what anyone thinks. Jamie's a fool to care about the Chatfields. For Pete's sake, who ever heard of them outside this hick burg?

MARY

With satisfaction.

No one. You're quite right, Edmund. Big frogs in a small puddle. It is stupid of Jamie.

She pauses, looking out the window—then with an undercurrent of lonely yearning.

Still, the Chatfields and people like them stand for something. I mean they have decent, presentable homes they don't have to be ashamed of. They have friends who entertain them and whom they entertain. They're not cut off from everyone.

She turns back from the window.

Not that I want anything to do with them. I've always hated this town and everyone in it. You know that. I never wanted to live here in the first place, but your father liked it and insisted on building this house, and I've had to come here every summer.

EDMUND

Well, it's better than spending the summer in a New York hotel, isn't it? And this town's not so bad. I like it well enough. I suppose because it's the only home we've had.

MARY

I've never felt it was my home. It was wrong from the start. Everything was done in the cheapest way. Your father would never spend the money to make it right. It's just as well we haven't any friends here. I'd be ashamed to have them step in the door. But he's never wanted family friends. He hates calling on people, or receiving them. All he likes is to hobnob with men at the Club or in a barroom. Jamie and you are the same way, but you're not to blame. You've never had a chance to meet decent people here. I know you both would have been so different if you'd been able to associate with nice girls instead of— You'd never have disgraced yourselves as you have, so that now no respectable parents will let their daughters be seen with you.

EDMUND

Irritably.

Oh, Mama, forget it! Who cares? Jamie and I would be bored stiff. And about the Old Man, what's the use of talking? You can't change him.

MARY

Mechanically rebuking.

Don't call your father the Old Man. You should have more respect.
Then dully.

I know it's useless to talk. But sometimes I feel so lonely.
Her lips quiver and she keeps her head turned away.

EDMUND

Anyway, you've got to be fair, Mama. It may have been all his fault in the beginning, but you know that later on, even if he'd wanted to, we couldn't have had people here—

He flounders guiltily.

I mean, you wouldn't have wanted them.

MARY

Wincing—her lips quivering pitifully.

Don't. I can't bear having you remind me.

EDMUND

Don't take it that way! Please, Mama! I'm trying to help. Because it's bad for you to forget. The right way is to remember. So you'll always be on your guard. You know what's happened before.

Miserably.

God, Mama, you know I hate to remind you. I'm doing it because it's been so wonderful having you home the way you've been, and it would be terrible—

MARY

Strickenly.

Please, dear. I know you mean it for the best, but—

A defensive uneasiness comes into her voice again.

I don't understand why you should suddenly say such things. What put it in your mind this morning?

EDMUND

Evasively.

Nothing. Just because I feel rotten and blue, I suppose.

MARY

Tell me the truth. Why are you so suspicious all of a sudden?

EDMUND

I'm not!

MARY

Oh, yes you are. I can feel it. Your father and Jamie, too—particularly Jamie.

EDMUND

Now don't start imagining things, Mama.

MARY

Her hands fluttering.

It makes it so much harder, living in this atmosphere of constant suspicion, knowing everyone is spying on me, and none of you believe in me, or trust me.

EDMUND

That's crazy, Mama. We do trust you.

MARY

If there was only some place I could go to get away for a day, or even an afternoon, some woman friend I could talk to—not about anything serious, simply laugh and gossip and forget for a while—someone besides the servants—that stupid Cathleen!

EDMUND

Gets up worriedly and puts his arm around her.

Stop it, Mama. You're getting yourself worked up over nothing.

MARY

Your father goes out. He meets his friends in barrooms or at the Club. You and Jamie have the boys you know. You go out. But I am alone. I've always been alone.

EDMUND

Soothingly.

Come now! You know that's a fib. One of us always stays around to keep you company, or goes with you in the automobile when you take a drive.

MARY

Bitterly.

Because you're afraid to trust me alone!

She turns on him—sharply.

I insist you tell me why you act so differently this morning—why you felt you had to remind me—

EDMUND

Hesitates—then blurts out guiltily.

It's stupid. It's just that I wasn't asleep when you came in my room last night. You didn't go back to your and Papa's room. You went in the spare room for the rest of the night.

MARY

Because your father's snoring was driving me crazy! For heaven's sake, haven't I often used the spare room as my bedroom?
Bitterly.
But I see what you thought. That was when—

EDMUND

Too vehemently.
I didn't think anything!

MARY

So you pretended to be asleep in order to spy on me!

EDMUND

No! I did it because I knew if you found out I was feverish and couldn't sleep, it would upset you.

MARY

Jamie was pretending to be asleep, too, I'm sure, and I suppose your father—

EDMUND

Stop it, Mama!

MARY

Oh, I can't bear it, Edmund, when even you—!
Her hands flutter up to pat her hair in their aimless, distracted way. Suddenly a strange undercurrent of revengefulness comes into her voice.
It would serve all of you right if it was true!

EDMUND

Mama! Don't say that! That's the way you talk when—

MARY

Stop suspecting me! Please, dear! You hurt me! I couldn't sleep because I was thinking about you. That's the real reason! I've been so worried ever since you've been sick.
She puts her arms around him and hugs him with a frightened, protective tenderness.

EDMUND
Soothingly.
That's foolishness. You know it's only a bad cold.

MARY
Yes, of course, I know that!

EDMUND
But listen, Mama. I want you to promise me that even if it should turn out to be something worse, you'll know I'll soon be all right again, anyway, and you won't worry yourself sick, and you'll keep on taking care of yourself—

MARY
Frightenedly.
I won't listen when you're so silly! There's absolutely no reason to talk as if you expected something dreadful! Of course, I promise you. I give you my sacred word of honor!
Then with a sad bitterness.
But I suppose you're remembering I've promised before on my word of honor.

EDMUND
No!

MARY
Her bitterness receding into a resigned helplessness.
I'm not blaming you, dear. How can you help it? How can any one of us forget?
Strangely.
That's what makes it so hard—for all of us. We can't forget.

EDMUND
Grabs her shoulder.
Mama! Stop it!

MARY
Forcing a smile.
All right, dear. I didn't mean to be so gloomy. Don't mind me. Here. Let me feel your head. Why, it's nice and cool. You certainly haven't any fever now.

EDMUND
Forget! It's you—

MARY
But I'm quite all right, dear.
With a quick, strange, calculating, almost sly glance at him.
Except I naturally feel tired and nervous this morning, after such a bad night. I really ought to go upstairs and lie down until lunch time and take a nap.
He gives her an instinctive look of suspicion—then, ashamed of himself, looks quickly away. She hurries on nervously.
What are you going to do? Read here? It would be much better for you to go out in the fresh air and sunshine. But don't get overheated, remember. Be sure and wear a hat.
She stops, looking straight at him now. He avoids her eyes. There is a tense pause. Then she speaks jeeringly.
Or are you afraid to trust me alone?

EDMUND
Tormentedly.
No! Can't you stop talking like that! I think you ought to take a nap.
He goes to the screen door—forcing a joking tone.
I'll go down and help Jamie bear up. I love to lie in the shade and watch him work.
He forces a laugh in which she makes herself join. Then he goes out on the porch and disappears down the steps. Her first reaction is one of relief. She appears to relax. She sinks down in one of the wicker armchairs at rear of table and leans her head back, closing her eyes. But suddenly she grows terribly tense again. Her eyes open and she strains forward,

seized by a fit of nervous panic. She begins a desperate battle with her-self. Her long fingers, warped and knotted by rheumatism, drum on the arms of the chair, driven by an insistent life of their own, without her consent.

CURTAIN

Act Two, Scene One

SCENE

The same. It is around quarter to one. No sunlight comes into the room now through the windows at right. Outside the day is still fine but increasingly sultry, with a faint haziness in the air which softens the glare of the sun.

Edmund sits in the armchair at left of table, reading a book. Or rather he is trying to concentrate on it but cannot. He seems to be listening for some sound from upstairs. His manner is nervously apprehensive and he looks more sickly than in the previous act.

The second girl, CATHLEEN, *enters from the back parlor. She carries a tray on which is a bottle of bonded Bourbon, several whiskey glasses, and a pitcher of ice water. She is a buxom Irish peasant, in her early twenties, with a red-cheeked comely face, black hair and blue eyes— amiable, ignorant, clumsy, and possessed by a dense, well-meaning stupidity. She puts the tray on the table. Edmund pretends to be so absorbed in his book he does not notice her, but she ignores this.*

CATHLEEN
With garrulous familiarity.
Here's the whiskey. It'll be lunch time soon. Will I call your father and Mister Jamie, or will you?

EDMUND
Without looking up from his book.
You do it.

CATHLEEN

It's a wonder your father wouldn't look at his watch once in a while.
He's a divil for making the meals late, and then Bridget curses me as
if I was to blame. But he's a grand handsome man, if he is old. You'll
never see the day you're as good looking—nor Mister Jamie, either.
She chuckles.

I'll wager Mister Jamie wouldn't miss the time to stop work and
have his drop of whiskey if he had a watch to his name!

EDMUND

Gives up trying to ignore her and grins.
You win that one.

CATHLEEN

And here's another I'd win, that you're making me call them so you
can sneak a drink before they come.

EDMUND

Well, I hadn't thought of that—

CATHLEEN

Oh no, not you! Butter wouldn't melt in your mouth, I suppose.

EDMUND

But now you suggest it—

CATHLEEN

Suddenly primly virtuous.
I'd never suggest a man or a woman touch drink, Mister Edmund.
Sure, didn't it kill an uncle of mine in the old country.
Relenting.
Still, a drop now and then is no harm when you're in low spirits, or
have a bad cold.

EDMUND

Thanks for handing me a good excuse.
Then with forced casualness.
You'd better call my mother, too.

CATHLEEN

What for? She's always on time without any calling. God bless her, she has some consideration for the help.

EDMUND

She's been taking a nap.

CATHLEEN

She wasn't asleep when I finished my work upstairs a while back. She was lying down in the spare room with her eyes wide open. She'd a terrible headache, she said.

EDMUND

His casualness more forced.
Oh well then, just call my father.

CATHLEEN

Goes to the screen door, grumbling good-naturedly.
No wonder my feet kill me each night. I won't walk out in this heat and get sunstroke. I'll call from the porch.
She goes out on the side porch, letting the screen door slam behind her, and disappears on her way to the front porch. A moment later she is heard shouting.
Mister Tyrone! Mister Jamie! It's time!
Edmund, who has been staring frightenedly before him, forgetting his book, springs to his feet nervously.

EDMUND

God, what a wench!
He grabs the bottle and pours a drink, adds ice water and drinks. As he does so, he hears someone coming in the front door. He puts the glass hastily on the tray and sits down again, opening his book. Jamie comes in from the front parlor, his coat over his arm. He has taken off collar and tie and carries them in his hand. He is wiping sweat from his forehead with a handkerchief. Edmund looks up as if his reading was interrupted. Jamie takes one look at the bottle and glasses and smiles cynically.

JAMIE

Sneaking one, eh? Cut out the bluff, Kid. You're a rottener actor than I am.

EDMUND

Grins.

Yes, I grabbed one while the going was good.

JAMIE

Puts a hand affectionately on his shoulder.

That's better. Why kid me? We're pals, aren't we?

EDMUND

I wasn't sure it was you coming.

JAMIE

I made the Old Man look at his watch. I was halfway up the walk when Cathleen burst into song. Our wild Irish lark! She ought to be a train announcer.

EDMUND

That's what drove me to drink. Why don't you sneak one while you've got a chance?

JAMIE

I was thinking of that little thing.

He goes quickly to the window at right.

The Old Man was talking to old Captain Turner. Yes, he's still at it.

He comes back and takes a drink.

And now to cover up from his eagle eye. He memorizes the level in the bottle after every drink.

He measures two drinks of water and pours them in the whiskey bottle and shakes it up.

There. That fixes it.

He pours water in the glass and sets it on the table by Edmund.

And here's the water you've been drinking.

EDMUND

Fine! You don't think it will fool him, do you?

JAMIE

Maybe not, but he can't prove it.

Putting on his collar and tie.

I hope he doesn't forget lunch listening to himself talk. I'm hungry.

He sits across the table from Edmund—irritably.

That's what I hate about working down in front. He puts on an act for every damned fool that comes along.

EDMUND

Gloomily.

You're in luck to be hungry. The way I feel I don't care if I ever eat again.

JAMIE

Gives him a glance of concern.

Listen, Kid. You know me. I've never lectured you, but Doctor Hardy was right when he told you to cut out the redeye.

EDMUND

Oh, I'm going to after he hands me the bad news this afternoon. A few before then won't make any difference.

JAMIE

Hesitates—then slowly.

I'm glad you've got your mind prepared for bad news. It won't be such a jolt.

He catches Edmund staring at him.

I mean, it's a cinch you're really sick, and it would be wrong dope to kid yourself.

EDMUND

Disturbed.

I'm not. I know how rotten I feel, and the fever and chills I get at night are no joke. I think Doctor Hardy's last guess was right. It must be the damned malaria come back on me.

JAMIE

Maybe, but don't be too sure.

EDMUND
Why? What do you think it is?

JAMIE
Hell, how would I know? I'm no Doc.
Abruptly.
Where's Mama?

EDMUND
Upstairs.

JAMIE
Looks at him sharply.
When did she go up?

EDMUND
Oh, about the time I came down to the hedge, I guess. She said she was going to take a nap.

JAMIE
You didn't tell me—

EDMUND
Defensively.
Why should I? What about it? She was tired out. She didn't get much sleep last night.

JAMIE
I know she didn't.
A pause. The brothers avoid looking at each other.

EDMUND
That damned foghorn kept me awake, too.
Another pause.

JAMIE
She's been upstairs alone all morning, eh? You haven't seen her?

EDMUND
No. I've been reading here. I wanted to give her a chance to sleep.

JAMIE
Is she coming down to lunch?

EDMUND
Of course.

JAMIE
Dryly.
No of course about it. She might not want any lunch. Or she might start having most of her meals alone upstairs. That's happened, hasn't it?

EDMUND
With frightened resentment.
Cut it out, Jamie! Can't you think anything but—?
Persuasively.
You're all wrong to suspect anything. Cathleen saw her not long ago. Mama didn't tell her she wouldn't be down to lunch.

JAMIE
Then she wasn't taking a nap?

EDMUND
Not right then, but she was lying down, Cathleen said.

JAMIE
In the spare room?

EDMUND
Yes. For Pete's sake, what of it?

JAMIE
Bursts out.
You damned fool! Why did you leave her alone so long? Why didn't you stick around?

EDMUND
Because she accused me—and you and Papa—of spying on her all the time and not trusting her. She made me feel ashamed. I know how rotten it must be for her. And she promised on her sacred word of honor—

JAMIE

With a bitter weariness.

You ought to know that doesn't mean anything.

EDMUND

It does this time!

JAMIE

That's what we thought the other times.

He leans over the table to give his brother's arm an affectionate grasp.

Listen, Kid, I know you think I'm a cynical bastard, but remember I've seen a lot more of this game than you have. You never knew what was really wrong until you were in prep school. Papa and I kept it from you. But I was wise ten years or more before we had to tell you. I know the game backwards and I've been thinking all morning of the way she acted last night when she thought we were asleep. I haven't been able to think of anything else. And now you tell me she got you to leave her alone upstairs all morning.

EDMUND

She didn't! You're crazy!

JAMIE

Placatingly.

All right, Kid. Don't start a battle with me. I hope as much as you do I'm crazy. I've been as happy as hell because I'd really begun to believe that this time—

He stops—looking through the front parlor toward the hall—lowering his voice, hurriedly.

She's coming downstairs. You win on that. I guess I'm a damned suspicious louse.

They grow tense with a hopeful, fearful expectancy. Jamie mutters.

Damn! I wish I'd grabbed another drink.

EDMUND

Me, too.

He coughs nervously and this brings on a real fit of coughing. Jamie glances at him with worried pity. Mary enters from the front parlor. At first one notices no change except that she appears to be less nervous, to be more as she was when we first saw her after breakfast, but then one becomes aware that her eyes are brighter, and there is a peculiar detachment in her voice and manner, as if she were a little withdrawn from her words and actions.

MARY

Goes worriedly to Edmund and puts her arm around him.
You mustn't cough like that. It's bad for your throat. You don't want to get a sore throat on top of your cold.
She kisses him. He stops coughing and gives her a quick apprehensive glance, but if his suspicions are aroused her tenderness makes him renounce them and he believes what he wants to believe for the moment. On the other hand, Jamie knows after one probing look at her that his suspicions are justified. His eyes fall to stare at the floor, his face sets in an expression of embittered, defensive cynicism. Mary goes on, half sitting on the arm of Edmund's chair, her arm around him, so her face is above and behind his and he cannot look into her eyes.
But I seem to be always picking on you, telling you don't do this and don't do that. Forgive me, dear. It's just that I want to take care of you.

EDMUND

I know, Mama. How about you? Do you feel rested?

MARY

Yes, ever so much better. I've been lying down ever since you went out. It's what I needed after such a restless night. I don't feel nervous now.

EDMUND

That's fine.
He pats her hand on his shoulder. Jamie gives him a strange, almost contemptuous glance, wondering if his brother can really mean this. Edmund does not notice but his mother does.

MARY

In a forced teasing tone.
Good heavens, how down in the mouth you look, Jamie. What's the matter now?

JAMIE
Without looking at her.
Nothing.

MARY
Oh, I'd forgotten you've been working on the front hedge. That accounts for your sinking into the dumps, doesn't it?

JAMIE
If you want to think so, Mama.

MARY
Keeping her tone.
Well, that's the effect it always has, isn't it? What a big baby you are! Isn't he, Edmund?

EDMUND
He's certainly a fool to care what anyone thinks.

MARY
Strangely.
Yes, the only way is to make yourself not care.
She catches Jamie giving her a bitter glance and changes the subject.
Where is your father? I heard Cathleen call him.

EDMUND
Gabbing with old Captain Turner, Jamie says. He'll be late, as usual.
Jamie gets up and goes to the windows at right, glad of an excuse to turn his back.

MARY
I've told Cathleen time and again she must go wherever he is and tell him. The idea of screaming as if this were a cheap boardinghouse!

JAMIE
Looking out the window.
She's down there now.
Sneeringly.
Interrupting the famous Beautiful Voice! She should have more respect.

MARY

Sharply—letting her resentment toward him come out.

It's you who should have more respect! Stop sneering at your father! I won't have it! You ought to be proud you're his son! He may have his faults. Who hasn't? But he's worked hard all his life. He made his way up from ignorance and poverty to the top of his profession! Everyone else admires him and you should be the last one to sneer— you, who, thanks to him, have never had to work hard in your life! *Stung, Jamie has turned to stare at her with accusing antagonism. Her eyes waver guiltily and she adds in a tone which begins to placate.* Remember your father is getting old, Jamie. You really ought to show more consideration.

JAMIE

I ought to?

EDMUND

Uneasily.

Oh, dry up, Jamie!

Jamie looks out the window again.

And, for Pete's sake, Mama, why jump on Jamie all of a sudden?

MARY

Bitterly.

Because he's always sneering at someone else, always looking for the worst weakness in everyone.

Then with a strange, abrupt change to a detached, impersonal tone.

But I suppose life has made him like that, and he can't help it. None of us can help the things life has done to us. They're done before you realize it, and once they're done they make you do other things until at last everything comes between you and what you'd like to be, and you've lost your true self forever.

Edmund is made apprehensive by her strangeness. He tries to look up in her eyes but she keeps them averted. Jamie turns to her—then looks quickly out of the window again.

JAMIE

Dully.

I'm hungry. I wish the Old Man would get a move on. It's a rotten trick the way he keeps meals waiting, and then beefs because they're spoiled.

MARY

With a resentment that has a quality of being automatic and on the surface while inwardly she is indifferent.

Yes, it's very trying, Jamie. You don't know how trying. You don't have to keep house with summer servants who don't care because they know it isn't a permanent position. The really good servants are all with people who have homes and not merely summer places. And your father won't even pay the wages the best summer help ask. So every year I have stupid, lazy greenhorns to deal with. But you've heard me say this a thousand times. So has he, but it goes in one ear and out the other. He thinks money spent on a home is money wasted. He's lived too much in hotels. Never the best hotels, of course. Second-rate hotels. He doesn't understand a home. He doesn't feel at home in it. And yet, he wants a home. He's even proud of having this shabby place. He loves it here.

She laughs—a hopeless and yet amused laugh.

It's really funny, when you come to think of it. He's a peculiar man.

EDMUND

Again attempting uneasily to look up in her eyes.

What makes you ramble on like that, Mama?

MARY

Quickly casual—patting his cheek.

Why, nothing in particular, dear. It *is* foolish.

As she speaks, Cathleen enters from the back parlor.

CATHLEEN

Volubly.

Lunch is ready, Ma'am, I went down to Mister Tyrone, like you ordered, and he said he'd come right away, but he kept on talking to that man, telling him of the time when—

MARY

Indifferently.

All right, Cathleen. Tell Bridget I'm sorry but she'll have to wait a few minutes until Mister Tyrone is here.

Cathleen mutters, "Yes, Ma'am," and goes off through the back parlor, grumbling to herself.

JAMIE

Damn it! Why don't you go ahead without him? He's told us to.

MARY

With a remote, amused smile.

He doesn't mean it. Don't you know your father yet? He'd be so terribly hurt.

EDMUND

Jumps up — as if he was glad of an excuse to leave.

I'll make him get a move on.

He goes out on the side porch. A moment later he is heard calling from the porch exasperatedly.

Hey! Papa! Come on! We can't wait all day!

Mary has risen from the arm of the chair. Her hands play restlessly over the table top. She does not look at Jamie but she feels the cynically appraising glance he gives her face and hands.

MARY

Tensely.

Why do you stare like that?

JAMIE

You know.

He turns back to the window.

MARY

I don't know.

JAMIE

Oh, for God's sake, do you think you can fool me, Mama? I'm not blind.

MARY

Looks directly at him now, her face set again in an expression of blank, stubborn denial.

I don't know what you're talking about.

JAMIE

No? Take a look at your eyes in the mirror!

EDMUND

Coming in from the porch.

I got Papa moving. He'll be here in a minute.

With a glance from one to the other, which his mother avoids—uneasily.

What's happened? What's the matter, Mama?

MARY

Disturbed by his coming, gives way to a flurry of guilty, nervous excitement.

Your brother ought to be ashamed of himself. He's been insinuating I don't know what.

EDMUND

Turns on Jamie.

God damn you!

He takes a threatening step toward him. Jamie turns his back with a shrug and looks out the window.

MARY

More upset, grabs Edmund's arm—excitedly.

Stop this at once, do you hear me? How dare you use such language before me!

Abruptly her tone and manner change to the strange detachment she has shown before.

It's wrong to blame your brother. He can't help being what the past has made him. Any more than your father can. Or you. Or I.

EDMUND

Frightenedly—with a desperate hoping against hope.

He's a liar! It's a lie, isn't it, Mama?

MARY

Keeping her eyes averted.

What is a lie? Now you're talking in riddles like Jamie.

Then her eyes meet his stricken, accusing look. She stammers.

Edmund! Don't!

She looks away and her manner instantly regains the quality of strange detachment—calmly.

There's your father coming up the steps now. I must tell Bridget.

She goes through the back parlor. Edmund moves slowly to his chair. He looks sick and hopeless.

JAMIE

From the window, without looking around.

Well?

EDMUND

Refusing to admit anything to his brother yet—weakly defiant.

Well, what? You're a liar.

Jamie again shrugs his shoulders. The screen door on the front porch is heard closing. Edmund says dully.

Here's Papa. I hope he loosens up with the old bottle.

Tyrone comes in through the front parlor. He is putting on his coat.

TYRONE

Sorry I'm late. Captain Turner stopped to talk and once he starts gabbing you can't get away from him.

JAMIE

Without turning—dryly.

You mean once he starts listening.

His father regards him with dislike. He comes to the table with a quick measuring look at the bottle of whiskey. Without turning, Jamie senses this.

It's all right. The level in the bottle hasn't changed.

TYRONE

I wasn't noticing that.

He adds caustically.

As if it proved anything with you around. I'm on to your tricks.

67

EDMUND

Dully.

Did I hear you say, let's all have a drink?

TYRONE

Frowns at him.

Jamie is welcome after his hard morning's work, but I won't invite you. Doctor Hardy—

EDMUND

To hell with Doctor Hardy! One isn't going to kill me. I feel—all in, Papa.

TYRONE

With a worried look at him—putting on a fake heartiness.

Come along, then. It's before a meal and I've always found that good whiskey, taken in moderation as an appetizer, is the best of tonics.

Edmund gets up as his father passes the bottle to him. He pours a big drink. Tyrone frowns admonishingly.

I said, in moderation.

He pours his own drink and passes the bottle to Jamie, grumbling.

It'd be a waste of breath mentioning moderation to you.

Ignoring the hint, Jamie pours a big drink. His father scowls—then, giving it up, resumes his hearty air, raising his glass.

Well, here's health and happiness!

Edmund gives a bitter laugh.

EDMUND

That's a joke!

TYRONE

What is?

EDMUND

Nothing. Here's how.

They drink.

TYRONE

Becoming aware of the atmosphere.

What's the matter here? There's gloom in the air you could cut with a knife.

Turns on Jamie resentfully.

You got the drink you were after, didn't you? Why are you wearing that gloomy look on your mug?

JAMIE

Shrugging his shoulders.

You won't be singing a song yourself soon.

EDMUND

Shut up, Jamie.

TYRONE

Uneasy now—changing the subject.

I thought lunch was ready. I'm hungry as a hunter. Where is your mother?

MARY

Returning through the back parlor, calls.

Here I am.

She comes in. She is excited and self-conscious. As she talks, she glances everywhere except at any of their faces.

I've had to calm down Bridget. She's in a tantrum over your being late again, and I don't blame her. If your lunch is dried up from waiting in the oven, she said it served you right, you could like it or leave it for all she cared.

With increasing excitement.

Oh, I'm so sick and tired of pretending this is a home! You won't help me! You won't put yourself out the least bit! You don't know how to act in a home! You don't really want one! You never have wanted one—never since the day we were married! You should have remained a bachelor and lived in second-rate hotels and entertained your friends in barrooms!

She adds strangely, as if she were now talking aloud to herself rather than to Tyrone.

Then nothing would ever have happened.

They stare at her. Tyrone knows now. He suddenly looks a tired, bitterly sad old man. Edmund glances at his father and sees that he knows, but he still cannot help trying to warn his mother.

EDMUND

Mama! Stop talking. Why don't we go in to lunch.

MARY

Starts and at once the quality of unnatural detachment settles on her face again. She even smiles with an ironical amusement to herself.

Yes, it is inconsiderate of me to dig up the past, when I know your father and Jamie must be hungry.

Putting her arm around Edmund's shoulder—with a fond solicitude which is at the same time remote.

I do hope you have an appetite, dear. You really must eat more.

Her eyes become fixed on the whiskey glass on the table beside him—sharply.

Why is that glass there? Did you take a drink? Oh, how can you be such a fool? Don't you know it's the worst thing?

She turns on Tyrone.

You're to blame, James. How could you let him? Do you want to kill him? Don't you remember my father? He wouldn't stop after he was stricken. He said doctors were fools! He thought, like you, that whiskey is a good tonic!

A look of terror comes into her eyes and she stammers.

But, of course, there's no comparison at all. I don't know why I— Forgive me for scolding you, James. One small drink won't hurt Edmund. It might be good for him, if it gives him an appetite.

She pats Edmund's cheek playfully, the strange detachment again in her manner. He jerks his head away. She seems not to notice, but she moves instinctively away.

JAMIE

Roughly, to hide his tense nerves.

For God's sake, let's eat. I've been working in the damned dirt under the hedge all morning. I've earned my grub.

He comes around in back of his father, not looking at his mother, and grabs Edmund's shoulder.

Come on, Kid. Let's put on the feed bag.

Edmund gets up, keeping his eyes averted from his mother. They pass her, heading for the back parlor.

TYRONE
Dully.
Yes, you go in with your mother, lads. I'll join you in a second.
But they keep on without waiting for her. She looks at their backs with a helpless hurt and, as they enter the back parlor, starts to follow them. Tyrone's eyes are on her, sad and condemning. She feels them and turns sharply without meeting his stare.

MARY
Why do you look at me like that?
Her hands flutter up to pat her hair.
Is it my hair coming down? I was so worn out from last night. I thought I'd better lie down this morning. I drowsed off and had a nice refreshing nap. But I'm sure I fixed my hair again when I woke up.
Forcing a laugh.
Although, as usual, I couldn't find my glasses.
Sharply.
Please stop staring! One would think you were accusing me—
Then pleadingly.
James! You don't understand!

TYRONE
With dull anger.
I understand that I've been a God-damned fool to believe in you!
He walks away from her to pour himself a big drink.

MARY
Her face again sets in stubborn defiance.
I don't know what you mean by "believing in me." All I've felt was distrust and spying and suspicion.
Then accusingly.
Why are you having another drink? You never have more than one before lunch.
Bitterly.

I know what to expect. You will be drunk tonight. Well, it won't be the first time, will it—or the thousandth?

Again she bursts out pleadingly.

Oh, James, please! You don't understand! I'm so worried about Edmund! I'm so afraid he—

TYRONE

I don't want to listen to your excuses, Mary.

MARY

Strickenly.

Excuses? You mean— ? Oh, you can't believe that of me! You mustn't believe that, James!

Then slipping away into her strange detachment—quite casually.

Shall we not go into lunch, dear? I don't want anything but I know you're hungry.

He walks slowly to where she stands in the doorway. He walks like an old man. As he reaches her she bursts out piteously.

James! I tried so hard! I tried so hard! Please believe—!

TYRONE

Moved in spite of himself—helplessly.

I suppose you did, Mary.

Then grief-strickenly.

For the love of God, why couldn't you have the strength to keep on?

MARY

Her face setting into that stubborn denial again.

I don't know what you're talking about. Have the strength to keep on what?

TYRONE

Hopelessly.

Never mind. It's no use now.

He moves on and she keeps beside him as they disappear in the back parlor.

CURTAIN

Act Two, Scene Two

SCENE

The same, about a half hour later. The tray with the bottle of whiskey has been removed from the table. The family are returning from lunch as the curtain rises. Mary is the first to enter from the back parlor. Her husband follows. He is not with her as he was in the similar entrance after breakfast at the opening of Act One. He avoids touching her or looking at her. There is condemnation in his face, mingled now with the beginning of an old weary, helpless resignation. Jamie and Edmund follow their father. Jamie's face is hard with defensive cynicism. Edmund tries to copy this defense but without success. He plainly shows he is heartsick as well as physically ill.

Mary is terribly nervous again, as if the strain of sitting through lunch with them had been too much for her. Yet at the same time, in contrast to this, her expression shows more of that strange aloofness which seems to stand apart from her nerves and the anxieties which harry them.

She is talking as she enters—a stream of words that issues casually, in a routine of family conversation, from her mouth. She appears indifferent to the fact that their thoughts are not on what she is saying any more than her own are. As she talks, she comes to the left of the table and stands, facing front, one hand fumbling with the bosom of her dress, the other playing over the table top. Tyrone lights a cigar and goes to the screen door, staring out. Jamie fills a pipe from a jar on top of the bookcase at rear. He lights it as he goes to look out the window at right. Edmund sits in a chair by the table, turned half away from his mother so he does not have to watch her.

MARY

It's no use finding fault with Bridget. She doesn't listen. I can't

73

threaten her, or she'd threaten she'd leave. And she does do her best at times. It's too bad they seem to be just the times you're sure to be late, James. Well, there's this consolation: it's difficult to tell from her cooking whether she's doing her best or her worst.

She gives a little laugh of detached amusement—indifferently.

Never mind. The summer will soon be over, thank goodness. Your season will open again and we can go back to second-rate hotels and trains. I hate them, too, but at least I don't expect them to be like a home, and there's no housekeeping to worry about. It's unreasonable to expect Bridget or Cathleen to act as if this was a home. They know it isn't as well as we know it. It never has been and it never will be.

TYRONE

Bitterly without turning around.

No, it never can be now. But it was once, before you—

MARY

Her face instantly set in blank denial.

Before I what?

There is a dead silence. She goes on with a return of her detached air.

No, no. Whatever you mean, it isn't true, dear. It was never a home. You've always preferred the Club or a barroom. And for me it's always been as lonely as a dirty room in a one-night stand hotel. In a real home one is never lonely. You forget I know from experience what a home is like. I gave up one to marry you—my father's home.

At once, through an association of ideas she turns to Edmund. Her manner becomes tenderly solicitous, but there is the strange quality of detachment in it.

I'm worried about you, Edmund. You hardly touched a thing at lunch. That's no way to take care of yourself. It's all right for me not to have an appetite. I've been growing too fat. But you must eat.

Coaxingly maternal.

Promise me you will, dear, for my sake.

EDMUND

Dully.

Yes, Mama.

MARY
Pats his cheek as he tries not to shrink away.
That's a good boy.
There is another pause of dead silence. Then the telephone in the front hall rings and all of them stiffen startledly.

TYRONE
Hastily.
I'll answer. McGuire said he'd call me.
He goes out through the front parlor.

MARY
Indifferently.
McGuire. He must have another piece of property on his list that no one would think of buying except your father. It doesn't matter any more, but it's always seemed to me your father could afford to keep on buying property but never to give me a home.
She stops to listen as Tyrone's voice is heard from the hall.

TYRONE
Hello.
With forced heartiness.
Oh, how are you, Doctor?
Jamie turns from the window. Mary's fingers play more rapidly on the table top. Tyrone's voice, trying to conceal, reveals that he is hearing bad news.
I see—
Hurriedly.
Well, you'll explain all about it when you see him this afternoon. Yes, he'll be in without fail. Four o'clock. I'll drop in myself and have a talk with you before that. I have to go uptown on business, anyway. Goodbye, Doctor.

EDMUND
Dully.
That didn't sound like glad tidings.
Jamie gives him a pitying glance—then looks out the window again. Mary's face is terrified and her hands flutter distractedly. Tyrone comes in. The strain is obvious in his casualness as he addresses Edmund.

TYRONE

It was Doctor Hardy. He wants you to be sure and see him at four.

EDMUND

Dully.

What did he say? Not that I give a damn now.

MARY

Bursts out excitedly.

I wouldn't believe him if he swore on a stack of Bibles. You mustn't pay attention to a word he says, Edmund.

TYRONE

Sharply.

Mary!

MARY

More excitedly.

Oh, we all realize why you like him, James! Because he's cheap! But please don't try to tell me! I know all about Doctor Hardy. Heaven knows I ought to after all these years. He's an ignorant fool! There should be a law to keep men like him from practicing. He hasn't the slightest idea— When you're in agony and half insane, he sits and holds your hand and delivers sermons on will power!

Her face is drawn in an expression of intense suffering by the memory. For the moment, she loses all caution. With bitter hatred.

He deliberately humiliates you! He makes you beg and plead! He treats you like a criminal! He understands nothing! And yet it was exactly the same type of cheap quack who first gave you the medicine—and you never knew what it was until too late!

Passionately.

I hate doctors! They'll do anything—anything to keep you coming to them. They'll sell their souls! What's worse, they'll sell yours, and you never know it till one day you find yourself in hell!

EDMUND

Mama! For God's sake, stop talking.

TYRONE
Shakenly.
Yes, Mary, it's no time—

MARY
Suddenly is overcome by guilty confusion—stammers.
I— Forgive me, dear. You're right. It's useless to be angry now.
There is again a pause of dead silence. When she speaks again, her face has cleared and is calm, and the quality of uncanny detachment is in her voice and manner.
I'm going upstairs for a moment, if you'll excuse me. I have to fix my hair.
She adds smilingly.
That is if I can find my glasses. I'll be right down.

TYRONE
As she starts through the doorway—pleading and rebuking.
Mary!

MARY
Turns to stare at him calmly.
Yes, dear? What is it?

TYRONE
Helplessly.
Nothing.

MARY
With a strange derisive smile.
You're welcome to come up and watch me if you're so suspicious.

TYRONE
As if that could do any good! You'd only postpone it. And I'm not your jailor. This isn't a prison.

MARY
No. I know you can't help thinking it's a home.
She adds quickly with a detached contrition.
I'm sorry, dear. I don't mean to be bitter. It's not your fault.
She turns and disappears through the back parlor. The three in the

room remain silent. It is as if they were waiting until she got upstairs before speaking.

JAMIE
Cynically brutal.
Another shot in the arm!

EDMUND
Angrily.
Cut out that kind of talk!

TYRONE
Yes! Hold your foul tongue and your rotten Broadway loafer's lingo! Have you no pity or decency?
Losing his temper.
You ought to be kicked out in the gutter! But if I did it, you know damned well who'd weep and plead for you, and excuse you and complain till I let you come back.

JAMIE
A spasm of pain crosses his face.
Christ, don't I know that? No pity? I have all the pity in the world for her. I understand what a hard game to beat she's up against—which is more than you ever have! My lingo didn't mean I had no feeling. I was merely putting bluntly what we all know, and have to live with now, again.
Bitterly.
The cures are no damned good except for a while. The truth is there is no cure and we've been saps to hope—
Cynically.
They never come back!

EDMUND
Scornfully parodying his brother's cynicism.
They never come back! Everything is in the bag! It's all a frame-up! We're all fall guys and suckers and we can't beat the game!
Disdainfully.
Christ, if I felt the way you do—!

JAMIE

Stung for a moment—then shrugging his shoulders, dryly.

I thought you did. Your poetry isn't very cheery. Nor the stuff you read and claim you admire.

He indicates the small bookcase at rear.

Your pet with the unpronounceable name, for example.

EDMUND

Nietzsche. You don't know what you're talking about. You haven't read him.

JAMIE

Enough to know it's a lot of bunk!

TYRONE

Shut up, both of you! There's little choice between the philosophy you learned from Broadway loafers, and the one Edmund got from his books. They're both rotten to the core. You've both flouted the faith you were born and brought up in—the one true faith of the Catholic Church—and your denial has brought nothing but self-destruction!

His two sons stare at him contemptuously. They forget their quarrel and are as one against him on this issue.

EDMUND

That's the bunk, Papa!

JAMIE

We don't pretend, at any rate.

Caustically.

I don't notice you've worn any holes in the knees of your pants going to Mass.

TYRONE

It's true I'm a bad Catholic in the observance, God forgive me. But I believe!

Angrily.

And you're a liar! I may not go to church but every night and morning of my life I get on my knees and pray!

EDMUND
Bitingly.
Did you pray for Mama?

TYRONE
I did. I've prayed to God these many years for her.

EDMUND
Then Nietzsche must be right.
He quotes from Thus Spake Zarathustra.
"God is dead: of His pity for man hath God died."

TYRONE
Ignores this.
If your mother had prayed, too— She hasn't denied her faith, but
she's forgotten it, until now there's no strength of the spirit left in
her to fight against her curse.
Then dully resigned.
But what's the good of talk? We've lived with this before and now
we must again. There's no help for it.
Bitterly.
Only I wish she hadn't led me to hope this time. By God, I never
will again!

EDMUND
That's a rotten thing to say, Papa!
Defiantly.
Well, I'll hope! She's just started. It can't have got a hold on her yet.
She can still stop. I'm going to talk to her.

JAMIE
Shrugs his shoulders.
You can't talk to her now. She'll listen but she won't listen. She'll be
here but she won't be here. You know the way she gets.

TYRONE
Yes, that's the way the poison acts on her always. Every day from
now on, there'll be the same drifting away from us until by the end
of each night—

EDMUND

Miserably.

Cut it out, Papa!

He jumps up from his chair.

I'm going to get dressed.

Bitterly, as he goes.

I'll make so much noise she can't suspect I've come to spy on her.

He disappears through the front parlor and can be heard stamping noisily upstairs.

JAMIE

After a pause.

What did Doc Hardy say about the Kid?

TYRONE

Dully.

It's what you thought. He's got consumption.

JAMIE

God damn it!

TYRONE

There is no possible doubt, he said.

JAMIE

He'll have to go to a sanatorium.

TYRONE

Yes, and the sooner the better, Hardy said, for him and everyone around him. He claims that in six months to a year Edmund will be cured, if he obeys orders.

He sighs—gloomily and resentfully.

I never thought a child of mine—It doesn't come from my side of the family. There wasn't one of us that didn't have lungs as strong as an ox.

JAMIE

Who gives a damn about that part of it! Where does Hardy want to send him?

TYRONE

That's what I'm to see him about.

JAMIE

Well, for God's sake, pick out a good place and not some cheap dump!

TYRONE

Stung.

I'll send him wherever Hardy thinks best!

JAMIE

Well, don't give Hardy your old over-the-hills-to-the-poorhouse song about taxes and mortgages.

TYRONE

I'm no millionaire who can throw money away! Why shouldn't I tell Hardy the truth?

JAMIE

Because he'll think you want him to pick a cheap dump, and because he'll know it isn't the truth—especially if he hears afterwards you've seen McGuire and let that flannel-mouth, gold-brick merchant sting you with another piece of bum property!

TYRONE

Furiously.

Keep your nose out of my business!

JAMIE

This is Edmund's business. What I'm afraid of is, with your Irish bog-trotter idea that consumption is fatal, you'll figure it would be a waste of money to spend any more than you can help.

TYRONE

You liar!

JAMIE

All right. Prove I'm a liar. That's what I want. That's why I brought it up.

TYRONE

His rage still smouldering.

I have every hope Edmund will be cured. And keep your dirty tongue off Ireland! You're a fine one to sneer, with the map of it on your face!

JAMIE

Not after I wash my face.

Then before his father can react to this insult to the Old Sod, he adds dryly, shrugging his shoulders.

Well, I've said all I have to say. It's up to you.

Abruptly.

What do you want me to do this afternoon, now you're going uptown? I've done all I can do on the hedge until you cut more of it. You don't want me to go ahead with your clipping, I know that.

TYRONE

No. You'd get it crooked, as you get everything else.

JAMIE

Then I'd better go uptown with Edmund. The bad news coming on top of what's happened to Mama may hit him hard.

TYRONE

Forgetting his quarrel.

Yes, go with him, Jamie. Keep up his spirits, if you can.

He adds caustically.

If you can without making it an excuse to get drunk!

JAMIE

What would I use for money? The last I heard they were still selling booze, not giving it away.

He starts for the front-parlor doorway.

I'll get dressed.

He stops in the doorway as he sees his mother approaching from the hall, and moves aside to let her come in. Her eyes look brighter, and her manner is more detached. This change becomes more marked as the scene goes on.

MARY

Vaguely.

You haven't seen my glasses anywhere, have you, Jamie?

She doesn't look at him. He glances away, ignoring her question but she doesn't seem to expect an answer. She comes forward, addressing her husband without looking at him.

You haven't seen them, have you, James?

Behind her Jamie disappears through the front parlor.

TYRONE

Turns to look out the screen door.

No, Mary.

MARY

What's the matter with Jamie? Have you been nagging at him again? You shouldn't treat him with such contempt all the time. He's not to blame. If he'd been brought up in a real home, I'm sure he would have been different.

She comes to the windows at right—lightly.

You're not much of a weather prophet, dear. See how hazy it's getting. I can hardly see the other shore.

TYRONE

Trying to speak naturally.

Yes, I spoke too soon. We're in for another night of fog, I'm afraid.

MARY

Oh, well, I won't mind it tonight.

TYRONE

No, I don't imagine you will, Mary.

MARY

Flashes a glance at him—after a pause.

I don't see Jamie going down to the hedge. Where did he go?

TYRONE

He's going with Edmund to the Doctor's. He went up to change his clothes.

Then, glad of an excuse to leave her.

I'd better do the same or I'll be late for my appointment at the Club. *He makes a move toward the front-parlor doorway, but with a swift impulsive movement she reaches out and clasps his arm.*

MARY
A note of pleading in her voice.
Don't go yet, dear. I don't want to be alone.
Hastily.
I mean, you have plenty of time. You know you boast you can dress in one-tenth the time it takes the boys.
Vaguely.
There is something I wanted to say. What is it? I've forgotten. I'm glad Jamie is going uptown. You didn't give him any money, I hope.

TYRONE
I did not.

MARY
He'd only spend it on drink and you know what a vile, poisonous tongue he has when he's drunk. Not that I would mind anything he said tonight, but he always manages to drive you into a rage, especially if you're drunk, too, as you will be.

TYRONE
Resentfully.
I won't. I never get drunk.

MARY
Teasing indifferently.
Oh, I'm sure you'll hold it well. You always have. It's hard for a stranger to tell, but after thirty-five years of marriage—

TYRONE
I've never missed a performance in my life. That's the proof!
Then bitterly.
If I did get drunk it is not you who should blame me. No man has ever had a better reason.

MARY
Reason? What reason? You always drink too much when you go to

85

the Club, don't you? Particularly when you meet McGuire. He sees to that. Don't think I'm finding fault, dear. You must do as you please. I won't mind.

TYRONE

I know you won't.
He turns toward the front parlor, anxious to escape.
I've got to get dressed.

MARY

Again she reaches out and grasps his arm—pleadingly.
No, please wait a little while, dear. At least, until one of the boys comes down. You will all be leaving me so soon.

TYRONE

With bitter sadness.
It's you who are leaving us, Mary.

MARY

I? That's a silly thing to say, James. How could I leave? There is no-where I could go. Who would I go to see? I have no friends.

TYRONE

It's your own fault—
He stops and sighs helplessly—persuasively.
There's surely one thing you can do this afternoon that will be good for you, Mary. Take a drive in the automobile. Get away from the house. Get a little sun and fresh air.
Injuredly.
I bought the automobile for you. You know I don't like the damned things. I'd rather walk any day, or take a trolley.
With growing resentment.
I had it here waiting for you when you came back from the sana-torium. I hoped it would give you pleasure and distract your mind. You used to ride in it every day, but you've hardly used it at all lately. I paid a lot of money I couldn't afford, and there's the chauffeur I have to board and lodge and pay high wages whether he drives you or not.
Bitterly.

Waste! The same old waste that will land me in the poorhouse in my old age! What good did it do you? I might as well have thrown the money out the window.

MARY
With detached calm.
Yes, it was a waste of money, James. You shouldn't have bought a secondhand automobile. You were swindled again as you always are, because you insist on secondhand bargains in everything.

TYRONE
It's one of the best makes! Everyone says it's better than any of the new ones!

MARY
Ignoring this.
It was another waste to hire Smythe, who was only a helper in a garage and had never been a chauffeur. Oh, I realize his wages are less than a real chauffeur's, but he more than makes up for that, I'm sure, by the graft he gets from the garage on repair bills. Something is always wrong. Smythe sees to that, I'm afraid.

TYRONE
I don't believe it! He may not be a fancy millionaire's flunky but he's honest! You're as bad as Jamie, suspecting everyone!

MARY
You mustn't be offended, dear. I wasn't offended when you gave me the automobile. I knew you didn't mean to humiliate me. I knew that was the way you had to do everything. I was grateful and touched. I knew buying the car was a hard thing for you to do, and it proved how much you loved me, in your way, especially when you couldn't really believe it would do me any good.

TYRONE
Mary!
He suddenly hugs her to him — brokenly.
Dear Mary! For the love of God, for my sake and the boys' sake and your own, won't you stop now?

MARY

Stammers in guilty confusion for a second.

I—James! Please!

Her strange, stubborn defense comes back instantly.

Stop what? What are you talking about?

He lets his arm fall to his side brokenly. She impulsively puts her arm around him.

James! We've loved each other! We always will! Let's remember only that, and not try to understand what we cannot understand, or help things that cannot be helped—the things life has done to us we cannot excuse or explain.

TYRONE

As if he hadn't heard—bitterly.

You won't even try?

MARY

Her arms drop hopelessly and she turns away—with detachment.

Try to go for a drive this afternoon, you mean? Why, yes, if you wish me to, although it makes me feel lonelier than if I stayed here. There is no one I can invite to drive with me, and I never know where to tell Smythe to go. If there was a friend's house where I could drop in and laugh and gossip awhile. But, of course, there isn't. There never has been.

Her manner becoming more and more remote.

At the Convent I had so many friends. Girls whose families lived in lovely homes. I used to visit them and they'd visit me in my father's home. But, naturally, after I married an actor—you know how actors were considered in those days—a lot of them gave me the cold shoulder. And then, right after we were married, there was the scandal of that woman who had been your mistress, suing you. From then on, all my old friends either pitied me or cut me dead. I hated the ones who cut me much less than the pitiers.

TYRONE

With guilty resentment.

For God's sake, don't dig up what's long forgotten. If you're that far gone in the past already, when it's only the beginning of the afternoon, what will you be tonight?

MARY
Stares at him defiantly now.
Come to think of it, I do have to drive uptown. There's something I must get at the drugstore.

TYRONE
Bitterly scornful.
Leave it to you to have some of the stuff hidden, and prescriptions for more! I hope you'll lay in a good stock ahead so we'll never have another night like the one when you screamed for it, and ran out of the house in your nightdress half crazy, to try and throw yourself off the dock!

MARY
Tries to ignore this.
I have to get tooth powder and toilet soap and cold cream—
She breaks down pitiably.
James! You mustn't remember! You mustn't humiliate me so!

TYRONE
Ashamed.
I'm sorry. Forgive me, Mary!

MARY
Defensively detached again.
It doesn't matter. Nothing like that ever happened. You must have dreamed it.
He stares at her hopelessly. Her voice seems to drift farther and farther away.
I was so healthy before Edmund was born. You remember, James. There wasn't a nerve in my body. Even traveling with you season after season, with week after week of one-night stands, in trains without Pullmans, in dirty rooms of filthy hotels, eating bad food, bearing children in hotel rooms, I still kept healthy. But bearing Edmund was the last straw. I was so sick afterwards, and that igno-

rant quack of a cheap hotel doctor—All he knew was I was in pain.
It was easy for him to stop the pain.

TYRONE

Mary! For God's sake, forget the past!

MARY

With strange objective calm.

Why? How can I? The past is the present, isn't it? It's the future,
too. We all try to lie out of that but life won't let us.

Going on.

I blame only myself. I swore after Eugene died I would never have
another baby. I was to blame for his death. If I hadn't left him with
my mother to join you on the road, because you wrote telling me
you missed me and were so lonely, Jamie would never have been
allowed, when he still had measles, to go in the baby's room.

Her face hardening.

I've always believed Jamie did it on purpose. He was jealous of the
baby. He hated him.

As Tyrone starts to protest.

Oh, I know Jamie was only seven, but he was never stupid. He'd
been warned it might kill the baby. He knew. I've never been able
to forgive him for that.

TYRONE

With bitter sadness.

Are you back with Eugene now? Can't you let our dead baby rest in
peace?

MARY

As if she hadn't heard him.

It was my fault. I should have insisted on staying with Eugene and
not have let you persuade me to join you, just because I loved you.
Above all, I shouldn't have let you insist I have another baby to take
Eugene's place, because you thought that would make me forget his
death. I knew from experience by then that children should have
homes to be born in, if they are to be good children, and women
need homes, if they are to be good mothers. I was afraid all the
time I carried Edmund. I knew something terrible would happen. I

knew I'd proved by the way I'd left Eugene that I wasn't worthy to have another baby, and that God would punish me if I did. I never should have borne Edmund.

TYRONE

With an uneasy glance through the front parlor.
Mary! Be careful with your talk. If he heard you he might think you never wanted him. He's feeling bad enough already without—

MARY

Violently.
It's a lie! I did want him! More than anything in the world! You don't understand! I meant, for his sake. He has never been happy. He never will be. Nor healthy. He was born nervous and too sensitive, and that's my fault. And now, ever since he's been so sick I've kept remembering Eugene and my father and I've been so frightened and guilty—
Then, catching herself, with an instant change to stubborn denial.
Oh, I know it's foolish to imagine dreadful things when there's no reason for it. After all, everyone has colds and gets over them.
Tyrone stares at her and sighs helplessly. He turns away toward the front parlor and sees Edmund coming down the stairs in the hall.

TYRONE

Sharply, in a low voice.
Here's Edmund. For God's sake try and be yourself—at least until he goes! You can do that much for him!
He waits, forcing his face into a pleasantly paternal expression. She waits frightenedly, seized again by a nervous panic, her hands fluttering over the bosom of her dress, up to her throat and hair, with a distracted aimlessness. Then, as Edmund approaches the doorway, she cannot face him. She goes swiftly away to the windows at left and stares out with her back to the front parlor. Edmund enters. He has changed to a ready-made blue serge suit, high stiff collar and tie, black shoes.

With an actor's heartiness.
Well! You look spic and span. I'm on my way up to change, too.
He starts to pass him.

EDMUND

Dryly.

Wait a minute, Papa. I hate to bring up disagreeable topics, but there's the matter of carfare. I'm broke.

TYRONE

Starts automatically on a customary lecture.

You'll always be broke until you learn the value—

Checks himself guiltily, looking at his son's sick face with worried pity.

But you've been learning, lad. You worked hard before you took ill. You've done splendidly. I'm proud of you.

He pulls out a small roll of bills from his pants pocket and carefully selects one. Edmund takes it. He glances at it and his face expresses astonishment. His father again reacts customarily—sarcastically.

Thank you.

He quotes.

"How sharper than a serpent's tooth it is—"

EDMUND

"To have a thankless child." I know. Give me a chance, Papa. I'm knocked speechless. This isn't a dollar. It's a ten spot.

TYRONE

Embarrassed by his generosity.

Put it in your pocket. You'll probably meet some of your friends uptown and you can't hold your end up and be sociable with nothing in your jeans.

EDMUND

You meant it? Gosh, thank you, Papa.

He is genuinely pleased and grateful for a moment—then he stares at his father's face with uneasy suspicion.

But why all of a sudden—?

Cynically.

Did Doc Hardy tell you I was going to die?

Then he sees his father is bitterly hurt.

No! That's a rotten crack. I was only kidding, Papa.

He puts an arm around his father impulsively and gives him an affectionate hug.

I'm very grateful. Honest, Papa.

TYRONE
Touched, returns his hug.
You're welcome, lad.

MARY
Suddenly turns to them in a confused panic of frightened anger.
I won't have it!
She stamps her foot.
Do you hear, Edmund! Such morbid nonsense! Saying you're going to die! It's the books you read! Nothing but sadness and death! Your father shouldn't allow you to have them. And some of the poems you've written yourself are even worse! You'd think you didn't want to live! A boy of your age with everything before him! It's just a pose you get out of books! You're not really sick at all!

TYRONE
Mary! Hold your tongue!

MARY
Instantly changing to a detached tone.
But, James, it's absurd of Edmund to be so gloomy and make such a great to-do about nothing.
Turning to Edmund but avoiding his eyes — teasingly affectionate.
Never mind, dear. I'm on to you.
She comes to him.
You want to be petted and spoiled and made a fuss over, isn't that it? You're still such a baby.
She puts her arm around him and hugs him. He remains rigid and un-yielding. Her voice begins to tremble.
But please don't carry it too far, dear. Don't say horrible things. I know it's foolish to take them seriously but I can't help it. You've got me — so frightened.
She breaks and hides her face on his shoulder, sobbing. Edmund is moved in spite of himself. He pats her shoulder with an awkward tenderness.

EDMUND

Don't, mother.

His eyes meet his father's.

TYRONE

Huskily—clutching at hopeless hope.

Maybe if you asked your mother now what you said you were going to—

He fumbles with his watch.

By God, look at the time! I'll have to shake a leg.

He hurries away through the front parlor. Mary lifts her head. Her manner is again one of detached motherly solicitude. She seems to have forgotten the tears which are still in her eyes.

MARY

How do you feel, dear?

She feels his forehead.

Your head is a little hot, but that's just from going out in the sun. You look ever so much better than you did this morning.

Taking his hand.

Come and sit down. You musn't stand on your feet so much. You must learn to husband your strength.

She gets him to sit and she sits sideways on the arm of his chair, an arm around his shoulder, so he cannot meet her eyes.

EDMUND

Starts to blurt out the appeal he now feels is quite hopeless.

Listen, Mama—

MARY

Interrupting quickly.

Now, now! Don't talk. Lean back and rest.

Persuasively.

You know, I think it would be much better for you if you stayed home this afternoon and let me take care of you. It's such a tiring trip uptown in the dirty old trolley on a hot day like this. I'm sure you'd be much better off here with me.

EDMUND
Dully.
You forget I have an appointment with Hardy.
Trying again to get his appeal started.
Listen, Mama—

MARY
Quickly.
You can telephone and say you don't feel well enough.
Excitedly.
It's simply a waste of time and money seeing him. He'll only tell you some lie. He'll pretend he's found something serious the matter because that's his bread and butter.
She gives a hard sneering little laugh.
The old idiot! All he knows about medicine is to look solemn and preach will power!

EDMUND
Trying to catch her eyes.
Mama! Please listen! I want to ask you something! You— You're only just started. You can still stop. You've got the will power! We'll all help you. I'll do anything! Won't you, Mama?

MARY
Stammers pleadingly.
Please don't—talk about things you don't understand!

EDMUND
Dully.
All right, I give up. I knew it was no use.

MARY
In blank denial now.
Anyway, I don't know what you're referring to. But I do know you should be the last one— Right after I returned from the sanatorium, you began to be ill. The doctor there had warned me I must have peace at home with nothing to upset me, and all I've done is worry about you.
Then distractedly.

But that's no excuse! I'm only trying to explain. It's not an excuse!
She hugs him to her—pleadingly.
Promise me, dear, you won't believe I made you an excuse.

EDMUND
Bitterly.
What else can I believe?

MARY
Slowly takes her arm away—her manner remote and objective again.
Yes, I suppose you can't help suspecting that.

EDMUND
Ashamed but still bitter.
What do you expect?

MARY
Nothing, I don't blame you. How could you believe me—when I can't believe myself? I've become such a liar. I never lied about anything once upon a time. Now I have to lie, especially to myself. But how can you understand, when I don't myself. I've never understood anything about it, except that one day long ago I found I could no longer call my soul my own.
She pauses—then lowering her voice to a strange tone of whispered confidence.
But some day, dear, I will find it again—some day when you're all well, and I see you healthy and happy and successful, and I don't have to feel guilty any more—some day when the Blessed Virgin Mary forgives me and gives me back the faith in Her love and pity I used to have in my convent days, and I can pray to Her again—when She sees no one in the world can believe in me even for a moment any more, then She will believe in me, and with Her help it will be so easy. I will hear myself scream with agony, and at the same time I will laugh because I will be so sure of myself.
Then as Edmund remains hopelessly silent, she adds sadly.
Of course, you can't believe that, either.
She rises from the arm of his chair and goes to stare out the windows at right with her back to him—casually.

Now I think of it, you might as well go uptown. I forgot I'm taking a drive. I have to go to the drugstore. You would hardly want to go there with me. You'd be so ashamed.

EDMUND
Brokenly.
Mama! Don't!

MARY
I suppose you'll divide that ten dollars your father gave you with Jamie. You always divide with each other, don't you? Like good sports. Well, I know what he'll do with his share. Get drunk someplace where he can be with the only kind of woman he understands or likes.
She turns to him, pleading frightenedly.
Edmund! Promise me you won't drink! It's so dangerous! You know Doctor Hardy told you—

EDMUND
Bitterly.
I thought he was an old idiot. Anyway, by tonight, what will you care?

MARY
Pitifully.
Edmund!
Jamie's voice is heard from the front hall, "Come on, Kid, let's beat it."
Mary's manner at once becomes detached again.
Go on, Edmund. Jamie's waiting.
She goes to the front-parlor doorway.
There comes your father downstairs, too.
Tyrone's voice calls, "Come on, Edmund."

EDMUND
Jumping up from his chair.
I'm coming.
He stops beside her—without looking at her.
Goodbye, Mama.

MARY

Kisses him with detached affection.

Goodbye, dear. If you're coming home for dinner, try not to be late. And tell your father. You know what Bridget is.

He turns and hurries away. Tyrone calls from the hall, "Goodbye, Mary," and then Jamie, "Goodbye, Mama."

She calls back.

Goodbye.

The front screen door is heard closing after them. She comes and stands by the table, one hand drumming on it, the other fluttering up to pat her hair. She stares about the room with frightened, forsaken eyes and whispers to herself.

It's so lonely here.

Then her face hardens into bitter self-contempt.

You're lying to yourself again. You wanted to get rid of them. Their contempt and disgust aren't pleasant company. You're glad they're gone.

She gives a little despairing laugh.

Then Mother of God, why do I feel so lonely?

CURTAIN

Act Three

The same. It is around half past six in the evening. Dusk is gathering in the living room, an early dusk due to the fog which has rolled in from the Sound and is like a white curtain drawn down outside the windows. From a lighthouse beyond the harbor's mouth, a foghorn is heard at regular intervals, moaning like a mournful whale in labor, and from the harbor itself, intermittently, comes the warning ringing of bells on yachts at anchor.

The tray with the bottle of whiskey, glasses, and pitcher of ice water is on the table, as it was in the pre-luncheon scene of the previous act.

Mary and the second girl, Cathleen, are discovered. The latter is standing at left of table. She holds an empty whiskey glass in her hand as if she'd forgotten she had it. She shows the effects of drink. Her stupid, good-humored face wears a pleased and flattered simper.

Mary is paler than before and her eyes shine with unnatural brilliance. The strange detachment in her manner has intensified. She has hidden deeper within herself and found refuge and release in a dream where present reality is but an appearance to be accepted and dismissed unfeelingly—even with a hard cynicism—or entirely ignored. There is at times an uncanny gay, free youthfulness in her manner, as if in spirit she were released to become again, simply and without self-consciousness, the naive, happy, chattering schoolgirl of her convent days. She wears the dress into which she had changed for her drive to town, a simple, fairly expensive affair, which would be extremely becoming if it were not for the careless, almost slovenly way she wears it. Her hair is no longer fastidiously in place. It has a slightly disheveled, lopsided look.

She talks to Cathleen with a confiding familiarity, as if the second girl were an old, intimate friend. As the curtain rises, she is standing by the screen door looking out. A moan of the foghorn is heard.

MARY
Amused—girlishly.
That foghorn! Isn't it awful, Cathleen?

CATHLEEN
Talks more familiarly than usual but never with intentional impertinence because she sincerely likes her mistress.
It is indeed, Ma'am. It's like a banshee.

MARY
Goes on as if she hadn't heard. In nearly all the following dialogue there is the feeling that she has Cathleen with her merely as an excuse to keep talking.
I don't mind it tonight. Last night it drove me crazy. I lay awake worrying until I couldn't stand it any more.

CATHLEEN
Bad cess to it. I was scared out of my wits riding back from town. I thought that ugly monkey, Smythe, would drive us in a ditch or against a tree. You couldn't see your hand in front of you. I'm glad you had me sit in back with you, Ma'am. If I'd been in front with that monkey— He can't keep his dirty hands to himself. Give him half a chance and he's pinching me on the leg or you-know-where— asking your pardon, Ma'am, but it's true.

MARY
Dreamily.
It wasn't the fog I minded, Cathleen. I really love fog.

CATHLEEN
They say it's good for the complexion.

MARY
It hides you from the world and the world from you. You feel that everything has changed, and nothing is what it seemed to be. No one can find or touch you any more.

CATHLEEN

I wouldn't care so much if Smythe was a fine, handsome man like some chauffeurs I've seen—I mean, if it was all in fun, for I'm a decent girl. But for a shriveled runt like Smythe—! I've told him, you must think I'm hard up that I'd notice a monkey like you. I've warned him, one day I'll give a clout that'll knock him into next week. And so I will!

MARY

It's the foghorn I hate. It won't let you alone. It keeps reminding you, and warning you, and calling you back.
She smiles strangely.
But it can't tonight. It's just an ugly sound. It doesn't remind me of anything.
She gives a teasing, girlish laugh.
Except, perhaps, Mr. Tyrone's snores. I've always had such fun teasing him about it. He has snored ever since I can remember, especially when he's had too much to drink, and yet he's like a child, he hates to admit it.
She laughs, coming to the table.
Well, I suppose I snore at times, too, and I don't like to admit it. So I have no right to make fun of him, have I?
She sits in the rocker at right of table.

CATHLEEN

Ah, sure, everybody healthy snores. It's a sign of sanity, they say.
Then, worriedly.
What time is it, Ma'am? I ought to go back in the kitchen. The damp is in Bridget's rheumatism and she's like a raging divil. She'll bite my head off.
She puts her glass on the table and makes a movement toward the back parlor.

MARY

With a flash of apprehension.
No, don't go, Cathleen. I don't want to be alone, yet.

CATHLEEN

You won't be for long. The Master and the boys will be home soon.

MARY

I doubt if they'll come back for dinner. They have too good an excuse to remain in the barrooms where they feel at home.
Cathleen stares at her, stupidly puzzled. Mary goes on smilingly.
Don't worry about Bridget. I'll tell her I kept you with me, and you
can take a big drink of whiskey to her when you go. She won't mind
then.

CATHLEEN

Grins—at her ease again.
No, Ma'am. That's the one thing can make her cheerful. She loves
her drop.

MARY

Have another drink yourself, if you wish, Cathleen.

CATHLEEN

I don't know if I'd better, Ma'am. I can feel what I've had already.
Reaching for the bottle.
Well, maybe one more won't harm.
She pours a drink.
Here's your good health, Ma'am.
She drinks without bothering about a chaser.

MARY

Dreamily.
I really did have good health once, Cathleen. But that was long ago.

CATHLEEN

Worried again.
The Master's sure to notice what's gone from the bottle. He has the
eye of a hawk for that.

MARY

Amusedly.
Oh, we'll play Jamie's trick on him. Just measure a few drinks of
water and pour them in.

CATHLEEN

Does this — with a silly giggle.

God save me, it'll be half water. He'll know by the taste.

MARY

Indifferently.

No, by the time he comes home he'll be too drunk to tell the difference. He has such a good excuse, he believes, to drown his sorrows.

CATHLEEN

Philosophically.

Well, it's a good man's failing. I wouldn't give a trauneen for a teetotaler. They've no high spirits.

Then, stupidly puzzled.

Good excuse? You mean Master Edmund, Ma'am? I can tell the Master is worried about him.

MARY

Stiffens defensively — but in a strange way the reaction has a mechanical quality, as if it did not penetrate to real emotion.

Don't be silly, Cathleen. Why should he be? A touch of grippe is nothing. And Mr. Tyrone never is worried about anything, except money and property and the fear he'll end his days in poverty. I mean, deeply worried. Because he cannot really understand anything else.

She gives a little laugh of detached, affectionate amusement.

My husband is a very peculiar man, Cathleen.

CATHLEEN

Vaguely resentful.

Well, he's a fine, handsome, kind gentleman just the same, Ma'am. Never mind his weakness.

MARY

Oh, I don't mind. I've loved him dearly for thirty-six years. That proves I know he's lovable at heart and can't help being what he is, doesn't it?

CATHLEEN

Hazily reassured.

That's right, Ma'am. Love him dearly, for any fool can see he worships the ground you walk on.

Fighting the effect of her last drink and trying to be soberly conversational.

Speaking of acting, Ma'am, how is it you never went on the stage?

MARY

Resentfully.

I? What put that absurd notion in your head? I was brought up in a respectable home and educated in the best convent in the Middle West. Before I met Mr. Tyrone I hardly knew there was such a thing as a theater. I was a very pious girl. I even dreamed of becoming a nun. I've never had the slightest desire to be an actress.

CATHLEEN

Bluntly.

Well, I can't imagine you a holy nun, Ma'am. Sure, you never darken the door of a church, God forgive you.

MARY

Ignores this.

I've never felt at home in the theater. Even though Mr. Tyrone has made me go with him on all his tours, I've had little to do with the people in his company, or with anyone on the stage. Not that I have anything against them. They have always been kind to me, and I to them. But I've never felt at home with them. Their life is not my life. It has always stood between me and—

She gets up—abruptly.

But let's not talk of old things that couldn't be helped.

She goes to the porch door and stares out.

How thick the fog is. I can't see the road. All the people in the world could pass by and I would never know. I wish it was always that way. It's getting dark already. It will soon be night, thank goodness.

She turns back—vaguely.

It was kind of you to keep me company this afternoon, Cathleen. I would have been lonely driving uptown alone.

CATHLEEN

Sure, wouldn't I rather ride in a fine automobile than stay here and listen to Bridget's lies about her relations? It was like a vacation, Ma'am.
She pauses — then stupidly.
There was only one thing I didn't like.

MARY

Vaguely.
What was that, Cathleen?

CATHLEEN

The way the man in the drugstore acted when I took in the prescription for you.
Indignantly.
The impidence of him!

MARY

With stubborn blankness.
What are you talking about? What drugstore? What prescription?
Then hastily, as Cathleen stares in stupid amazement.
Oh, of course, I'd forgotten. The medicine for the rheumatism in my hands. What did the man say?
Then with indifference.
Not that it matters, as long as he filled the prescription.

CATHLEEN

It mattered to me, then! I'm not used to being treated like a thief. He gave me a long look and says insultingly, "Where did you get hold of this?" and I says, "It's none of your damned business, but if you must know, it's for the lady I work for, Mrs. Tyrone, who's sitting out in the automobile." That shut him up quick. He gave a look out at you and said, "Oh," and went to get the medicine.

MARY

Vaguely.
Yes, he knows me.
She sits in the armchair at right rear of table. She adds in a calm, detached voice.

It's a special kind of medicine. I have to take it because there is no other that can stop the pain—*all* the pain—I mean, in my hands.

She raises her hands and regards them with melancholy sympathy. There is no tremor in them now.

Poor hands! You'd never believe it, but they were once one of my good points, along with my hair and eyes, and I had a fine figure, too.

Her tone has become more and more far-off and dreamy.

They were a musician's hands. I used to love the piano. I worked so hard at my music in the Convent—if you can call it work when you do something you love. Mother Elizabeth and my music teacher both said I had more talent than any student they remembered. My father paid for special lessons. He spoiled me. He would do anything I asked. He would have sent me to Europe to study after I graduated from the Convent. I might have gone—if I hadn't fallen in love with Mr. Tyrone. Or I might have become a nun. I had two dreams. To be a nun, that was the more beautiful one. To become a concert pianist, that was the other.

She pauses, regarding her hands fixedly. Cathleen blinks her eyes to fight off drowsiness and a tipsy feeling.

I haven't touched a piano in so many years. I couldn't play with such crippled fingers, even if I wanted to. For a time after my marriage I tried to keep up my music. But it was hopeless. One-night stands, cheap hotels, dirty trains, leaving children, never having a home—

She stares at her hands with fascinated disgust.

See, Cathleen, how ugly they are! So maimed and crippled! You would think they'd been through some horrible accident!

She gives a strange little laugh.

So they have, come to think of it.

She suddenly thrusts her hands behind her back.

I won't look at them. They're worse than the foghorn for reminding me—

Then with defiant self-assurance.

But even they can't touch me now.

She brings her hands from behind her back and deliberately stares at them—calmly.

They're far away. I see them, but the pain has gone.

CATHLEEN
Stupidly puzzled.
You've taken some of the medicine? It made you act funny, Ma'am.
If I didn't know better, I'd think you'd a drop taken.

MARY
Dreamily.
It kills the pain. You go back until at last you are beyond its reach.
Only the past when you were happy is real.
*She pauses—then as if her words had been an evocation which called
back happiness she changes in her whole manner and facial expression.
She looks younger. There is a quality of an innocent convent girl about
her, and she smiles shyly.*
If you think Mr. Tyrone is handsome now, Cathleen, you should
have seen him when I first met him. He had the reputation of being
one of the best looking men in the country. The girls in the Convent
who had seen him act, or seen his photographs, used to rave about
him. He was a great matinee idol then, you know. Women used to
wait at the stage door just to see him come out. You can imagine
how excited I was when my father wrote me he and James Tyrone
had become friends, and that I was to meet him when I came home
for Easter vacation. I showed the letter to all the girls, and how
envious they were! My father took me to see him act first. It was a
play about the French Revolution and the leading part was a nobleman. I couldn't take my eyes off him. I wept when he was thrown
in prison—and then was so mad at myself because I was afraid my
eyes and nose would be red. My father had said we'd go backstage
to his dressing room right after the play, and so we did.
She gives a little excited, shy laugh.
I was so bashful all I could do was stammer and blush like a little
fool. But he didn't seem to think I was a fool. I know he liked me
the first moment we were introduced.
Coquettishly.
I guess my eyes and nose couldn't have been red, after all. I was
really very pretty then, Cathleen. And he was handsomer than my
wildest dream, in his make-up and his nobleman's costume that was
so becoming to him. He was different from all ordinary men, like

someone from another world. At the same time he was simple, and kind, and unassuming, not a bit stuck-up or vain. I fell in love right then. So did he, he told me afterwards. I forgot all about becoming a nun or a concert pianist. All I wanted was to be his wife.

She pauses, staring before her with unnaturally bright, dreamy eyes, and a rapt, tender, girlish smile.

Thirty-six years ago, but I can see it as clearly as if it were tonight! We've loved each other ever since. And in all those thirty-six years, there has never been a breath of scandal about him. I mean, with any other woman. Never since he met me. That has made me very happy, Cathleen. It has made me forgive so many other things.

CATHLEEN

Fighting tipsy drowsiness—sentimentally.

He's a fine gentleman and you're a lucky woman.

Then, fidgeting.

Can I take the drink to Bridget, Ma'am? It must be near dinner-time and I ought to be in the kitchen helping her. If she don't get something to quiet her temper, she'll be after me with the cleaver.

MARY

With a vague exasperation at being brought back from her dream.

Yes, yes, go. I don't need you now.

CATHLEEN

With relief.

Thank you, Ma'am.

She pours out a big drink and starts for the back parlor with it.

You won't be alone long. The Master and the boys—

MARY

Impatiently.

No, no, they won't come. Tell Bridget I won't wait. You can serve dinner promptly at half past six. I'm not hungry but I'll sit at the table and we'll get it over with.

CATHLEEN

You ought to eat something, Ma'am. It's a queer medicine if it takes away your appetite.

MARY

Has begun to drift into dreams again—reacts mechanically.

What medicine? I don't know what you mean.

In dismissal.

You better take the drink to Bridget.

CATHLEEN

Yes, Ma'am.

She disappears through the back parlor. Mary waits until she hears the pantry door close behind her. Then she settles back in relaxed dreaminess, staring fixedly at nothing. Her arms rest limply along the arms of the chair, her hands with long, warped, swollen-knuckled, sensitive fingers drooping in complete calm. It is growing dark in the room. There is a pause of dead quiet. Then from the world outside comes the melancholy moan of the foghorn, followed by a chorus of bells, muffled by the fog, from the anchored craft in the harbor. Mary's face gives no sign she has heard, but her hands jerk and the fingers automatically play for a moment on the air. She frowns and shakes her head mechanically as if a fly had walked across her mind. She suddenly loses all the girlish quality and is an aging, cynically sad, embittered woman.

MARY

Bitterly.

You're a sentimental fool. What is so wonderful about that first meeting between a silly romantic schoolgirl and a matinee idol? You were much happier before you knew he existed, in the Convent when you used to pray to the Blessed Virgin.

Longingly.

If I could only find the faith I lost, so I could pray again!

She pauses—then begins to recite the Hail Mary in a flat, empty tone.

"Hail, Mary, full of grace! The Lord is with Thee; blessed art Thou among women."

Sneeringly.

You expect the Blessed Virgin to be fooled by a lying dope fiend reciting words! You can't hide from her!

She springs to her feet. Her hands fly up to pat her hair distractedly.

I must go upstairs. I haven't taken enough. When you start again you never know exactly how much you need.

She goes toward the front parlor—then stops in the doorway as she hears the sound of voices from the front path. She starts guiltily.

That must be them—

She hurries back to sit down. Her face sets in stubborn defensiveness—resentfully.

Why are they coming back? They don't want to. And I'd much rather be alone.

Suddenly her whole manner changes. She becomes pathetically relieved and eager.

Oh, I'm so glad they've come! I've been so horribly lonely!

The front door is heard closing and Tyrone calls uneasily from the hall.

TYRONE

Are you there, Mary?

The light in the hall is turned on and shines through the front parlor to fall on Mary.

MARY

Rises from her chair, her face lighting up lovingly—with excited eagerness.

I'm here, dear. In the living room. I've been waiting for you.

Tyrone comes in through the front parlor. Edmund is behind him. Tyrone has had a lot to drink but beyond a slightly glazed look in his eyes and a trace of blur in his speech, he does not show it. Edmund has also had more than a few drinks without much apparent effect, except that his sunken cheeks are flushed and his eyes look bright and feverish. They stop in the doorway to stare appraisingly at her. What they see fulfills their worst expectations. But for the moment Mary is unconscious of their condemning eyes. She kisses her husband and then Edmund. Her manner is unnaturally effusive. They submit shrinkingly. She talks excitedly.

I'm so happy you've come. I had given up hope. I was afraid you wouldn't come home. It's such a dismal, foggy evening. It must be much more cheerful in the barrooms uptown, where there are people you can talk and joke with. No, don't deny it. I know how you feel. I don't blame you a bit. I'm all the more grateful to you for coming home. I was sitting here so lonely and blue. Come and sit down.

She sits at left rear of table, Edmund at left of table, and Tyrone in the rocker at right of it.

Dinner won't be ready for a minute. You're actually a little early. Will wonders never cease. Here's the whiskey, dear. Shall I pour a drink for you?

Without waiting for a reply she does so.

And you, Edmund? I don't want to encourage you, but one before dinner, as an appetizer, can't do any harm.

She pours a drink for him. They make no move to take the drinks. She talks on as if unaware of their silence.

Where's Jamie? But, of course, he'll never come home so long as he has the price of a drink left.

She reaches out and clasps her husband's hand—sadly.

I'm afraid Jamie has been lost to us for a long time, dear.

Her face hardens.

But we mustn't allow him to drag Edmund down with him, as he'd like to do. He's jealous because Edmund has always been the baby—just as he used to be of Eugene. He'll never be content until he makes Edmund as hopeless a failure as he is.

EDMUND
Miserably.
Stop talking, Mama.

TYRONE
Dully.
Yes, Mary, the less you say now—
Then to Edmund, a bit tipsily.
All the same there's truth in your mother's warning. Beware of that brother of yours, or he'll poison life for you with his damned sneering serpent's tongue!

EDMUND
As before.
Oh, cut it out, Papa.

MARY
Goes on as if nothing had been said.
It's hard to believe, seeing Jamie as he is now, that he was ever my

baby. Do you remember what a healthy, happy baby he was, James? The one-night stands and filthy traïns and cheap hotels and bad food never made him cross or sick. He was always smiling or laughing. He hardly ever cried. Eugene was the same, too, happy and healthy, during the two years he lived before I let him die through my neglect.

TYRONE
Oh, for the love of God! I'm a fool for coming home!

EDMUND
Papa! Shut up!

MARY
Smiles with detached tenderness at Edmund.
It was Edmund who was the crosspatch when he was little, always getting upset and frightened about nothing at all.
She pats his hand—teasingly.
Everyone used to say, dear, you'd cry at the drop of a hat.

EDMUND
Cannot control his bitterness.
Maybe I guessed there was a good reason not to laugh.

TYRONE
Reproving and pitying.
Now, now, lad. You know better than to pay attention—

MARY
As if she hadn't heard—sadly again.
Who would have thought Jamie would grow up to disgrace us. You remember, James, for years after he went to boarding school, we received such glowing reports. Everyone liked him. All his teachers told us what a fine brain he had, and how easily he learned his lessons. Even after he began to drink and they had to expel him, they wrote us how sorry they were, because he was so likable and such a brilliant student. They predicted a wonderful future for him if he would only learn to take life seriously.
She pauses—then adds with a strange, sad detachment.
It's such a pity. Poor Jamie! It's hard to understand—

Abruptly a change comes over her. Her face hardens and she stares at her husband with accusing hostility.

No, it isn't at all. You brought him up to be a boozer. Since he first opened his eyes, he's seen you drinking. Always a bottle on the bureau in the cheap hotel rooms! And if he had a nightmare when he was little, or a stomach-ache, your remedy was to give him a teaspoonful of whiskey to quiet him.

TYRONE
Stung.
So I'm to blame because that lazy hulk has made a drunken loafer of himself? Is that what I came home to listen to? I might have known! When you have the poison in you, you want to blame everyone but yourself!

EDMUND
Papa! You told me not to pay attention.
Then, resentfully.
Anyway it's true. You did the same thing with me. I can remember that teaspoonful of booze every time I woke up with a nightmare.

MARY
In a detached reminiscent tone.
Yes, you were continually having nightmares as a child. You were born afraid. Because I was so afraid to bring you into the world.
She pauses — then goes on with the same detachment.
Please don't think I blame your father, Edmund. He didn't know any better. He never went to school after he was ten. His people were the most ignorant kind of poverty-stricken Irish. I'm sure they honestly believed whiskey is the healthiest medicine for a child who is sick or frightened.
Tyrone is about to burst out in angry defense of his family but Edmund intervenes.

EDMUND
Sharply.
Papa!
Changing the subject.
Are we going to have this drink, or aren't we?

TYRONE

Controlling himself—dully.

You're right. I'm a fool to take notice.

He picks up his glass listlessly.

Drink hearty, lad.

Edmund drinks but Tyrone remains staring at the glass in his hand. Edmund at once realizes how much the whiskey has been watered. He frowns, glancing from the bottle to his mother—starts to say something but stops.

MARY

In a changed tone—repentently.

I'm sorry if I sounded bitter, James. I'm not. It's all so far away. But I did feel a little hurt when you wished you hadn't come home. I was so relieved and happy when you came, and grateful to you. It's very dreary and sad to be here alone in the fog with night falling.

TYRONE

Moved.

I'm glad I came, Mary, when you act like your real self.

MARY

I was so lonesome I kept Cathleen with me just to have someone to talk to.

Her manner and quality drift back to the shy convent girl again.

Do you know what I was telling her, dear? About the night my father took me to your dressing room and I first fell in love with you. Do you remember?

TYRONE

Deeply moved—his voice husky.

Can you think I'd ever forget, Mary?

Edmund looks away from them, sad and embarrassed.

MARY

Tenderly.

No. I know you still love me, James, in spite of everything.

TYRONE

His face works and he blinks back tears—with quiet intensity.
Yes! As God is my judge! Always and forever, Mary!

MARY

And I love you, dear, in spite of everything.
There is a pause in which Edmund moves embarrassedly. The strange detachment comes over her manner again as if she were speaking impersonally of people seen from a distance.
But I must confess, James, although I couldn't help loving you, I would never have married you if I'd known you drank so much. I remember the first night your barroom friends had to help you up to the door of our hotel room, and knocked and then ran away before I came to the door. We were still on our honeymoon, do you remember?

TYRONE

With guilty vehemence.
I don't remember! It wasn't on our honeymoon! And I never in my life had to be helped to bed, or missed a performance!

MARY

As though he hadn't spoken.
I had waited in that ugly hotel room hour after hour. I kept making excuses for you. I told myself it must be some business connected with the theater. I knew so little about the theater. Then I became terrified. I imagined all sorts of horrible accidents. I got on my knees and prayed that nothing had happened to you—and then they brought you up and left you outside the door.
She gives a little, sad sigh.
I didn't know how often that was to happen in the years to come, how many times I was to wait in ugly hotel rooms. I became quite used to it.

EDMUND

Bursts out with a look of accusing hate at his father.
Christ! No wonder— !
He controls himself—gruffly.
When is dinner, Mama? It must be time.

TYRONE

Overwhelmed by shame which he tries to hide, fumbles with his watch.
Yes. It must be. Let's see.
He stares at his watch without seeing it. Pleadingly.
Mary! Can't you forget—?

MARY

With detached pity.
No, dear. But I forgive. I always forgive you. So don't look so guilty.
I'm sorry I remembered out loud. I don't want to be sad, or to make
you sad. I want to remember only the happy part of the past.
Her manner drifts back to the shy, gay convent girl.
Do you remember our wedding, dear? I'm sure you've completely
forgotten what my wedding gown looked like. Men don't notice
such things. They don't think they're important. But it was important to me, I can tell you! How I fussed and worried! I was so excited
and happy! My father told me to buy anything I wanted and never
mind what it cost. The best is none too good, he said. I'm afraid
he spoiled me dreadfully. My mother didn't. She was very pious
and strict. I think she was a little jealous. She didn't approve of my
marrying—especially an actor. I think she hoped I would become
a nun. She used to scold my father. She'd grumble, "You never tell
me, never mind what it costs, when I buy anything! You've spoiled
that girl so, I pity her husband if she ever marries. She'll expect him
to give her the moon. She'll never make a good wife."
She laughs affectionately.
Poor mother!
She smiles at Tyrone with a strange, incongruous coquetry.
But she was mistaken, wasn't she, James? I haven't been such a bad
wife, have I?

TYRONE

Huskily, trying to force a smile.
I'm not complaining, Mary.

A shadow of vague guilt crosses her face.

At least, I've loved you dearly, and done the best I could—under the circumstances.

The shadow vanishes and her shy, girlish expression returns.

That wedding gown was nearly the death of me and the dressmaker, too!

She laughs.

I was so particular. It was never quite good enough. At last she said she refused to touch it any more or she might spoil it, and I made her leave so I could be alone to examine myself in the mirror. I was so pleased and vain. I thought to myself, "Even if your nose and mouth and ears are a trifle too large, your eyes and hair and figure, and your hands, make up for it. You're just as pretty as any actress he's ever met, and you don't have to use paint."

She pauses, wrinkling her brow in an effort of memory.

Where is my wedding gown now, I wonder? I kept it wrapped up in tissue paper in my trunk. I used to hope I would have a daughter and when it came time for her to marry— She couldn't have bought a lovelier gown, and I knew, James, you'd never tell her, never mind the cost. You'd want her to pick up something at a bargain. It was made of soft, shimmering satin, trimmed with wonderful old duchesse lace, in tiny ruffles around the neck and sleeves, and worked in with the folds that were draped round in a bustle effect at the back. The basque was boned and very tight. I remember I held my breath when it was fitted, so my waist would be as small as possible. My father even let me have duchesse lace on my white satin slippers, and lace with the orange blossoms in my veil. Oh, how I loved that gown! It was so beautiful! Where is it now, I wonder? I used to take it out from time to time when I was lonely, but it always made me cry, so finally a long while ago—

She wrinkles her forehead again.

I wonder where I hid it? Probably in one of the old trunks in the attic. Some day I'll have to look.

She stops, staring before her. Tyrone sighs, shaking his head hopelessly, and attempts to catch his son's eye, looking for sympathy, but Edmund is staring at the floor.

TYRONE

Forces a casual tone.

Isn't it dinner time, dear?

With a feeble attempt at teasing.

You're forever scolding me for being late, but now I'm on time for once, it's dinner that's late.

She doesn't appear to hear him. He adds, still pleasantly.

Well, if I can't eat yet, I can drink. I'd forgotten I had this.

He drinks his drink. Edmund watches him. Tyrone scowls and looks at his wife with sharp suspicion—roughly.

Who's been tampering with my whiskey? The damned stuff is half water! Jamie's been away and he wouldn't overdo his trick like this, anyway. Any fool could tell— Mary, answer me!

With angry disgust.

I hope to God you haven't taken to drink on top of—

EDMUND

Shut up, Papa!

To his mother, without looking at her.

You treated Cathleen and Bridget, isn't that it, Mama?

MARY

With indifferent casualness.

Yes, of course. They work hard for poor wages. And I'm the house-keeper, I have to keep them from leaving. Besides, I wanted to treat Cathleen because I had her drive uptown with me, and sent her to get my prescription filled.

EDMUND

For God's sake, Mama! You can't trust her! Do you want everyone on earth to know?

MARY

Her face hardening stubbornly.

Know what? That I suffer from rheumatism in my hands and have to take medicine to kill the pain? Why should I be ashamed of that? *Turns on Edmund with a hard, accusing antagonism—almost a revengeful enmity.*

I never knew what rheumatism was before you were born! Ask your father!

Edmund looks away, shrinking into himself.

TYRONE

Don't mind her, lad. It doesn't mean anything. When she gets to the stage where she gives the old crazy excuse about her hands she's gone far away from us.

MARY

Turns on him—with a strangely triumphant, taunting smile.

I'm glad you realize that, James! Now perhaps you'll give up trying to remind me, you and Edmund!

Abruptly, in a detached, matter-of-fact tone.

Why don't you light the light, James? It's getting dark. I know you hate to, but Edmund has proved to you that one bulb burning doesn't cost much. There's no sense letting your fear of the poor-house make you too stingy.

TYRONE

Reacts mechanically.

I never claimed one bulb cost much! It's having them on, one here and one there, that makes the Electric Light Company rich.

He gets up and turns on the reading lamp—roughly.

But I'm a fool to talk reason to you.

To Edmund.

I'll get a fresh bottle of whiskey, lad, and we'll have a real drink.

He goes through the back parlor.

MARY

With detached amusement.

He'll sneak around to the outside cellar door so the servants won't see him. He's really ashamed of keeping his whiskey padlocked in the cellar. Your father is a strange man, Edmund. It took many years before I understood him. You must try to understand and forgive him, too, and not feel contempt because he's close-fisted. His father deserted his mother and their six children a year or so after they came to America. He told them he had a premonition he would die soon, and he was homesick for Ireland, and wanted to go back there to die. So he went and he did die. He must have been a peculiar man, too. Your father had to go to work in a machine shop when he was only ten years old.

EDMUND
Protests dully.
Oh, for Pete's sake, Mama. I've heard Papa tell that machine shop story ten thousand times.

MARY
Yes, dear, you've had to listen, but I don't think you've ever tried to understand.

EDMUND
Ignoring this—miserably.
Listen, Mama! You're not so far gone yet you've forgotten everything. You haven't asked me what I found out this afternoon. Don't you care a damn?

MARY
Shakenly.
Don't say that! You hurt me, dear!

EDMUND
What I've got is serious, Mama. Doc Hardy knows for sure now.

MARY
Stiffens into scornful, defensive stubbornness.
That lying old quack! I warned you he'd invent— !

EDMUND
Miserably dogged.
He called in a specialist to examine me, so he'd be absolutely sure.

MARY
Ignoring this.
Don't tell me about Hardy! If you heard what the doctor at the sanatorium, who really knows something, said about how he'd treated me! He said he ought to be locked up! He said it was a wonder I hadn't gone mad! I told him I had once, that time I ran down in my nightdress to throw myself off the dock. You remember that, don't

you? And yet you want me to pay attention to what Doctor Hardy says. Oh, no!

EDMUND
Bitterly.
I remember, all right. It was right after that Papa and Jamie decided they couldn't hide it from me any more. Jamie told me. I called him a liar! I tried to punch him in the nose. But I knew he wasn't lying.
His voice trembles, his eyes begin to fill with tears.
God, it made everything in life seem rotten!

MARY
Pitiably.
Oh, don't. My baby! You hurt me so dreadfully!

EDMUND
Dully.
I'm sorry, Mama. It was you who brought it up.
Then with a bitter, stubborn persistence.
Listen, Mama. I'm going to tell you whether you want to hear or not. I've got to go to a sanatorium.

MARY
Dazedly, as if this was something that had never occurred to her.
Go away?
Violently.
No! I won't have it! How dare Doctor Hardy advise such a thing without consulting me! How dare your father allow him! What right has he? You are my baby! Let him attend to Jamie!
More and more excited and bitter.
I know why he wants you sent to a sanatorium. To take you from me! He's always tried to do that. He's been jealous of every one of my babies! He kept finding ways to make me leave them. That's what caused Eugene's death. He's been jealous of you most of all. He knew I loved you most because—

EDMUND
Miserably.
Oh, stop talking crazy, can't you, Mama! Stop trying to blame him.

And why are you so against my going away now? I've been away a lot, and I've never noticed it broke your heart!

MARY
Bitterly.
I'm afraid you're not very sensitive, after all.
Sadly.
You might have guessed, dear, that after I knew you knew—about me—I had to be glad whenever you were where you couldn't see me.

EDMUND
Brokenly.
Mama! Don't!
He reaches out blindly and takes her hand—but he drops it immediately, overcome by bitterness again.
All this talk about loving me—and you won't even listen when I try to tell you how sick—

MARY
With an abrupt transformation into a detached bullying motherliness.
Now, now. That's enough! I don't care to hear because I know it's nothing but Hardy's ignorant lies.
He shrinks back into himself. She keeps on in a forced, teasing tone but with an increasing undercurrent of resentment.
You're so like your father, dear. You love to make a scene out of nothing so you can be dramatic and tragic.
With a belittling laugh.
If I gave you the slightest encouragement, you'd tell me next you were going to die—

EDMUND
People do die of it. Your own father—

MARY
Sharply.
Why do you mention him? There's no comparison at all with you. He had consumption.
Angrily.

I hate you when you become gloomy and morbid! I forbid you to remind me of my father's death, do you hear me?

EDMUND
His face hard—grimly.
Yes, I hear you, Mama. I wish to God I didn't!
He gets up from his chair and stands staring condemningly at her—bitterly.
It's pretty hard to take at times, having a dope fiend for a mother!
She winces—all life seeming to drain from her face, leaving it with the appearance of a plaster cast. Instantly Edmund wishes he could take back what he has said. He stammers miserably.
Forgive me, Mama. I was angry. You hurt me.
There is a pause in which the foghorn and the ships' bells are heard.

MARY
Goes slowly to the windows at right like an automaton—looking out, a blank, far-off quality in her voice.
Just listen to that awful foghorn. And the bells. Why is it fog makes everything sound so sad and lost, I wonder?

EDMUND
Brokenly.
I—I can't stay here. I don't want any dinner.
He hurries away through the front parlor. She keeps staring out the window until she hears the front door close behind him. Then she comes back and sits in her chair, the same blank look on her face.

MARY
Vaguely.
I must go upstairs. I haven't taken enough.
She pauses—then longingly.
I hope, sometime, without meaning it, I will take an overdose. I never could do it deliberately. The Blessed Virgin would never forgive me, then.
She hears Tyrone returning and turns as he comes in, through the back parlor, with a bottle of whiskey he has just uncorked. He is fuming.

TYRONE

Wrathfully.

The padlock is all scratched. That drunken loafer has tried to pick the lock with a piece of wire, the way he's done before.

With satisfaction, as if this was a perpetual battle of wits with his elder son.

But I've fooled him this time. It's a special padlock a professional burglar couldn't pick.

He puts the bottle on the tray and suddenly is aware of Edmund's absence.

Where's Edmund?

MARY

With a vague far-away air.

He went out. Perhaps he's going uptown again to find Jamie. He still has some money left, I suppose, and it's burning a hole in his pocket. He said he didn't want any dinner. He doesn't seem to have any appetite these days.

Then stubbornly.

But it's just a summer cold.

Tyrone stares at her and shakes his head helplessly and pours himself a big drink and drinks it. Suddenly it is too much for her and she breaks out and sobs.

Oh, James, I'm so frightened!

She gets up and throws her arms around him and hides her face on his shoulder—sobbingly.

I know he's going to die!

TYRONE

Don't say that! It's not true! They promised me in six months he'd be cured.

MARY

You don't believe that! I can tell when you're acting! And it will be my fault. I should never have borne him. It would have been better for his sake. I could never hurt him then. He wouldn't have had to know his mother was a dope fiend—and hate her!

TYRONE

His voice quivering.

Hush, Mary, for the love of God! He loves you. He knows it was a curse put on you without your knowing or willing it. He's proud you're his mother!

Abruptly as he hears the pantry door opening.

Hush, now! Here comes Cathleen. You don't want her to see you crying.

She turns quickly away from him to the windows at right, hastily wiping her eyes. A moment later Cathleen appears in the back-parlor doorway. She is uncertain in her walk and grinning woozily.

CATHLEEN

Starts guiltily when she sees Tyrone—with dignity.

Dinner is served, Sir.

Raising her voice unnecessarily.

Dinner is served, Ma'am.

She forgets her dignity and addresses Tyrone with good-natured familiarity.

So you're here, are you? Well, well. Won't Bridget be in a rage! I told her the Madame said you wouldn't be home.

Then reading accusation in his eye.

Don't be looking at me that way. If I've a drop taken, I didn't steal it. I was invited.

She turns with huffy dignity and disappears through the back parlor.

TYRONE

Sighs—then summoning his actor's heartiness.

Come along, dear. Let's have our dinner. I'm hungry as a hunter.

MARY

Comes to him—her face is composed in plaster again and her tone is remote.

I'm afraid you'll have to excuse me, James. I couldn't possibly eat anything. My hands pain me dreadfully. I think the best thing for me is to go to bed and rest. Good night, dear.

She kisses him mechanically and turns toward the front parlor.

TYRONE

Harshly.

Up to take more of that God-damned poison, is that it? You'll be like a mad ghost before the night's over!

MARY

Starts to walk away — blankly.

I don't know what you're talking about, James. You say such mean, bitter things when you've drunk too much. You're as bad as Jamie or Edmund.

She moves off through the front parlor. He stands a second as if not knowing what to do. He is a sad, bewildered, broken old man. He walks wearily off through the back parlor toward the dining room.

CURTAIN

Act Four

SCENE

The same. It is around midnight. The lamp in the front hall has been turned out, so that now no light shines through the front parlor. In the living room only the reading lamp on the table is lighted. Outside the windows the wall of fog appears denser than ever. As the curtain rises, the foghorn is heard, followed by the ships' bells from the harbor.

Tyrone is seated at the table. He wears his pince-nez, and is playing solitaire. He has taken off his coat and has on an old brown dressing gown. The whiskey bottle on the tray is three-quarters empty. There is a fresh full bottle on the table, which he has brought from the cellar so there will be an ample reserve at hand. He is drunk and shows it by the owlish, deliberate manner in which he peers at each card to make certain of its identity, and then plays it as if he wasn't certain of his aim. His eyes have a misted, oily look and his mouth is slack. But despite all the whiskey in him, he has not escaped, and he looks as he appeared at the close of the preceding act, a sad, defeated old man, possessed by hopeless resignation.

As the curtain rises, he finishes a game and sweeps the cards together. He shuffles them clumsily, dropping a couple on the floor. He retrieves them with difficulty, and starts to shuffle again, when he hears someone entering the front door. He peers over his pince-nez through the front parlor.

TYRONE
His voice thick.
Who's that? Is it you, Edmund?
Edmund's voice answers curtly, "Yes." Then he evidently collides with

something in the dark hall and can be heard cursing. A moment later the hall lamp is turned on. Tyrone frowns and calls.

Turn that light out before you come in.

But Edmund doesn't. He comes in through the front parlor. He is drunk now, too, but like his father he carries it well, and gives little physical sign of it except in his eyes and a chip-on-the-shoulder aggressiveness in his manner. Tyrone speaks, at first with a warm, relieved welcome.

I'm glad you've come, lad. I've been damned lonely.

Then resentfully.

You're a fine one to run away and leave me to sit alone here all night when you know—

With sharp irritation.

I told you to turn out that light! We're not giving a ball. There's no reason to have the house ablaze with electricity at this time of night, burning up money!

EDMUND

Angrily.

Ablaze with electricity! One bulb! Hell, everyone keeps a light on in the front hall until they go to bed.

He rubs his knee.

I damned near busted my knee on the hat stand.

TYRONE

The light from here shows in the hall. You could see your way well enough if you were sober.

EDMUND

If *I* was sober? I like that!

TYRONE

I don't give a damn what other people do. If they want to be wasteful fools, for the sake of show, let them be!

EDMUND

One bulb! Christ, don't be such a cheap skate! I've proved by figures if you left the light bulb on all night it wouldn't be as much as one drink!

TYRONE

To hell with your figures! The proof is in the bills I have to pay!

EDMUND

Sits down opposite his father—contemptuously.

Yes, facts don't mean a thing, do they? What you want to believe, that's the only truth!

Derisively.

Shakespeare was an Irish Catholic, for example.

TYRONE

Stubbornly.

So he was. The proof is in his plays.

EDMUND

Well he wasn't, and there's no proof of it in his plays, except to you!

Jeeringly.

The Duke of Wellington, there was another good Irish Catholic!

TYRONE

I never said he was a good one. He was a renegade but a Catholic just the same.

EDMUND

Well, he wasn't. You just want to believe no one but an Irish Catholic general could beat Napoleon.

TYRONE

I'm not going to argue with you. I asked you to turn out that light in the hall.

EDMUND

I heard you, and as far as I'm concerned it stays on.

TYRONE

None of your damned insolence! Are you going to obey me or not?

EDMUND

Not! If you want to be a crazy miser put it out yourself!

TYRONE

With threatening anger.

Listen to me! I've put up with a lot from you because from the mad things you've done at times I've thought you weren't quite right in your head. I've excused you and never lifted my hand to you. But there's a straw that breaks the camel's back. You'll obey me and put out that light or, big as you are, I'll give you a thrashing that'll teach you— !

Suddenly he remembers Edmund's illness and instantly becomes guilty and shamefaced.

Forgive me, lad. I forgot— You shouldn't goad me into losing my temper.

EDMUND

Ashamed himself now.

Forget it, Papa. I apologize, too. I had no right being nasty about nothing. I am a bit soused, I guess. I'll put out the damned light.

He starts to get up.

TYRONE

No, stay where you are. Let it burn.

He stands up abruptly—and a bit drunkenly—and begins turning on the three bulbs in the chandelier, with a childish, bitterly dramatic self-pity.

We'll have them all on! Let them burn! To hell with them! The poorhouse is the end of the road, and it might as well be sooner as later!

He finishes turning on the lights.

EDMUND

Has watched this proceeding with an awakened sense of humor—now he grins, teasing affectionately.

That's a grand curtain.

He laughs.

You're a wonder, Papa.

TYRONE

Sits down sheepishly—grumbles pathetically.

That's right, laugh at the old fool! The poor old ham! But the final curtain will be in the poorhouse just the same, and that's not comedy!

Then as Edmund is still grinning, he changes the subject.

Well, well, let's not argue. You've got brains in that head of yours, though you do your best to deny them. You'll live to learn the value of a dollar. You're not like your damned tramp of a brother. I've given up hope he'll ever get sense. Where is he, by the way?

EDMUND

How would I know?

TYRONE

I thought you'd gone back uptown to meet him.

EDMUND

No. I walked out to the beach. I haven't seen him since this afternoon.

TYRONE

Well, if you split the money I gave you with him, like a fool—

EDMUND

Sure I did. He's always staked me when he had anything.

TYRONE

Then it doesn't take a soothsayer to tell he's probably in the whorehouse.

EDMUND

What of it if he is? Why not?

TYRONE

Contemptuously.

Why not, indeed. It's the fit place for him. If he's ever had a loftier dream than whores and whiskey, he's never shown it.

EDMUND

Oh, for Pete's sake, Papa! If you're going to start that stuff, I'll beat it.

He starts to get up.

TYRONE
Placatingly.
All right, all right, I'll stop. God knows, I don't like the subject either. Will you join me in a drink?

EDMUND
Ah! Now you're talking!

TYRONE
Passes the bottle to him—mechanically.
I'm wrong to treat you. You've had enough already.

EDMUND
Pouring a big drink—a bit drunkenly.
Enough is *not* as good as a feast.
He hands back the bottle.

TYRONE
It's too much in your condition.

EDMUND
Forget my condition!
He raises his glass.
Here's how.

TYRONE
Drink hearty.
They drink.
If you walked all the way to the beach you must be damp and chilled.

EDMUND
Oh, I dropped in at the Inn on the way out and back.

TYRONE
It's not a night I'd pick for a long walk.

EDMUND
I loved the fog. It was what I needed.
He sounds more tipsy and looks it.

TYRONE

You should have more sense than to risk—

EDMUND

To hell with sense! We're all crazy. What do we want with sense?
He quotes from Dowson sardonically.

"They are not long, the weeping and the laughter,
  Love and desire and hate:
  I think they have no portion in us after
  We pass the gate.

  They are not long, the days of wine and roses:
  Out of a misty dream
  Our path emerges for a while, then closes
  Within a dream."

Staring before him.

The fog was where I wanted to be. Halfway down the path you can't see this house. You'd never know it was here. Or any of the other places down the avenue. I couldn't see but a few feet ahead. I didn't meet a soul. Everything looked and sounded unreal. Nothing was what it is. That's what I wanted—to be alone with myself in another world where truth is untrue and life can hide from itself. Out beyond the harbor, where the road runs along the beach, I even lost the feeling of being on land. The fog and the sea seemed part of each other. It was like walking on the bottom of the sea. As if I had drowned long ago. As if I was a ghost belonging to the fog, and the fog was the ghost of the sea. It felt damned peaceful to be nothing more than a ghost within a ghost.

He sees his father staring at him with mingled worry and irritated disapproval. He grins mockingly.

Don't look at me as if I'd gone nutty. I'm talking sense. Who wants to see life as it is, if they can help it? It's the three Gorgons in one. You look in their faces and turn to stone. Or it's Pan. You see him and you die—that is, inside you—and have to go on living as a ghost.

TYRONE

Impressed and at the same time revolted.

You have a poet in you but it's a damned morbid one!

Forcing a smile.

Devil take your pessimism. I feel low-spirited enough.

He sighs.

Why can't you remember your Shakespeare and forget the third-raters. You'll find what you're trying to say in him—as you'll find everything else worth saying.

He quotes, using his fine voice.

"We are such stuff as dreams are made on, and our little life is rounded with a sleep."

EDMUND

Ironically.

Fine! That's beautiful. But I wasn't trying to say that. We are such stuff as manure is made on, so let's drink up and forget it. That's more my idea.

TYRONE

Disgustedly.

Ach! Keep such sentiments to yourself. I shouldn't have given you that drink.

EDMUND

It did pack a wallop, all right. On you, too.

He grins with affectionate teasing.

Even if you've never missed a performance!

Aggressively.

Well, what's wrong with being drunk? It's what we're after, isn't it? Let's not kid each other, Papa. Not tonight. We know what we're trying to forget.

Hurriedly.

But let's not talk about it. It's no use now.

TYRONE

Dully.

No. All we can do is try to be resigned—again.

EDMUND

Or be so drunk you can forget.

He recites, and recites well, with bitter, ironical passion, the Symons'
translation of Baudelaire's prose poem.
"Be always drunken. Nothing else matters: that is the only question.
If you would not feel the horrible burden of Time weighing on your
shoulders and crushing you to the earth, be drunken continually.

Drunken with what? With wine, with poetry, or with virtue, as
you will. But be drunken.

And if sometimes, on the stairs of a palace, or on the green side
of a ditch, or in the dreary solitude of your own room, you should
awaken and the drunkenness be half or wholly slipped away from
you, ask of the wind, or of the wave, or of the star, or of the bird, or
of the clock, of whatever flies, or sighs, or rocks, or sings, or speaks,
ask what hour it is; and the wind, wave, star, bird, clock, will answer
you: 'It is the hour to be drunken! Be drunken, if you would not be
martyred slaves of Time; be drunken continually! With wine, with
poetry, or with virtue, as you will.'"
He grins at his father provocatively.

TYRONE
Thickly humorous.
I wouldn't worry about the virtue part of it, if I were you.
Then disgustedly.
Pah! It's morbid nonsense! What little truth is in it you'll find nobly
said in Shakespeare.
Then appreciatively.
But you recited it well, lad. Who wrote it?

EDMUND
Baudelaire.

TYRONE
Never heard of him.

EDMUND
Grins provocatively.
He also wrote a poem about Jamie and the Great White Way.

TYRONE

That loafer! I hope to God he misses the last car and has to stay up-town!

EDMUND

Goes on, ignoring this.

Although he was French and never saw Broadway and died before Jamie was born. He knew him and Little Old New York just the same.

He recites the Symons' translation of Baudelaire's "Epilogue."

  "With heart at rest I climbed the citadel's
    Steep height, and saw the city as from a tower,
    Hospital, brothel, prison, and such hells,

  Where evil comes up softly like a flower.
    Thou knowest, O Satan, patron of my pain,
    Not for vain tears I went up at that hour;

  But like an old sad faithful lecher, fain
    To drink delight of that enormous trull
    Whose hellish beauty makes me young again.

  Whether thou sleep, with heavy vapours full,
    Sodden with day, or, new apparelled, stand
    In gold-laced veils of evening beautiful,

  I love thee, infamous city! Harlots and
    Hunted have pleasures of their own to give,
    The vulgar herd can never understand."

TYRONE

With irritable disgust.

Morbid filth! Where the hell do you get your taste in literature? Filth and despair and pessimism! Another atheist, I suppose. When you deny God, you deny hope. That's the trouble with you. If you'd get down on your knees—

EDMUND

As if he hadn't heard—sardonically.

It's a good likeness of Jamie, don't you think, hunted by himself

and whiskey, hiding in a Broadway hotel room with some fat tart—
he likes them fat—reciting Dowson's Cynara to her.
He recites derisively, but with deep feeling.

"All night upon mine heart I felt her warm heart beat,
  Night-long within mine arms in love and sleep she lay;
  Surely the kisses of her bought red mouth were sweet;
  But I was desolate and sick of an old passion,
  When I awoke and found the dawn was gray:
  I have been faithful to thee, Cynara! in my fashion."

Jeeringly.
And the poor fat burlesque queen doesn't get a word of it, but sus-
pects she's being insulted! And Jamie never loved any Cynara, and
was never faithful to a woman in his life, even in his fashion! But he
lies there, kidding himself he is superior and enjoys pleasures "the
vulgar herd can never understand"!
He laughs.
It's nuts—completely nuts!

TYRONE
Vaguely—his voice thick.
It's madness, yes. If you'd get on your knees and pray. When you
deny God, you deny sanity.

EDMUND
Ignoring this.
But who am I to feel superior? I've done the same damned thing.
And it's no more crazy than Dowson himself, inspired by an ab-
sinthe hangover, writing it to a dumb barmaid, who thought he was
a poor crazy souse, and gave him the gate to marry a waiter!
He laughs—then soberly, with genuine sympathy.
Poor Dowson. Booze and consumption got him.
*He starts and for a second looks miserable and frightened. Then with
defensive irony.*
Perhaps it would be tactful of me to change the subject.

TYRONE
Thickly.
Where you get your taste in authors— That damned library of
yours!

He indicates the small bookcase at rear.

Voltaire, Rousseau, Schopenhauer, Nietzsche, Ibsen! Atheists, fools, and madmen! And your poets! This Dowson, and this Baudelaire, and Swinburne and Oscar Wilde, and Whitman and Poe! Whore-mongers and degenerates! Pah! When I've three good sets of Shake-speare there (*he nods at the large bookcase*) you could read.

EDMUND
Provocatively.
They say he was a souse, too.

TYRONE
They lie! I don't doubt he liked his glass — it's a good man's failing — but he knew how to drink so it didn't poison his brain with morbid-ness and filth. Don't compare him with the pack you've got in there.
He indicates the small bookcase again.
Your dirty Zola! And your Dante Gabriel Rossetti who was a dope fiend!
He starts and looks guilty.

EDMUND
With defensive dryness.
Perhaps it would be wise to change the subject.
A pause.
You can't accuse me of not knowing Shakespeare. Didn't I win five dollars from you once when you bet me I couldn't learn a leading part of his in a week, as you used to do in stock in the old days. I learned Macbeth and recited it letter perfect, with you giving me the cues.

TYRONE
Approvingly.
That's true. So you did.
He smiles teasingly and sighs.
It was a terrible ordeal, I remember, hearing you murder the lines. I kept wishing I'd paid over the bet without making you prove it.
He chuckles and Edmund grins. Then he starts as he hears a sound from upstairs — with dread.

Did you hear? She's moving around. I was hoping she'd gone to sleep.

EDMUND

Forget it! How about another drink?

He reaches out and gets the bottle, pours a drink and hands it back. Then with a strained casualness, as his father pours a drink.

When did Mama go to bed?

TYRONE

Right after you left. She wouldn't eat any dinner. What made you run away?

EDMUND

Nothing.

Abruptly raising his glass.

Well, here's how.

TYRONE

Mechanically.

Drink hearty, lad.

They drink. Tyrone again listens to sounds upstairs—with dread.

She's moving around a lot. I hope to God she doesn't come down.

EDMUND

Dully.

Yes. She'll be nothing but a ghost haunting the past by this time.

He pauses—then miserably.

Back before I was born—

TYRONE

Doesn't she do the same with me? Back before she ever knew me. You'd think the only happy days she's ever known were in her father's home, or at the Convent, praying and playing the piano.

Jealous resentment in his bitterness.

As I've told you before, you must take her memories with a grain of salt. Her wonderful home was ordinary enough. Her father wasn't the great, generous, noble Irish gentleman she makes out. He was a nice enough man, good company and a good talker. I liked him and he liked me. He was prosperous enough, too, in his wholesale grocery business, an able man. But he had his weakness. She condemns my drinking but she forgets his. It's true he never touched a drop till he was forty, but after that he made up for lost time. He became a steady champagne drinker, the worst kind. That was his grand pose, to drink only champagne. Well, it finished him quick— that and the consumption—

He stops with a guilty glance at his son.

EDMUND
Sardonically.
We don't seem able to avoid unpleasant topics, do we?

TYRONE
Sighs sadly.
No.
Then with a pathetic attempt at heartiness.
What do you say to a game or two of Casino, lad?

EDMUND
All right.

TYRONE
Shuffling the cards clumsily.
We can't lock up and go to bed till Jamie comes on the last trolley— which I hope he won't—and I don't want to go upstairs, anyway, till she's asleep.

EDMUND
Neither do I.

TYRONE
Keeps shuffling the cards fumblingly, forgetting to deal them.
As I was saying, you must take her tales of the past with a grain of salt. The piano playing and her dream of becoming a concert pianist. That was put in her head by the nuns flattering her. She was their pet. They loved her for being so devout. They're innocent women, anyway, when it comes to the world. They don't know that not one in a million who shows promise ever rises to concert playing. Not that your mother didn't play well for a schoolgirl, but that's no reason to take it for granted she could have—

EDMUND
Sharply.
Why don't you deal, if we're going to play.

TYRONE
Eh? I am.
Dealing with very uncertain judgment of distance.
And the idea she might have become a nun. That's the worst. Your mother was one of the most beautiful girls you could ever see. She knew it, too. She was a bit of a rogue and a coquette, God bless her, behind all her shyness and blushes. She was never made to renounce the world. She was bursting with health and high spirits and the love of loving.

EDMUND
For God's sake, Papa! Why don't you pick up your hand?

TYRONE
Picks it up—dully.
Yes, let's see what I have here.
They both stare at their cards unseeingly. Then they both start. Tyrone whispers.
Listen!

EDMUND
She's coming downstairs.

TYRONE
Hurriedly.
We'll play our game. Pretend not to notice and she'll soon go up again.

EDMUND
Staring through the front parlor—with relief.
I don't see her. She must have started down and then turned back.

TYRONE
Thank God.

EDMUND
Yes. It's pretty horrible to see her the way she must be now.

With bitter misery.

The hardest thing to take is the blank wall she builds around her. Or it's more like a bank of fog in which she hides and loses herself. Deliberately, that's the hell of it! You know something in her does it deliberately—to get beyond our reach, to be rid of us, to forget we're alive! It's as if, in spite of loving us, she hated us!

TYRONE

Remonstrates gently.

Now, now, lad. It's not her. It's the damned poison.

EDMUND

Bitterly.

She takes it to get that effect. At least, I know she did this time!
Abruptly.
My play, isn't it? Here.
He plays a card.

TYRONE

Plays mechanically—gently reproachful.

She's been terribly frightened about your illness, for all her pretending. Don't be too hard on her, lad. Remember she's not responsible. Once that cursed poison gets a hold on anyone—

EDMUND

His face grows hard and he stares at his father with bitter accusation.

It never should have gotten a hold on her! I know damned well she's not to blame! And I know who is! You are! Your damned stinginess! If you'd spent money for a decent doctor when she was so sick after I was born, she'd never have known morphine existed! Instead you put her in the hands of a hotel quack who wouldn't admit his ignorance and took the easiest way out, not giving a damn what happened to her afterwards! All because his fee was cheap! Another one of your bargains!

TYRONE

Stung—angrily.

Be quiet! How dare you talk of something you know nothing about!
Trying to control his temper.

You must try to see my side of it, too, lad. How was I to know he was that kind of a doctor? He had a good reputation—

EDMUND
Among the souses in the hotel bar, I suppose!

TYRONE
That's a lie! I asked the hotel proprietor to recommend the best—

EDMUND
Yes! At the same time crying poorhouse and making it plain you wanted a cheap one! I know your system! By God, I ought to after this afternoon!

TYRONE
Guiltily defensive.
What about this afternoon?

EDMUND
Never mind now. We're talking about Mama! I'm saying no matter how you excuse yourself you know damned well your stinginess is to blame—

TYRONE
And I say you're a liar! Shut your mouth right now, or—

EDMUND
Ignoring this.
After you found out she'd been made a morphine addict, why didn't you send her to a cure then, at the start, while she still had a chance? No, that would have meant spending some money! I'll bet you told her all she had to do was use a little will power! That's what you still believe in your heart, in spite of what doctors, who really know something about it, have told you!

TYRONE
You lie again! I know better than that now! But how was I to know then? What did I know of morphine? It was years before I discovered what was wrong. I thought she'd never got over her sickness, that's all. Why didn't I send her to a cure, you say?
Bitterly.

Haven't I? I've spent thousands upon thousands in cures! A waste. What good have they done her? She always started again.

EDMUND

Because you've never given her anything that would help her want to stay off it! No home except this summer dump in a place she hates and you've refused even to spend money to make this look decent, while you keep buying more property, and playing sucker for every con man with a gold mine, or a silver mine, or any kind of get-rich-quick swindle! You've dragged her around on the road, season after season, on one-night stands, with no one she could talk to, waiting night after night in dirty hotel rooms for you to come back with a bun on after the bars closed! Christ, is it any wonder she didn't want to be cured. Jesus, when I think of it I hate your guts!

TYRONE
Strickenly.
Edmund!
Then in a rage.
How dare you talk to your father like that, you insolent young cub! After all I've done for you.

EDMUND

We'll come to that, what you're doing for me!

TYRONE
Looking guilty again—ignores this.
Will you stop repeating your mother's crazy accusations, which she never makes unless it's the poison talking? I never dragged her on the road against her will. Naturally, I wanted her with me. I loved her. And she came because she loved me and wanted to be with me. That's the truth, no matter what she says when she's not herself. And she needn't have been lonely. There was always the members of my company to talk to, if she'd wanted. She had her children, too, and I insisted, in spite of the expense, on having a nurse to travel with her.

EDMUND
Bitterly.
Yes, your one generosity, and that because you were jealous of her paying too much attention to us, and wanted us out of your way! It was another mistake, too! If she'd had to take care of me all by herself, and had that to occupy her mind, maybe she'd have been able—

TYRONE
Goaded into vindictiveness.
Or for that matter, if you insist on judging things by what she says when she's not in her right mind, if you hadn't been born she'd never—
He stops ashamed.

EDMUND
Suddenly spent and miserable.
Sure. I know that's what she feels, Papa.

TYRONE
Protests penitently.
She doesn't! She loves you as dearly as ever mother loved a son! I only said that because you put me in such a God-damned rage, raking up the past, and saying you hate me—

EDMUND
Dully.
I didn't mean it, Papa.
He suddenly smiles—kidding a bit drunkenly.
I'm like Mama, I can't help liking you, in spite of everything.

TYRONE
Grins a bit drunkenly in return.
I might say the same of you. You're no great shakes as a son. It's a case of "A poor thing but mine own."
They both chuckle with real, if alcoholic, affection. Tyrone changes the subject.
What's happened to our game? Whose play is it?

EDMUND

Yours, I guess.

*Tyrone plays a card which Edmund takes and the game gets forgotten
again.*

TYRONE

You mustn't let yourself be too downhearted, lad, by the bad news
you had today. Both the doctors promised me, if you obey orders
at this place you're going, you'll be cured in six months, or a year at
most.

EDMUND

His face hard again.

Don't kid me. You don't believe that.

TYRONE

Too vehemently.

Of course I believe it! Why shouldn't I believe it when both Hardy
and the specialist—?

EDMUND

You think I'm going to die.

TYRONE

That's a lie! You're crazy!

EDMUND

More bitterly.

So why waste money? That's why you're sending me to a state
farm—

TYRONE

In guilty confusion.

What state farm? It's the Hilltown Sanatorium, that's all I know,
and both doctors said it was the best place for you.

EDMUND

Scathingly.

For the money! That is, for nothing, or practically nothing. Don't
lie, Papa! You know damned well Hilltown Sanatorium is a state

institution! Jamie suspected you'd cry poorhouse to Hardy and he wormed the truth out of him.

TYRONE
Furiously.
That drunken loafer! I'll kick him out in the gutter! He's poisoned your mind against me ever since you were old enough to listen!

EDMUND
You can't deny it's the truth about the state farm, can you?

TYRONE
It's not true the way you look at it! What if it is run by the state? That's nothing against it. The state has the money to make a better place than any private sanatorium. And why shouldn't I take advantage of it? It's my right—and yours. We're residents. I'm a property owner. I help to support it. I'm taxed to death—

EDMUND
With bitter irony.
Yes, on property valued at a quarter of a million.

TYRONE
Lies! It's all mortgaged!

EDMUND
Hardy and the specialist know what you're worth. I wonder what they thought of you when they heard you moaning poorhouse and showing you wanted to wish me on charity!

TYRONE
It's a lie! All I told them was I couldn't afford any millionaire's sanatorium because I was land poor. That's the truth!

EDMUND
And then you went to the Club to meet McGuire and let him stick you with another bum piece of property!
As Tyrone starts to deny.
Don't lie about it! We met McGuire in the hotel bar after he left you. Jamie kidded him about hooking you, and he winked and laughed!

TYRONE
Lying feebly.
He's a liar if he said—

EDMUND
Don't lie about it!
With gathering intensity.
God, Papa, ever since I went to sea and was on my own, and found
out what hard work for little pay was, and what it felt like to be
broke, and starve, and camp on park benches because I had no
place to sleep, I've tried to be fair to you because I knew what you'd
been up against as a kid. I've tried to make allowances. Christ, you
have to make allowances in this damned family or go nuts! I have
tried to make allowances for myself when I remember all the rotten stuff I've pulled! I've tried to feel like Mama that you can't help
being what you are where money is concerned. But God Almighty,
this last stunt of yours is too much! It makes me want to puke!
Not because of the rotten way you're treating me. To hell with that!
I've treated you rottenly, in my way, more than once. But to think
when it's a question of your son having consumption, you can show
yourself up before the whole town as such a stinking old tightwad!
Don't you know Hardy will talk and the whole damned town will
know! Jesus, Papa, haven't you any pride or shame?
Bursting with rage.
And don't think I'll let you get away with it! I won't go to any
damned state farm just to save you a few lousy dollars to buy more
bum property with! You stinking old miser—!
*He chokes huskily, his voice trembling with rage, and then is shaken by
a fit of coughing.*

TYRONE
*Has shrunk back in his chair under this attack, his guilty contrition
greater than his anger. He stammers.*
Be quiet! Don't say that to me! You're drunk! I won't mind you.
Stop coughing, lad. You've got yourself worked up over nothing.
Who said you had to go to this Hilltown place? You can go any-
where you like. I don't give a damn what it costs. All I care about is

to have you get well. Don't call me a stinking miser, just because I don't want doctors to think I'm a millionaire they can swindle.

Edmund has stopped coughing. He looks sick and weak. His father stares at him frightenedly.

You look weak, lad. You'd better take a bracer.

EDMUND

Grabs the bottle and pours his glass brimfull—weakly.

Thanks.

He gulps down the whiskey.

TYRONE

Pours himself a big drink, which empties the bottle, and drinks it. His head bows and he stares dully at the cards on the table—vaguely.

Whose play is it?

He goes on dully, without resentment.

A stinking old miser. Well, maybe you're right. Maybe I can't help being, although all my life since I had anything I've thrown money over the bar to buy drinks for everyone in the house, or loaned money to sponges I knew would never pay it back—

With a loose-mouthed sneer of self-contempt.

But, of course, that was in barrooms, when I was full of whiskey. I can't feel that way about it when I'm sober in my home. It was at home I first learned the value of a dollar and the fear of the poorhouse. I've never been able to believe in my luck since. I've always feared it would change and everything I had would be taken away. But still, the more property you own, the safer you think you are. That may not be logical, but it's the way I have to feel. Banks fail, and your money's gone, but you think you can keep land beneath your feet.

Abruptly his tone becomes scornfully superior.

You said you realized what I'd been up against as a boy. The hell you do! How could you? You've had everything—nurses, schools, college, though you didn't stay there. You've had food, clothing. Oh, I know I had a fling of hard work with your back and hands, a bit of being homeless and penniless in a foreign land, and I respect you for it. But it was a game of romance and adventure to you. It was play.

EDMUND

Dully sarcastic.

Yes, particularly the time I tried to commit suicide at Jimmie the Priest's, and almost did.

TYRONE

You weren't in your right mind. No son of mine would ever — You were drunk.

EDMUND

I was stone cold sober. That was the trouble. I'd stopped to think too long.

TYRONE

With drunken peevishness.

Don't start your damned atheist morbidness again! I don't care to listen. I was trying to make plain to you —
Scornfully.

What do you know of the value of a dollar? When I was ten my father deserted my mother and went back to Ireland to die. Which he did soon enough, and deserved to, and I hope he's roasting in hell. He mistook rat poison for flour, or sugar, or something. There was gossip it wasn't by mistake but that's a lie. No one in my family ever —

EDMUND

My bet is, it wasn't by mistake.

TYRONE

More morbidness! Your brother put that in your head. The worst he can suspect is the only truth for him. But never mind. My mother was left, a stranger in a strange land, with four small children, me and a sister a little older and two younger than me. My two older brothers had moved to other parts. They couldn't help. They were hard put to it to keep themselves alive. There was no damned romance in our poverty. Twice we were evicted from the miserable hovel we called home, with my mother's few sticks of furniture thrown out in the street, and my mother and sisters crying. I cried, too, though I tried hard not to, because I was the man of the family.

At ten years old! There was no more school for me. I worked twelve hours a day in a machine shop, learning to make files. A dirty barn of a place where rain dripped through the roof, where you roasted in summer, and there was no stove in winter, and your hands got numb with cold, where the only light came through two small filthy windows, so on grey days I'd have to sit bent over with my eyes almost touching the files in order to see! You talk of work! And what do you think I got for it? Fifty cents a week! It's the truth! Fifty cents a week! And my poor mother washed and scrubbed for the Yanks by the day, and my older sister sewed, and my two younger stayed at home to keep the house. We never had clothes enough to wear, nor enough food to eat. Well I remember one Thanksgiving, or maybe it was Christmas, when some Yank in whose house mother had been scrubbing gave her a dollar extra for a present, and on the way home she spent it all on food. I can remember her hugging and kissing us and saying with tears of joy running down her tired face: "Glory be to God, for once in our lives we'll have enough for each of us!"

He wipes tears from his eyes.

A fine, brave, sweet woman. There never was a braver or finer.

EDMUND
Moved.
Yes, she must have been.

TYRONE
Her one fear was she'd get old and sick and have to die in the poor-house.

He pauses — then adds with grim humor.

It was in those days I learned to be a miser. A dollar was worth so much then. And once you've learned a lesson, it's hard to unlearn it. You have to look for bargains. If I took this state farm sanatorium for a good bargain, you'll have to forgive me. The doctors did tell me it's a good place. You must believe that, Edmund. And I swear I never meant you to go there if you didn't want to.

Vehemently.

You can choose any place you like! Never mind what it costs! Any place I can afford. Any place you like — within reason.

At this qualification, a grin twitches Edmund's lips. His resentment has gone. His father goes on with an elaborately offhand, casual air.

There was another sanatorium the specialist recommended. He said it had a record as good as any place in the country. It's endowed by a group of millionaire factory owners, for the benefit of their workers principally, but you're eligible to go there because you're a resident. There's such a pile of money behind it, they don't have to charge much. It's only seven dollars a week but you get ten times that value.
Hastily.

I don't want to persuade you to anything, understand. I'm simply repeating what I was told.

EDMUND

Concealing his smile — casually.

Oh, I know that. It sounds like a good bargain to me. I'd like to go there. So that settles that.
Abruptly he is miserably desperate again — dully.

It doesn't matter a damn now, anyway. Let's forget it!
Changing the subject.

How about our game? Whose play is it?

TYRONE

Mechanically.

I don't know. Mine, I guess. No, it's yours.
Edmund plays a card. His father takes it. Then about to play from his hand, he again forgets the game.

Yes, maybe life overdid the lesson for me, and made a dollar worth too much, and the time came when that mistake ruined my career as a fine actor.
Sadly.

I've never admitted this to anyone before, lad, but tonight I'm so heartsick I feel at the end of everything, and what's the use of fake pride and pretense. That God-damned play I bought for a song and made such a great success in — a great money success — it ruined me with its promise of an easy fortune. I didn't want to do anything else, and by the time I woke up to the fact I'd become a slave to the damned thing and did try other plays, it was too late. They had identified me with that one part, and didn't want me in anything else. They were right, too. I'd lost the great talent I once had through years of easy repetition, never learning a new part, never really working hard. Thirty-five to forty thousand dollars net profit a season like snapping your fingers! It was too great a temptation. Yet before I bought the damned thing I was considered one of the three or four young actors with the greatest artistic promise in America. I'd worked like hell. I'd left a good job as a machinist to take supers' parts because I loved the theater. I was wild with ambition. I read all the plays ever written. I studied Shakespeare as you'd study the Bible. I educated myself. I got rid of an Irish brogue you could cut with a knife. I loved Shakespeare. I would have acted in any of his plays for nothing, for the joy of being alive in his great poetry. And I acted well in him. I felt inspired by him. I could have been a great Shakespearean actor, if I'd kept on. I know that! In 1874 when Edwin Booth came to the theater in Chicago where I was leading man, I played Cassius to his Brutus one night, Brutus to his Cassius the next, Othello to his Iago, and so on. The first night I played Othello, he said to our manager, "That young man is playing Othello better than I ever did!"

Proudly.

That from Booth, the greatest actor of his day or any other! And it was true! And I was only twenty-seven years old! As I look back on it now, that night was the high spot in my career. I had life where I wanted it! And for a time after that I kept on upward with ambition high. Married your mother. Ask her what I was like in those days. Her love was an added incentive to ambition. But a few years later my good bad luck made me find the big money-maker. It wasn't that in my eyes at first. It was a great romantic part I knew I could play better than anyone. But it was a great box office success from the start—and then life had me where it wanted me—at from thirty-five to forty thousand net profit a season! A fortune in those days—or even in these.

Bitterly.

What the hell was it I wanted to buy, I wonder, that was worth— Well, no matter. It's a late day for regrets.

He glances vaguely at his cards.

My play, isn't it?

EDMUND

Moved, stares at his father with understanding—slowly.
I'm glad you've told me this, Papa. I know you a lot better now.

TYRONE

With a loose, twisted smile.
Maybe I shouldn't have told you. Maybe you'll only feel more contempt for me. And it's a poor way to convince you of the value of a
dollar.
*Then as if this phrase automatically aroused an habitual association in
his mind, he glances up at the chandelier disapprovingly.*
The glare from those extra lights hurts my eyes. You don't mind if
I turn them out, do you? We don't need them, and there's no use
making the Electric Company rich.

EDMUND

Controlling a wild impulse to laugh—agreeably.
No, sure not. Turn them out.

TYRONE

*Gets heavily and a bit waveringly to his feet and gropes uncertainly for
the lights—his mind going back to its line of thought.*
No, I don't know what the hell it was I wanted to buy.
He clicks out one bulb.
On my solemn oath, Edmund, I'd gladly face not having an acre of
land to call my own, nor a penny in the bank—
He clicks out another bulb.
I'd be willing to have no home but the poorhouse in my old age if
I could look back now on having been the fine artist I might have
been.
*He turns out the third bulb, so only the reading lamp is on, and sits
down again heavily. Edmund suddenly cannot hold back a burst of
strained, ironical laughter. Tyrone is hurt.*
What the devil are you laughing at?

EDMUND

Not at you, Papa. At life. It's so damned crazy.

TYRONE

Growls.

More of your morbidness! There's nothing wrong with life. It's we
who—

He quotes.

"The fault, dear Brutus, is not in our stars, but in ourselves that we
are underlings."

He pauses—then sadly.

The praise Edwin Booth gave my Othello. I made the manager put
down his exact words in writing. I kept it in my wallet for years. I
used to read it every once in a while until finally it made me feel so
bad I didn't want to face it any more. Where is it now, I wonder?
Somewhere in this house. I remember I put it away carefully—

EDMUND

With a wry ironical sadness.

It might be in an old trunk in the attic, along with Mama's wedding dress.

Then as his father stares at him, he adds quickly.

For Pete's sake, if we're going to play cards, let's play.

*He takes the card his father had played and leads. For a moment, they
play the game, like mechanical chess players. Then Tyrone stops, listening to a sound upstairs.*

TYRONE

She's still moving around. God knows when she'll go to sleep.

EDMUND

Pleads tensely.

For Christ's sake, Papa, forget it!

*He reaches out and pours a drink. Tyrone starts to protest, then gives it
up. Edmund drinks. He puts down the glass. His expression changes.
When he speaks it is as if he were deliberately giving way to drunkenness and seeking to hide behind a maudlin manner.*

Yes, she moves above and beyond us, a ghost haunting the past, and
here we sit pretending to forget, but straining our ears listening for
the slightest sound, hearing the fog drip from the eaves like the un-
even tick of a rundown, crazy clock—or like the dreary tears of a

trollop spattering in a puddle of stale beer on a honky-tonk table top!

He laughs with maudlin appreciation.

Not so bad, that last, eh? Original, not Baudelaire. Give me credit!

Then with alcoholic talkativeness.

You've just told me some high spots in your memories. Want to hear mine? They're all connected with the sea. Here's one. When I was on the Squarehead square rigger, bound for Buenos Aires. Full moon in the Trades. The old hooker driving fourteen knots. I lay on the bowsprit, facing astern, with the water foaming into spume under me, the masts with every sail white in the moonlight, towering high above me. I became drunk with the beauty and singing rhythm of it, and for a moment I lost myself—actually lost my life. I was set free! I dissolved in the sea, became white sails and flying spray, became beauty and rhythm, became moonlight and the ship and the high dim-starred sky! I belonged, without past or future, within peace and unity and a wild joy, within something greater than my own life, or the life of Man, to Life itself! To God, if you want to put it that way. Then another time, on the American Line, when I was lookout on the crow's nest in the dawn watch. A calm sea, that time. Only a lazy ground swell and a slow drowsy roll of the ship. The passengers asleep and none of the crew in sight. No sound of man. Black smoke pouring from the funnels behind and beneath me. Dreaming, not keeping lookout, feeling alone, and above, and apart, watching the dawn creep like a painted dream over the sky and sea which slept together. Then the moment of ecstatic freedom came. The peace, the end of the quest, the last harbor, the joy of belonging to a fulfillment beyond men's lousy, pitiful, greedy fears and hopes and dreams! And several other times in my life, when I was swimming far out, or lying alone on a beach, I have had the same experience. Became the sun, the hot sand, green seaweed anchored to a rock, swaying in the tide. Like a saint's vision of beatitude. Like the veil of things as they seem drawn back by an unseen hand. For a second you see—and seeing the secret, are the secret. For a second there is meaning! Then the hand lets the veil fall and you are alone, lost in the fog again, and you stumble on toward nowhere, for no good reason!

He grins wryly.

It was a great mistake, my being born a man, I would have been much more successful as a sea gull or a fish. As it is, I will always be a stranger who never feels at home, who does not really want and is not really wanted, who can never belong, who must always be a little in love with death!

TYRONE

Stares at him — impressed.

Yes, there's the makings of a poet in you all right.

Then protesting uneasily.

But that's morbid craziness about not being wanted and loving death.

EDMUND

Sardonically.

The *makings* of a poet. No, I'm afraid I'm like the guy who is always panhandling for a smoke. He hasn't even got the makings. He's got only the habit. I couldn't touch what I tried to tell you just now. I just stammered. That's the best I'll ever do, I mean, if I live. Well, it will be faithful realism, at least. Stammering is the native eloquence of us fog people.

A pause. Then they both jump startledly as there is a noise from outside the house, as if someone had stumbled and fallen on the front steps. Edmund grins.

Well, that sounds like the absent brother. He must have a peach of a bun on.

TYRONE

Scowling.

That loafer! He caught the last car, bad luck to it.

He gets to his feet.

Get him to bed, Edmund. I'll go out on the porch. He has a tongue like an adder when he's drunk. I'd only lose my temper.

He goes out the door to the side porch as the front door in the hall bangs shut behind Jamie. Edmund watches with amusement Jamie's wavering progress through the front parlor. Jamie comes in. He is very drunk and woozy on his legs. His eyes are glassy, his face bloated, his speech blurred, his mouth slack like his father's, a leer on his lips.

JAMIE
Swaying and blinking in the doorway—in a loud voice.
What ho! What ho!

EDMUND
Sharply.
Nix on the loud noise!

JAMIE
Blinks at him.
Oh, hello, Kid.
With great seriousness.
I'm as drunk as a fiddler's bitch.

EDMUND
Dryly.
Thanks for telling me your great secret.

JAMIE
Grins foolishly.
Yes. Unneshesary information Number One, eh?
He bends and slaps at the knees of his trousers.
Had serious accident. The front steps tried to trample on me. Took advantage of fog to waylay me. Ought to be a lighthouse out there. Dark in here, too.
Scowling.
What the hell is this, the morgue? Lesh have some light on subject.
He sways forward to the table, reciting Kipling.
  "Ford, ford, ford o' Kabul river,
    Ford o' Kabul river in the dark!
    Keep the crossing-stakes beside you, an' they will surely guide you
    'Cross the ford o' Kabul river in the dark."
He fumbles at the chandelier and manages to turn on the three bulbs.
Thash more like it. To hell with old Gaspard. Where is the old tight-wad?

EDMUND

Out on the porch.

JAMIE

Can't expect us to live in the Black Hole of Calcutta.
His eyes fix on the full bottle of whiskey.
Say! Have I got the d.t.'s?
He reaches out fumblingly and grabs it.
By God, it's real. What's matter with the Old Man tonight? Must be ossified to forget he left this out. Grab opportunity by the fore-lock. Key to my success.
He slops a big drink into a glass.

EDMUND

You're stinking now. That will knock you stiff.

JAMIE

Wisdom from the mouth of babes. Can the wise stuff, Kid. You're still wet behind the ears.
He lowers himself into a chair, holding the drink carefully aloft.

EDMUND

All right. Pass out if you want to.

JAMIE

Can't, that's trouble. Had enough to sink a ship, but can't sink. Well, here's hoping.
He drinks.

EDMUND

Shove over the bottle. I'll have one, too.

JAMIE

With sudden, big-brotherly solicitude, grabbing the bottle.
No, you don't. Not while I'm around. Remember doctor's orders. Maybe no one else gives a damn if you die, but I do. My kid brother. I love your guts, Kid. Everything else is gone. You're all I've got left.
Pulling bottle closer to him.
So no booze for you, if I can help it.
Beneath his drunken sentimentality there is a genuine sincerity.

EDMUND
Irritably.
Oh, lay off it.

JAMIE
Is hurt and his face hardens.
You don't believe I care, eh? Just drunken bull.
He shoves the bottle over.
All right. Go ahead and kill yourself.

EDMUND
Seeing he is hurt—affectionately.
Sure I know you care, Jamie, and I'm going on the wagon. But tonight doesn't count. Too many damned things have happened today.
He pours a drink.
Here's how.
He drinks.

JAMIE
Sobers up momentarily and with a pitying look.
I know, Kid. It's been a lousy day for you.
Then with sneering cynicism.
I'll bet old Gaspard hasn't tried to keep you off booze. Probably give you a case to take with you to the state farm for pauper patients. The sooner you kick the bucket, the less expense.
With contemptuous hatred.
What a bastard to have for a father! Christ, if you put him in a book, no one would believe it!

EDMUND
Defensively.
Oh, Papa's all right, if you try to understand him—and keep your sense of humor.

JAMIE
Cynically.
He's been putting on the old sob act for you, eh? He can always kid you. But not me. Never again.

Then slowly.

Although, in a way, I do feel sorry for him about one thing. But he has even that coming to him. He's to blame.

Hurriedly.

But to hell with that.

He grabs the bottle and pours another drink, appearing very drunk again.

That lash drink's getting me. This one ought to put the lights out. Did you tell Gaspard I got it out of Doc Hardy this sanatorium is a charity dump?

EDMUND

Reluctantly.

Yes. I told him I wouldn't go there. It's all settled now. He said I can go anywhere I want.

He adds, smiling without resentment.

Within reason, of course.

JAMIE

Drunkenly imitating his father.

Of course, lad. Anything within reason.

Sneering.

That means another cheap dump. Old Gaspard, the miser in "The Bells," that's a part he can play without make-up.

EDMUND

Irritably.

Oh, shut up, will you. I've heard that Gaspard stuff a million times.

JAMIE

Shrugs his shoulders—thickly.

Aw right, if you're shatisfied—let him get away with it. It's your funeral—I mean, I hope it won't be.

EDMUND

Changing the subject.

What did you do uptown tonight? Go to Mamie Burns?

JAMIE

Very drunk, his head nodding.

Sure thing. Where else could I find suitable feminine companion-
ship? And love. Don't forget love. What is a man without a good
woman's love? A God-damned hollow shell.

EDMUND

Chuckles tipsily, letting himself go now and be drunk.

You're a nut.

JAMIE

Quotes with gusto from Oscar Wilde's "The Harlot's House."

"Then, turning to my love, I said,
 'The dead are dancing with the dead,
 The dust is whirling with the dust.'

But she—she heard the violin,
And left my side and entered in:
Love passed into the house of lust.

Then suddenly the tune went false,
The dancers wearied of the waltz . . ."

He breaks off, thickly.

Not strictly accurate. If my love was with me, I didn't notice it. She
must have been a ghost.

He pauses.

Guess which one of Mamie's charmers I picked to bless me with
her woman's love. It'll hand you a laugh, Kid. I picked Fat Violet.

EDMUND

Laughs drunkenly.

No, honest? Some pick! God, she weighs a ton. What the hell for, a
joke?

JAMIE

No joke. Very serious. By the time I hit Mamie's dump I felt very
sad about myself and all the other poor bums in the world. Ready
for a weep on any old womanly bosom. You know how you get
when John Barleycorn turns on the soft music inside you. Then,
soon as I got in the door, Mamie began telling me all her troubles.

Beefed how rotten business was, and she was going to give Fat Violet the gate. Customers didn't fall for Vi. Only reason she'd kept her was she could play the piano. Lately Vi's gone on drunks and been too boiled to play, and was eating her out of house and home, and although Vi was a goodhearted dumbbell, and she felt sorry for her because she didn't know how the hell she'd make a living, still business was business, and she couldn't afford to run a home for fat tarts. Well, that made me feel sorry for Fat Violet, so I squandered two bucks of your dough to escort her upstairs. With no dishonorable intentions whatever. I like them fat, but not that fat. All I wanted was a little heart-to-heart talk concerning the infinite sorrow of life.

EDMUND
Chuckles drunkenly.
Poor Vi! I'll bet you recited Kipling and Swinburne and Dowson and gave her "I have been faithful to thee, Cynara, in my fashion."

JAMIE
Grins loosely.
Sure—with the Old Master, John Barleycorn, playing soft music. She stood it for a while. Then she got good and sore. Got the idea I took her upstairs for a joke. Gave me a grand bawling out. Said she was better than a drunken bum who recited poetry. Then she began to cry. So I had to say I loved her because she was fat, and she wanted to believe that, and I stayed with her to prove it, and that cheered her up, and she kissed me when I left, and said she'd fallen hard for me, and we both cried a little more in the hallway, and everything was fine, except Mamie Burns thought I'd gone bughouse.

EDMUND
Quotes derisively.

> "Harlots and
> Hunted have pleasures of their own to give,
> The vulgar herd can never understand."

JAMIE
Nods his head drunkenly.
Egzactly! Hell of a good time, at that. You should have stuck around

with me, Kid. Mamie Burns inquired after you. Sorry to hear you were sick. She meant it, too.

He pauses—then with maudlin humor, in a ham-actor tone.

This night has opened my eyes to a great career in store for me, my boy! I shall give the art of acting back to the performing seals, which are its most perfect expression. By applying my natural God-given talents in their proper sphere, I shall attain the pinnacle of success! I'll be the lover of the fat woman in Barnum and Bailey's circus!

Edmund laughs. Jamie's mood changes to arrogant disdain.

Pah! Imagine me sunk to the fat girl in a hick town hooker shop! Me! Who have made some of the best-lookers on Broadway sit up and beg!

He quotes from Kipling's "Sestina of the Tramp-Royal."

"Speakin' in general, I 'ave tried 'em all,

The 'appy roads that take you o'er the world."

With sodden melancholy.

Not so apt. Happy roads is bunk. Weary roads is right. Get you nowhere fast. That's where I've got—nowhere. Where everyone lands in the end, even if most of the suckers won't admit it.

EDMUND

Derisively.

Can it! You'll be crying in a minute.

JAMIE

Starts and stares at his brother for a second with bitter hostility—thickly.

Don't get—too damned fresh.

Then abruptly.

But you're right. To hell with repining! Fat Violet's a good kid. Glad I stayed with her. Christian act. Cured her blues. Hell of a good time. You should have stuck with me, Kid. Taken your mind off your troubles. What's the use coming home to get the blues over what can't be helped. All over—finished now—not a hope!

He stops, his head nodding drunkenly, his eyes closing—then suddenly he looks up, his face hard, and quotes jeeringly.

"If I were hanged on the highest hill,

Mother o' mine, O mother o' mine!
I know whose love would follow me still . . ."

EDMUND
Violently.
Shut up!

JAMIE
In a cruel, sneering tone with hatred in it.
Where's the hophead? Gone to sleep?
Edmund jerks as if he'd been struck. There is a tense silence. Edmund's face looks stricken and sick. Then in a burst of rage he springs from his chair.

EDMUND
You dirty bastard!
He punches his brother in the face, a blow that glances off the cheekbone. For a second Jamie reacts pugnaciously and half rises from his chair to do battle, but suddenly he seems to sober up to a shocked realization of what he has said and he sinks back limply.

JAMIE
Miserably.
Thanks, Kid. I certainly had that coming. Don't know what made me—booze talking—You know me, Kid.

EDMUND
His anger ebbing.
I know you'd never say that unless—But God, Jamie, no matter how drunk you are, it's no excuse!
He pauses—miserably.
I'm sorry I hit you. You and I never scrap—that bad.
He sinks back on his chair.

JAMIE
Huskily.
It's all right. Glad you did. My dirty tongue. Like to cut it out.
He hides his face in his hands—dully.
I suppose it's because I feel so damned sunk. Because this time

165

Mama had me fooled. I really believed she had it licked. She thinks I always believe the worst, but this time I believed the best.

His voice flutters.

I suppose I can't forgive her—yet. It meant so much. I'd begun to hope, if she'd beaten the game, I could, too.

He begins to sob, and the horrible part of his weeping is that it appears sober, not the maudlin tears of drunkenness.

EDMUND

Blinking back tears himself.

God, don't I know how you feel! Stop it, Jamie!

JAMIE

Trying to control his sobs.

I've known about Mama so much longer than you. Never forget the first time I got wise. Caught her in the act with a hypo. Christ, I'd never dreamed before that any women but whores took dope!

He pauses.

And then this stuff of you getting consumption. It's got me licked. We've been more than brothers. You're the only pal I've ever had. I love your guts. I'd do anything for you.

EDMUND

Reaches out and pats his arm.

I know that, Jamie.

JAMIE

His crying over—drops his hands from his face—with a strange bitterness.

Yet I'll bet you've heard Mama and old Gaspard spill so much bunk about my hoping for the worst, you suspect right now I'm thinking to myself that Papa is old and can't last much longer, and if you were to die, Mama and I would get all he's got, and so I'm probably hoping—

EDMUND

Indignantly.

Shut up, you damned fool! What the hell put that in your nut?

He stares at his brother accusingly.
Yes, that's what I'd like to know. What put that in your mind?

JAMIE
Confusedly—appearing drunk again.
Don't be a dumbbell! What I said! Always suspected of hoping for the worst. I've got so I can't help—
Then drunkenly resentful.
What are you trying to do, accuse me? Don't play the wise guy with me! I've learned more of life than you'll ever know! Just because you've read a lot of highbrow junk, don't think you can fool me! You're only an overgrown kid! Mama's baby and Papa's pet! The family White Hope! You've been getting a swelled head lately. About nothing! About a few poems in a hick town newspaper! Hell, I used to write better stuff for the Lit magazine in college! You better wake up! You're setting no rivers on fire! You let hick town boobs flatter you with bunk about your future—
Abruptly his tone changes to disgusted contrition. Edmund has looked away from him, trying to ignore this tirade.
Hell, Kid, forget it. That goes for Sweeny. You know I don't mean it. No one hopes more than I do you'll knock 'em all dead. No one is prouder you've started to make good.
Drunkenly assertive.
Why shouldn't I be proud? Hell, it's purely selfish. You reflect credit on me. I've had more to do with bringing you up than anyone. I wised you up about women, so you'd never be a fall guy, or make any mistakes you didn't want to make! And who steered you on to reading poetry first? Swinburne, for example? I did! And because I once wanted to write, I planted it in your mind that someday you'd write! Hell, you're more than my brother. I made you! You're my Frankenstein!
He has risen to a note of drunken arrogance. Edmund is grinning with amusement now.

EDMUND
All right, I'm your Frankenstein. So let's have a drink.
He laughs.
You crazy nut!

JAMIE

Thickly.

I'll have a drink. Not you. Got to take care of you.

He reaches out with a foolish grin of doting affection and grabs his brother's hand.

Don't be scared of this sanatorium business. Hell, you can beat that standing on your head. Six months and you'll be in the pink. Probably haven't got consumption at all. Doctors lot of fakers. Told me years ago to cut out booze or I'd soon be dead—and here I am. They're all con men. Anything to grab your dough. I'll bet this state farm stuff is political graft game. Doctors get a cut for every patient they send.

EDMUND

Disgustedly amused.

You're the limit! At the Last Judgment, you'll be around telling everyone it's in the bag.

JAMIE

And I'll be right. Slip a piece of change to the Judge and be saved, but if you're broke you can go to hell!

He grins at this blasphemy and Edmund has to laugh. Jamie goes on.

"Therefore put money in thy purse." That's the only dope.

Mockingly.

The secret of my success! Look what it's got me!

He lets Edmund's hand go to pour a big drink, and gulps it down. He stares at his brother with bleary affection—takes his hand again and begins to talk thickly but with a strange, convincing sincerity.

Listen, Kid, you'll be going away. May not get another chance to talk. Or might not be drunk enough to tell you truth. So got to tell you now. Something I ought to have told you long ago—for your own good.

He pauses—struggling with himself. Edmund stares, impressed and uneasy. Jamie blurts out.

Not drunken bull, but "in vino veritas" stuff. You better take it seriously. Want to warn you—against me. Mama and Papa are right. I've been rotten bad influence. And worst of it is, I did it on purpose.

EDMUND
Uneasily.
Shut up! I don't want to hear—

JAMIE
Nix, Kid! You listen! Did it on purpose to make a bum of you. Or
part of me did. A big part. That part that's been dead so long. That
hates life. My putting you wise so you'd learn from my mistakes.
Believed that myself at times, but it's a fake. Made my mistakes
look good. Made getting drunk romantic. Made whores fascinating vampires instead of poor, stupid, diseased slobs they really are.
Made fun of work as sucker's game. Never wanted you succeed
and make me look even worse by comparison. Wanted you to fail.
Always jealous of you. Mama's baby, Papa's pet!
He stares at Edmund with increasing enmity.
And it was your being born that started Mama on dope. I know
that's not your fault, but all the same, God damn you, I can't help
hating your guts—!

EDMUND
Almost frightenedly.
Jamie! Cut it out! You're crazy!

JAMIE
But don't get wrong idea, Kid. I love you more than I hate you.
My saying what I'm telling you now proves it. I run the risk you'll
hate me—and you're all I've got left. But I didn't mean to tell you
that last stuff—go that far back. Don't know what made me. What
I wanted to say is, I'd like to see you become the greatest success in
the world. But you'd better be on your guard. Because I'll do my
damnedest to make you fail. Can't help it. I hate myself. Got to take
revenge. On everyone else. Especially you. Oscar Wilde's "Reading
Gaol" has the dope twisted. The man was dead and so he had to kill
the thing he loved. That's what it ought to be. The dead part of me
hopes you won't get well. Maybe he's even glad the game has got
Mama again! He wants company, he doesn't want to be the only
corpse around the house!
He gives a hard, tortured laugh.

EDMUND

Jesus, Jamie! You really have gone crazy!

JAMIE

Think it over and you'll see I'm right. Think it over when you're away from me in the sanatorium. Make up your mind you've got to tie a can to me—get me out of your life—think of me as dead—tell people, "I had a brother, but he's dead." And when you come back, look out for me. I'll be waiting to welcome you with that "my old pal" stuff, and give you the glad hand, and at the first good chance I get stab you in the back.

EDMUND

Shut up! I'll be God-damned if I'll listen to you any more—

JAMIE

As if he hadn't heard.
Only don't forget me. Remember I warned you—for your sake. Give me credit. Greater love hath no man than this, that he saveth his brother from himself.
Very drunkenly, his head bobbing.
That's all. Feel better now. Gone to confession. Know you absolve me, don't you, Kid? You understand. You're a damned fine kid. Ought to be. I made you. So go and get well. Don't die on me. You're all I've got left. God bless you, Kid.
His eyes close. He mumbles.
That last drink—the old K. O.
He falls into a drunken doze, not completely asleep. Edmund buries his face in his hands miserably. Tyrone comes in quietly through the screen door from the porch, his dressing gown wet with fog, the collar turned up around his throat. His face is stern and disgusted but at the same time pitying. Edmund does not notice his entrance.

TYRONE

In a low voice.
Thank God he's asleep.
Edmund looks up with a start.
I thought he'd never stop talking.

He turns down the collar of his dressing gown.

We'd better let him stay where he is and sleep it off.

Edmund remains silent. Tyrone regards him—then goes on.

I heard the last part of his talk. It's what I've warned you. I hope you'll heed the warning, now it comes from his own mouth.

Edmund gives no sign of having heard.

Tyrone adds pityingly.

But don't take it too much to heart, lad. He loves to exaggerate the worst of himself when he's drunk. He's devoted to you. It's the one good thing left in him.

He looks down on Jamie with a bitter sadness.

A sweet spectacle for me! My first-born, who I hoped would bear my name in honor and dignity, who showed such brilliant promise!

EDMUND

Miserably.

Keep quiet, can't you, Papa?

TYRONE

Pours a drink.

A waste! A wreck, a drunken hulk, done with and finished!

He drinks. Jamie has become restless, sensing his father's presence, struggling up from his stupor. Now he gets his eyes open to blink up at Tyrone. The latter moves back a step defensively, his face growing hard.

JAMIE

Suddenly points a finger at him and recites with dramatic emphasis.

 Clarence is come, false, fleeting, perjured Clarence,

  That stabbed me in the field by Tewksbury.

  Seize on him, Furies, take him into torment."

Then resentfully.

What the hell are you staring at?

He recites sardonically from Rossetti.

 "Look in my face. My name is Might-Have-Been;

  I am also called No More, Too Late, Farewell."

TYRONE

I'm well aware of that, and God knows I don't want to look at it.

EDMUND

Papa! Quit it!

JAMIE

Derisively.

Got a great idea for you, Papa. Put on revival of "The Bells" this season. Great part in it you can play without make-up. Old Gaspard, the miser!

Tyrone turns away, trying to control his temper.

EDMUND

Shut up, Jamie!

JAMIE

Jeeringly.

I claim Edwin Booth never saw the day when he could give as good a performance as a trained seal. Seals are intelligent and honest. They don't put up any bluffs about the Art of Acting. They admit they're just hams earning their daily fish.

TYRONE

Stung, turns on him in a rage.

You loafer!

EDMUND

Papa! Do you want to start a row that will bring Mama down? Jamie, go back to sleep! You've shot off your mouth too much already.

Tyrone turns away.

JAMIE

Thickly.

All right, Kid. Not looking for argument. Too damned sleepy.

He closes his eyes, his head nodding. Tyrone comes to the table and sits down, turning his chair so he won't look at Jamie. At once he becomes sleepy, too.

TYRONE

Heavily.

I wish to God she'd go to bed so that I could, too.

Drowsily.

I'm dog tired. I can't stay up all night like I used to. Getting old—old and finished.

With a bone-cracking yawn.

Can't keep my eyes open. I think I'll catch a few winks. Why don't you do the same, Edmund? It'll pass the time until she—

His voice trails off. His eyes close, his chin sags, and he begins to breathe heavily through his mouth. Edmund sits tensely. He hears something and jerks nervously forward in his chair, staring through the front parlor into the hall. He jumps up with a hunted, distracted expression. It seems for a second he is going to hide in the back parlor. Then he sits down again and waits, his eyes averted, his hands gripping the arms of his chair. Suddenly all five bulbs of the chandelier in the front parlor are turned on from a wall switch, and a moment later someone starts playing the piano in there—the opening of one of Chopin's simpler waltzes, done with a forgetful, stiff-fingered groping, as if an awkward schoolgirl were practicing it for the first time. Tyrone starts to wide-awakeness and sober dread, and Jamie's head jerks back and his eyes open. For a moment they listen frozenly. The playing stops as abruptly as it began, and Mary appears in the doorway. She wears a sky-blue dressing gown over her nightdress, dainty slippers with pompons on her bare feet. Her face is paler than ever. Her eyes look enormous. They glisten like polished black jewels. The uncanny thing is that her face now appears so youthful. Experience seems ironed out of it. It is a marble mask of girlish innocence, the mouth caught in a shy smile. Her white hair is braided in two pigtails which hang over her breast. Over one arm, carried neglectfully, trailing on the floor, as if she had forgotten she held it, is an old-fashioned white satin wedding gown, trimmed with duchesse lace. She hesitates in the doorway, glancing round the room, her forehead puckered puzzledly, like someone who has come to a room to get something but has become absent-minded on the way and forgotten what it was. They stare at her. She seems aware of them merely as she is aware of other objects in the room, the furniture, the windows, familiar things she accepts automatically as naturally belonging there but which she is too preoccupied to notice.

JAMIE

Breaks the cracking silence—bitterly, self-defensively sardonic.
The Mad Scene. Enter Ophelia!
*His father and brother both turn on him fiercely. Edmund is quicker.
He slaps Jamie across the mouth with the back of his hand.*

TYRONE

His voice trembling with suppressed fury.
Good boy, Edmund. The dirty blackguard! His own mother!

JAMIE

Mumbles guiltily, without resentment.
All right, Kid. Had it coming. But I told you how much I'd hoped—
He puts his hands over his face and begins to sob.

TYRONE

I'll kick you out in the gutter tomorrow, so help me God.
But Jamie's sobbing breaks his anger, and he turns and shakes his shoulder, pleading.
Jamie, for the love of God, stop it!
*Then Mary speaks, and they freeze into silence again, staring at her.
She has paid no attention whatever to the incident. It is simply a part
of the familiar atmosphere of the room, a background which does not
touch her preoccupation; and she speaks aloud to herself, not to them.*

MARY

I play so badly now. I'm all out of practice. Sister Theresa will give
me a dreadful scolding. She'll tell me it isn't fair to my father when
he spends so much money for extra lessons. She's quite right, it isn't
fair, when he's so good and generous, and so proud of me. I'll practice every day from now on. But something horrible has happened
to my hands. The fingers have gotten so stiff—
She lifts her hands to examine them with a frightened puzzlement.
The knuckles are all swollen. They're so ugly. I'll have to go to the
Infirmary and show Sister Martha.
With a sweet smile of affectionate trust.
She's old and a little cranky, but I love her just the same, and she has
things in her medicine chest that'll cure anything. She'll give me

something to rub on my hands, and tell me to pray to the Blessed Virgin, and they'll be well again in no time.

She forgets her hands and comes into the room, the wedding gown trailing on the floor. She glances around vaguely, her forehead puckered again.

Let me see. What did I come here to find? It's terrible, how absentminded I've become. I'm always dreaming and forgetting.

TYRONE
In a stifled voice.
What's that she's carrying, Edmund?

EDMUND
Dully.
Her wedding gown, I suppose.

TYRONE
Christ!
He gets to his feet and stands directly in her path — in anguish.
Mary! Isn't it bad enough — ?
Controlling himself — gently persuasive.
Here, let me take it, dear. You'll only step on it and tear it and get it dirty dragging it on the floor. Then you'd be sorry afterwards.
She lets him take it, regarding him from somewhere far away within herself, without recognition, without either affection or animosity.

MARY
With the shy politeness of a well-bred young girl toward an elderly gentleman who relieves her of a bundle.
Thank you. You are very kind.
She regards the wedding gown with a puzzled interest.
It's a wedding gown. It's very lovely, isn't it?
A shadow crosses her face and she looks vaguely uneasy.
I remember now. I found it in the attic hidden in a trunk. But I don't know what I wanted it for. I'm going to be a nun — that is, if I can only find —
She looks around the room, her forehead puckered again.
What is it I'm looking for? I know it's something I lost.

She moves back from Tyrone, aware of him now only as some obstacle in her path.

TYRONE

In hopeless appeal.

Mary!

But it cannot penetrate her preoccupation. She doesn't seem to hear him. He gives up helplessly, shrinking into himself, even his defensive drunkenness taken from him, leaving him sick and sober. He sinks back on his chair, holding the wedding gown in his arms with an unconscious clumsy, protective gentleness.

JAMIE

Drops his hand from his face, his eyes on the table top. He has suddenly sobered up, too—dully.

It's no good, Papa.

He recites from Swinburne's "A Leave-taking" and does it well, simply but with a bitter sadness.

"Let us rise up and part; she will not know.
Let us go seaward as the great winds go,
Full of blown sand and foam; what help is here?
There is no help, for all these things are so,
And all the world is bitter as a tear.
And how these things are, though ye strove to show,
She would not know."

MARY

Looking around her.

Something I miss terribly. It can't be altogether lost.

She starts to move around in back of Jamie's chair.

JAMIE

Turns to look up into her face—and cannot help appealing pleadingly in his turn.

Mama!

She does not seem to hear. He looks away hopelessly.

Hell! What's the use? It's no good.

He recites from "A Leave-taking" again with increased bitterness.

"Let us go hence, my songs; she will not hear.

176

Let us go hence together without fear;
Keep silence now, for singing-time is over,
And over all old things and all things dear.
She loves not you nor me as all we love her.
Yea, though we sang as angels in her ear,
She would not hear."

MARY

Looking around her.

Something I need terribly. I remember when ·I had it I was never lonely nor afraid. I can't have lost it forever, I would die if I thought that. Because then there would be no hope.

She moves like a sleepwalker, around the back of Jamie's chair, then forward toward left front, passing behind Edmund.

EDMUND

Turns impulsively and grabs her arm. As he pleads he has the quality of a bewilderedly hurt little boy.

Mama! It isn't a summer cold! I've got consumption!

MARY

For a second he seems to have broken through to her. She trembles and her expression becomes terrified. She calls distractedly, as if giving a command to herself.

No!

And instantly she is far away again. She murmurs gently but impersonally.

You must not try to touch me. You must not try to hold me. It isn't right, when I am hoping to be a nun.

He lets his hand drop from her arm. She moves left to the front end of the sofa beneath the windows and sits down, facing front, her hands folded in her lap, in a demure schoolgirlish pose.

JAMIE

Gives Edmund a strange look of mingled pity and jealous gloating.

You damned fool. It's no good.

He recites again from the Swinburne poem.

   "Let us go hence, go hence; she will not see.
   Sing all once more together; surely she,

She too, remembering days and words that were,
Will turn a little toward us, sighing; but we,
We are hence, we are gone, as though we had not been there.
Nay, and though all men seeing had pity on me,
She would not see."

TYRONE

Trying to shake off his hopeless stupor.

Oh, we're fools to pay any attention. It's the damned poison. But I've never known her to drown herself in it as deep as this.

Gruffly.

Pass me that bottle, Jamie. And stop reciting that damned morbid poetry. I won't have it in my house!

Jamie pushes the bottle toward him. He pours a drink without disarranging the wedding gown he holds carefully over his other arm and on his lap, and shoves the bottle back. Jamie pours his and passes the bottle to Edmund, who, in turn, pours one. Tyrone lifts his glass and his sons follow suit mechanically, but before they can drink Mary speaks and they slowly lower their drinks to the table, forgetting them.

MARY

Staring dreamily before her. Her face looks extraordinarily youthful and innocent. The shyly eager, trusting smile is on her lips as she talks aloud to herself.

I had a talk with Mother Elizabeth. She is so sweet and good. A saint on earth. I love her dearly. It may be sinful of me but I love her better than my own mother. Because she always understands, even before you say a word. Her kind blue eyes look right into your heart. You can't keep any secrets from her. You couldn't deceive her, even if you were mean enough to want to.

She gives a little rebellious toss of her head—with girlish pique.

All the same, I don't think she was so understanding this time. I told her I wanted to be a nun. I explained how sure I was of my vocation, that I had prayed to the Blessed Virgin to make me sure, and to find me worthy. I told Mother I had had a true vision when I was praying in the shrine of Our Lady of Lourdes, on the little island in the lake. I said I knew, as surely as I knew I was kneeling there, that the Blessed Virgin had smiled and blessed me with her consent. But Mother Elizabeth told me I must be more sure than that, even, that I must prove it wasn't simply my imagination. She said, if I was so sure, then I wouldn't mind putting myself to a test by going home after I graduated, and living as other girls lived, going out to parties and dances and enjoying myself; and then if after a year or two I still felt sure, I could come back to see her and we would talk it over again.

She tosses her head—indignantly.

I never dreamed Holy Mother would give me such advice! I was really shocked. I said, of course, I would do anything she suggested, but I knew it was simply a waste of time. After I left her, I felt all mixed up, so I went to the shrine and prayed to the Blessed Virgin and found peace again because I knew she heard my prayer and would always love me and see no harm ever came to me so long as I never lost my faith in her.

She pauses and a look of growing uneasiness comes over her face. She passes a hand over her forehead as if brushing cobwebs from her brain— vaguely.

That was in the winter of senior year. Then in the spring something happened to me. Yes, I remember. I fell in love with James Tyrone and was so happy for a time.

She stares before her in a sad dream. Tyrone stirs in his chair. Edmund and Jamie remain motionless.

CURTAIN

Tao House
September 20, 1940

Notes and Context

By the time Eugene O'Neill wrote *Long Day's Journey Into Night,* he was deeply self-conscious of the historical and cultural circumstances shaping his life and work. He rarely went to the movies or the theater, but he listened to serious music, read avidly a wide range of books, and conversed or corresponded with some of the great minds of his era. He also thought deeply about his Irish ethnicity, his Catholic education, his political opinions, and his relationship with the changing social landscape of America. The play reflects much of this self-consciousness, using references and allusions that are specific to the circumstances of the characters and the playwright. The notes below are organized by topic, with relevant page numbers given in parentheses.

Literary and Cultural Orientation

The remarkably precise and detailed opening stage directions (11–14), which some have criticized as excessive, are meant for readers of the play, not directors, designers, and actors. O'Neill intended for the play to be published twenty-five years after his death but never produced. He aimed to represent context in the way that a novelist does, so that the action could be imagined—seen, heard, felt—from the published script alone. The same goes for the parenthetical line readings (for example, "*With a wry ironical sadness*"), which are meant not to coach actors but to help the reader imagine a performance. Descriptions of the setting and characters provide an exact portrait from memory of O'Neill's home in New London, Connecticut, in August 1912. The directive notes, in contrast, reflect a virtual performance of the play that he has constructed as drama.

The male Tyrones are all deeply invested in, or at least conditioned by, books. The catalogue of books on the Tyrone family's bookshelves (11) gives insight into how O'Neill understood the characters' orientation to literature and belief systems. They reflect a focus on the written word, as the many allusions and quotations throughout the play demonstrate. The characters also relish the effect of quoting words at a fitting moment, reflecting a performer's sensibility even among those (Jamie and Edmund, also Mary) who disparage the theater. The first set of books would be those favored mainly by Edmund, though Jamie seems familiar with the poets listed. Most of these poets are late Victorian English writers who flourished in the last decades of the nineteenth century and exhibited in their poems and their lives an attitude some called decadent, a fascination with the impolite facets of modern life. Some of those poets embraced the term as an alternative to the idealized worldview of their Victorian contemporaries. Most of them are quoted in the play.

The novelists are all French (read in English translation, presumably, since we have no evidence that the brothers know any foreign language) and pushed the novel in the direction of realism, even naturalism, implying a frank embrace of the facts of the modern world. The philosophical books come from the Germanic challenge to traditional metaphysics, including Christianity, capitalism, and liberalism. O'Neill took a strong interest in radical thinking around the time he entered Princeton, in 1906. In a New York bookstore, he found writings that would lead to his self-identification as a "philosophical anarchist," especially the books of Max Stirner (whose name is misspelled in the typescript and the first edition), including the 1844 treatise *The Ego and His Own: The Case of the Individual Against Authority.* (Stirner's title could serve as a subtitle to the play, even without the coincidence of O'Neill's initials being E.G.O.) O'Neill also took an interest in the antidoctrinal, proto-existentialist books of Friedrich Nietzsche; he especially admired *Thus Spake Zarathustra* (1885), a poetic development of Nietzsche's ideas about the Übermensch, which is an image of the individual released from the bonds of conventional thought and social controls.[1]

These writings all attempt to rethink the self and the place of the individual in society, and that project also engages Ibsen, Shaw, and Strindberg. O'Neill took up Henrik Ibsen, the great pioneer of modern dramatists, in 1906 after reading George Bernard Shaw's *Quintessence of Ibsenism* (1891). Both Ibsen and Shaw turned the conventional drama on its head by breaking the artificial patterns used by most playwrights to resolve their stories—disclosure of long-buried secrets leading to a happy ending with romantic fulfillment. Resistant to idealism (that is, adherence to assumed and learned ideas even when they fail to match reality), Ibsen and Shaw showed that the stage can be a place for analysis of the modern world, in all its contradictions and complexity, as opposed to a simple celebration of its assumed pleasures. In his 1936 Nobel Prize acceptance address, O'Neill counted the writings of the Swedish playwright August Strindberg as most influential of all. He mentioned that he read Strindberg a year or more after *Long Day's Journey*'s setting, in 1913–1914, when English translations first became available.[2] Strindberg took modern drama beyond realism such as a camera might record into the twists and turns of the human mind, even into madness. *Long Day's Journey* begins in a world such as you might find in Ibsen but then crosses into Strindberg's territory in the last act, when we get a glimpse into the emotional and spiritual abyss within each character.

The second set of books reflects the mindset of James Tyrone, though we learn that he has tried to instill those values in—to impose those books on—his sons. The novels in his library illustrate a romantic belief in the power of the heroic individual, which was a useful model for the actor in an era in which "star" acting required a performer who could electrify an audience of two or three thousand people. Alexandre Dumas completed his epic novel *The Count of Monte Cristo* in 1844. He later adapted it as a ten-act play, eventually whittled down to the three-hour version performed more than four thousand times from 1883 through 1912 by Eugene's father, James O'Neill. That title is not mentioned in *Long Day's Journey,* but when the fictional Mary tells Cathleen of first seeing the fictional Tyrone on the stage, she says it was "a play about the French Revolution and the leading part was a nobleman. . . . I wept when he was thrown in prison" (107). Those details loosely match what she would have seen in *Monte Cristo,* though the Revolution per se is not depicted, only its Napoleonic aftermath, and Edmond Dantès, who is thrown in prison, is not a nobleman by birth. He assumes the title of count after acquiring a large fortune from a fellow prisoner, an adopted father figure. The novel can be read as Dumas's fantasy of revenge over the loss of his own father in the Napoleonic era, ironically echoed in Tyrone's (and James O'Neill's) loss of a father at an early age.

The Tyrone family's frequent allusions to Irishness derive not just from the accident of lineage but from a studied engagement with that heritage.[3] Charles Lever (1806–1872) wrote popular comical novels of Irish life, and multiple histories of Ireland are at hand on the bookshelves. Yet Tyrone also investigates *The World's Best Literature* and even owns David Hume's six-volume *History of England,* a work criticized for its promotion of Tory values. The seemingly most important items in his library are the sets of Shakespeare, whose portrait hangs above Edmund's books, suggesting a common thread. Normand Berlin's *O'Neill's Shakespeare* argues for the importance of Shakespeare in O'Neill's literary universe.[4]

All of the characters in the play have a connection to Ireland, both in heritage and in characteristics. O'Neill named the family Tyrone after the Irish county once ruled by the ancestral O'Neills, who were great heroes in Irish lore. James Tyrone takes pride in all aspects of his heritage, though to become an actor he had to learn to speak without the accent ("an Irish brogue you could cut with a knife," 153). Mary's aspiration to be accepted in higher society places her in the category of lace-curtain Irish, which suggests an effort to leave her second-generation Irishness behind, though we hear that her laughter sometimes bears a trace of the Irish lilt. Many performers of both James and Mary have brought out traces of an Irish accent at various moments when the characters become submerged in the past. The sons also reflect an Irish self-consciousness and have the coloration of what is known as the Black Irish, a term that has quasi-racial connotations but is also sometimes associated with the stereotype of a hard-drinking, brutal masculinity, fallen from Catholic belief. Cathleen is a first-generation Irish immigrant who sometimes uses Gaelic words, such as "banshee" (a female fairy known for wailing at the approach of someone's death, 100), "cess" (luck, 100), and "trauneen" (a blade of grass or a person with a similar slimness, 103). The Ireland from which the immigrants came was a country of failing agriculture, and the former "bog-trotters" (82) like Shaughnessy were trying to have greater success in America with land that was less like a bog, or wetland.

No set of books is assigned to Mary Tyrone, but she refers frequently to the dogma of the Catholic Church, especially beliefs about her namesake in the Christian story, the Blessed Virgin Mary. She also recalls with pleasure the music she played as a student of the piano, especially the lushly sensual music of Frédéric Chopin (1810–1849), who was born in Poland but whose career flourished in Paris. The adaptation of a European peasant dance involving a sliding movement into the ballroom dance known as the waltz was a relatively recent innovation in Chopin's day. It was immediately associated with a more sensuous—and some thought shameless—mode of social interaction in the Romantic era.

The stage directions offer clues about what O'Neill understood to be the material status and class of this family. Mary and Tyrone sharply disagree about the quality of the house and its furnishings. O'Neill describes a house with a living room, two parlors, a dining room, and a kitchen on the first floor, a large porch outside, and four bedrooms, including a "spare room," on the second floor. For a mere summer cottage, that is a lot of space. Much of the furniture is wicker, which is more impermanent than hardwood furniture, but there are also oak pieces. The reading lamp on the center table is plugged into the chandelier, which might reflect that this older house has had to be retrofitted for electricity and that the job was not done well. We might interpret this as a sign of cheapness, but there are many windows, and the doors are of double width.

Little information is given about the characters' clothing except for Tyrone's "shabby" (13) dress, which seems notably in contrast to the handsome costumes he is accustomed to wearing onstage. The family can afford servants (chauffeur, cook, and housemaid), and no doubt a gardener might be found, but Tyrone seems to prefer to do this labor himself. It should be noted that O'Neill was working in his own garden in California nearly every afternoon following his mornings writing *Long Day's Journey*, though he also employed more than one gardener. O'Neill dressed well for dinner, but he enjoyed taking on the laborer's role and might thus have felt sympathy with the "peasant" streak in Tyrone. Jamie prefers a shirt with a collar and a tie for the same sort of work, and Edmund also wears a collar and tie (collars were detachable in those days so that they could be cleaned and pressed separately). That manner of dress was standard at the time for anyone other than the lowest laborer. Again, our questions about the class identification and material status of the characters will not be given a simple answer in O'Neill's stage directions.

The family exhibits a facility with language, which contributes to *Long Day's Journey*'s distinctive flavor. Some have criticized other O'Neill plays for perceived weaknesses in the dialogue, and the degree to which O'Neill had the "touch" (157) of a poet has been disputed. But few find fault in the rich display of language in this play.[5] O'Neill carefully delineates the forms of speech, so that we understand some modes as inherited, some as learned. Mary is an expert at affecting the pious phraseology of her Catholic upbringing, which is hers alone, but she has given lessons to the others in the rhetoric of accusation and the poetics of deception. Jamie has acquired a mode of speech that Tyrone characterizes as his "rotten Broadway loafer's lingo" (78), and Edmund has learned a little of that from Jamie. But Edmund has another mode he picked up from his days at sea, a working-class bluntness, missing only the four-letter words O'Neill favored in his own way of speaking. Both Jamie and Edmund turn frequently to the poetry they have read, often for ironic effect.

The slang associated with drinking finds colorful ways to name drunkenness: "boiled" (163) or having "a bun on" (22), both of which might come from the image of a drinker's enlarged and reddened nose, or "ossified" (159), meaning rendered bonelike or paralyzed from too much booze. Liquor is called "redeye" (57) or "John Barleycorn" (162); a drinker is a "souse" (138), and an extra drink is a "bracer" (149). O'Neill's brother Jamie was just as addicted to gambling, especially horse races ("the ponies," 21), as he was to alcohol, and in that seedy world it helps to have the "dope sheet" (21), a printed guide to make sure you don't get the "wrong dope" (57) like a "sucker" (144).

The gambler's "dope," intended to "wise you up," is not at all the same as that of the "dope fiend" (123) or "hophead" (165). The study of addiction grew largely out of observing the effect of opium products, such as the morphine taken by Mary. As late as 1912, these products were barely regulated by government authorities and still poorly understood by the medical community. But Jamie, the Broadway "sport" (34), understands that "the game" (166, 168) is a term that links the unfair worlds of drinking, gambling, and drug addiction, as well as a cruel metaphor for life. He also understands that the world of prostitution is another aspect of the game, where a "trollop"

(156), "trull" (136), "tart" (163), "harlot" (136), "hooker" (164), or "vampire" (169), so named because such women—and these are all synonyms for *whore*—seem to pull a man in in order to suck his blood (that is, his money), pursues whatever profit she can with her sexual allure. Broadway, or "the Great White Way" (135, so named for its defiance of the night with its bright lights), in those days designated not just a theater district but a continuum of many businesses to gratify the senses for profit. An actress can be someone who helps create the romantic visions of plays that feature a "matinee idol" (107, a male performer known to appeal to female audiences) like James Tyrone, but some actresses are sexualized by applying "paint" (117, heavy makeup), and they might even become a "burlesque queen" (137, a female performer in the most erotic form of theater in that day). The existence of that continuum is enough to make those whose sense of respectability was offended by such displays have suspicions about any aspect of the theater. Tyrone insists on an idealized understanding of the theatrical art, and he defends his record as a husband who has not been corrupted by it. But Mary has evidently had occasion to be alienated by his drinking, especially with men at "the Club" (23). James O'Neill was a founding member of the Players Club, which was intended initially for leading men in the theater, but there were many other clubs available for a sociable and well-to-do man like him, even in New London, where he was more highly regarded than *Long Day's Journey* might lead one to think.

Literary Allusions and Quotations

(21) "The Moor, I know his trumpet" (Shakespeare, *Othello*, 2.1.178). A military commander had a distinctive musical trumpet fanfare, blown to herald his arrival. Here the allusion is to the sound of Tyrone's snoring.

(33) "Ingratitude, the vilest weed that grows." This saying is of unknown origin, but it alludes to a sure way of spoiling a garden.

(80) "God is dead: of His pity for men hath God died." These are the most notorious words associated with the philosophy of Friedrich Nietzsche (from *Thus Spake Zarathustra,* a poetic restatement of an idea first put forward in *The Gay Science,* where it alludes to a new consciousness associated with the Übermensch, in which the notion of a transcendent deity is replaced by "the will to power"). O'Neill

quotes the Thomas Common translation, first published in 1909, which uses Elizabethan diction.

(92) "How sharper than a serpent's tooth . . ." (Shakespeare, *King Lear*, 1.4.312). These are the words spoken by Lear when he (mistakenly) thinks his daughter Cordelia has demonstrated a lack of love for him.

(132) "Enough is *not* as good as a feast." The English proverb is inverted here in order to contradict the idea that one should take only an adequate amount of something, not an excess.

(133) "They are not long, the weeping and the laughter" (Ernest Dowson, "Vitae summa brevis spem nos vetat incohare longam"). Dowson's title comes from a line of an ode by Horace: "The brief sum of life forbids us the hope of enduring long." His poem expresses a morbid regret at the passing of life, but his evocation of the "days of wine and roses" has been taken as a way of noting that life passes even more rapidly for those who indulge in its pleasures.

(133) "It's the three Gorgons. . . . Or it's Pan." According to Greek myth, one glance at any of the three female snake-haired Gorgons would turn a person to stone. The Greek word *gorgós* refers to anything that is terrifying—or petrifying. Similarly, the myth of Pan expresses the terrifying power of creatures that are wild.

(134) "We are such stuff as dreams are made on . . ." (Shakespeare, *The Tempest*, 4.1.156). These words, spoken by Prospero at the conclusion of the masque he has created, have long been taken as Shakespeare's expression of wonder at the capacity of the theater to summon up an illusion of life, which then passes. Thus, in a sense, Tyrone admires the way humans are godlike, a notion that Edmund directly skewers.

(135) "Be always drunken . . ." (Charles Baudelaire, translated by Arthur Symons). Baudelaire (1821–1867) has been called "the writer of modern life"; he found poetry not in a rustic landscape but in the streets of a city. This poem comes from Baudelaire's book *Le Spleen de Paris* ("spleen" referring to the impulse to malice). The Symons translation was not published until 1926.

(136) "With heart at rest . . ." (Baudelaire, "Epilogue," translated by Symons). This poem comes from Baudelaire's book *Les Fleurs du mal* ("The flowers of evil [or illness]"), which is a darkly ironic inversion of the sort of flowers associated with romantic poetry.

(137) "All night upon mine heart . . ." (Dowson, "Non sum qualis eram bonae sub Regno Cynarae," ca. 1896; title from a line of Catullus, "The days when Cynara was queen will not return for me"). The dream vision of a dead lover comes to an end with the poet awakening at dawn to his own mortality. Dowson was at the time in despair at the loss of a woman he loved, having also lost his father to tuberculosis (consumption) and his mother to suicide, and he was soon to succumb to tuberculosis at the age of thirty-two.

(145) "A poor thing but mine own" (variant of Shakespeare, *As You Like It*, 5.4.56). Tyrone misquotes the fool Touchstone's "an ill-favoured thing, sir, but mine own," which he says in reference to his own honesty.

(153) "Edwin Booth . . . Cassius to his Brutus . . . Othello to his Iago." Cassius and Brutus, in Shakespeare's *Julius Caesar*, stand on opposite sides of a great moral conflict concerning Caesar, and their arguments with each other offer memorable examples of Shakespearean rhetoric, including the speech Tyrone quotes on page 155. The traitorous Iago manipulates Othello to his doom, again in scenes of immense appeal to a great actor.

(155) "The fault, dear Brutus . . ." (Shakespeare, *Julius Caesar*, 1.2.140). See above.

(156) "Like the veil of things." Edmund alludes to a notion found in Indian religions that humans experience the world not directly but through a veil of illusion, which is conceived as the god Maya. O'Neill took a strong interest in Eastern religious concepts in the 1920s, but this line seems to give evidence that he was already thinking in these terms earlier.

(158) "Ford, ford, ford o' Kabul river . . ." (Rudyard Kipling, "Ford o' Kabul River"). Kipling (1865–1936) is mostly remembered as a writer of prose, especially stories that ranged throughout the British Empire (for example, *The Jungle Book*), but in his day he was thought of as a prodigious writer in all forms, a quintessential literary genius. This poem refers to a river in Afghanistan.

(158–161) "To hell with old Gaspard . . . 'The Bells.'" A popular 1877 French operetta, *Les Cloches de Corneville* by Robert Planquette, featured an old miser named Gaspard who oppresses his niece and servant. One dark night, when he is discovered retrieving the gold he has concealed in a castle, the bells are rung and he goes mad. The work was

The *Charles Racine,* the "old hooker," on which Eugene O'Neill sailed from Boston to Buenos Aires in 1910. (Louis Sheaffer–Eugene O'Neill Collection, Linda Lear Center for Special Collections & Archives, Connecticut College)

revived in New York in 1902, but James O'Neill would not have been involved as an actor because the parts must be played by trained singers. It is conceivable that O'Neill was confusing this operetta with *The Bells,* a translation of the 1867 play by Émile Erckmann and Alexandre Chatrian, *Le Juif polonais* (The Polish Jew), which the famous English actor Sir Henry Irving performed many hundreds of times from 1871 until the end of his life in 1905. The part of Matthias—the burgomaster who murders and robs a Polish Jew one snowy night in order to seize his gold, then escapes unnoticed, though he is haunted by the sound of sleigh bells—became the signature role of Irving's career, even after the play came to seem antiquated. Irving brought the play to the United States on numerous tours during the same decades when James O'Neill found himself trapped in *The Count of Monte Cristo.*

(162) "Then, turning to my love . . ." (Oscar Wilde, "The Harlot's House," ca. 1885). Wilde, who was known for his provocations in modern literature, gives a voyeur's impression of the prostitutes' world, which is inhuman, even deathly, but strangely entrancing. The poet's vision comes to an end with the dawn.

(164) "Speakin' in general, I 'ave tried 'em all . . ." (Kipling, "Sestina of the Tramp-Royal"). Kipling plays with the contrast between the elegant form of the troubadour's sestina and the working-class dialect of the speaker.

(164–65) "If I were hanged on the highest hill . . ." (Kipling, "Mother o' Mine"). Kipling's poem is unabashedly sentimental about the steadfast quality of maternal love.

(167) "That goes for Sweeny." The origin of this phrase is the world of horse racing. Sweeney (apparently misspelled by O'Neill) was a harness maker, a track announcer, or perhaps just a typical Irish name. The sense is "That's all nonsense." See George Monteiro, "That Goes for Sweeny: Jamie Tyrone's Slang Phrase from Act 4 of *Long Day's Journey Into Night,*" *Eugene O'Neill Review* 34 (2013): 233–235.

(167) "You're my Frankenstein." Mary Shelley's novel *Frankenstein; or, The Modern Prometheus* (1818) concerned a scientist, Dr. Frankenstein, using his knowledge to create new life, in the form of a nameless, humanlike "demon." Almost immediately after the book came out, people mistakenly referred to the "monster" as Frankenstein, as Jamie does here (Jamie the creator, Edmund the created), but in another sense, Edmund, as the figure of Eugene O'Neill, was the creator of the monstrous character named Jamie.

(168) "Therefore put money in thy purse" (Shakespeare, *Othello,* 1.3.352). Iago's repeated advice to Roderigo has a double edge: he's asking Roderigo to give him money, to enter into a bargain with the devil really, but he's also suggesting that this will be a sure investment to obtain what Roderigo desires, getting Othello out of the way as a rival for Desdemona.

(169) "Oscar Wilde's 'Reading Gaol.'" This long poem was written after Wilde's two years of imprisonment (1895–1897) for having a homosexual lover. It speaks of the tragic ironies one might find among the convicted, as in its most famous stanza:

> Yet each man kills the thing he loves
> By each let this be heard.
> Some do it with a bitter look,
> Some with a flattering word.
> The coward does it with a kiss,
> The brave man with a sword!

(170) "Greater love hath no man than this . . ." (variant of John 15:13). The second part of the verse actually reads: "that a man lay down his life for his friends." In the first play he ever wrote, *A Wife for a Life,* O'Neill also punningly played with this verse: ". . . that he giveth his wife for his friend."

(171) "Clarence is come . . ." (Shakespeare, *Richard III,* 1.4.55). The imprisoned Duke of Clarence describes a nightmare he has had in which a ghostly figure, seeing him, cries out these accusatory words. Later in the scene, he is murdered.

(171) "Look in my face. My name is Might-Have-Been . . ." (Dante Gabriel Rossetti, "A Superscription"). Rossetti (1828–1882) makes a mockery of the superscription, the words affixed above the crucified figure of Christ, to express the hollowness and failure he sees in his own life and death.

(172) "They don't put up any bluffs about the Art of Acting." As actors began to face a novel test of the truthfulness of their acting, the movie close-up, and as playwrights tried to elevate standards for realism, many began to theorize the actor's art and seek new ways of training. In 1913, William Gillette (1853–1937) gave a much-celebrated address called "The Illusion of the First Time in Acting."

(174) "The Mad Scene. Enter Ophelia!" In *Hamlet* 4.4, Gertrude hears that Ophelia, who had drawn the eye of a troubled Hamlet, has lost her sanity. Gertrude bids her enter, and Shakespeare's stage direction reads, "Enter Ophelia distracted."

(176) "Let us rise up and part . . ." (Algernon Charles Swinburne, "A Leave-Taking"). Jamie quotes first the second stanza, then the first, of this heart-wrenching poem. Here Jamie breaks through his cynicism to express the pure grief of loss.

(178) "Our Lady of Lourdes" refers to an image of the Virgin Mary specifically associated with her miraculous appearances in Lourdes, France, where a famous shrine for pilgrims to seek intercession has been in place since the late nineteenth century.

Notes

Editor's note: I wish to thank the staff of Yale University Press, especially Sarah Miller, Heather Gold, and Laura Jones Dooley, for their expert and genial help on this project, also Yasmine Jahanmir for overseeing the pictures, Brenda Murphy for her guidance and example, and Wendy Lukomski for her ear to my words, always loved.

1. See Eric Levin, "A Touch of the Postmodern: *Marco Millions* and Nietzschean Perspectivism," *Eugene O'Neill Review* 33 (2012): 14–23. On O'Neill and Stirner, see Robert M. Dowling, "On Eugene O'Neill's 'Philosophical Anarchism,'" *Eugene O'Neill Review* 29 (2007): 50–72. Jean Chothia lists all the books and authors known to have been read by O'Neill in an appendix of *Forging a Language: A Study of the Plays of Eugene O'Neill* (Cambridge: Cambridge University Press, 1979), 198–206.

2. Arthur and Barbara Gelb, *O'Neill* (New York: Harper and Brothers, 1962), 404.

3. The "Celtic Twilight" section of the online journal *Drunken Boat* (no. 12) presents numerous authors reflecting on the Irish American heritage of O'Neill: http://www.drunkenboat.com/db12/.

4. On the literary universe of the Tyrone and O'Neill families, see Laurin Porter, "Musical and Literary Allusions in O'Neill's Final Plays," *Eugene O'Neill Review* 28 (2006): 131–146; and Robert Combs, "Bohemians on the Bookcase: Quotations in *Long Day's Journey into Night* and *Ah! Wilderness*," *Eugene O'Neill Review* 33 (2012): 1–13.

5. Chothia's *Forging a Language* is an important examination of O'Neill's vocabulary, especially insightful in its discussion of *Long Day's Journey*. One of O'Neill's late plays, finished in 1942 but unproduced at the time of his death, is *A Touch of the Poet*. Harold Clurman, reviewing *Long Day's Journey* in 1956, quotes Tyrone telling Edmund that he has "the *makings* of a poet" in him, to which Edmund responds: "I just stammered. That's the best I'll ever do. . . . Well, it will be faithful realism, at least" (157). Clurman comments: "O'Neill's work is more than realism. And if it is stammering—it is still the most eloquent and significant stammer of the American theatre. We have not yet developed a cultivated speech that is either superior to it or as good." Review of *Long Day's Journey Into Night,* in the *Nation,* March 3, 1956, in *O'Neill and His Plays: Four Decades of Criticism,* ed. Oscar Cargill, N. Bryllion Fagin, and William J. Fisher (New York: New York University Press, 1961), 214.

An O'Neill Chronology

1846   Birth of James O'Neill, father of the playwright, in Kilkenny, Ireland. He moves to the United States with his family in 1855, and begins a career as an actor in 1866.

1857   Birth of Mary Ellen "Ella" Quinlan, mother of the playwright, in New Haven, Connecticut. She later moves with her family to Cleveland, Ohio, where she meets James O'Neill while still a student at St. Mary's Academy in Notre Dame, Indiana. They marry in 1877.

1878   Birth of James "Jamie" O'Neill, Jr., brother of the playwright, in San Francisco, where his father is the leading man in a theater company, having played important roles for the last decade, including Shakespearean roles opposite Edwin Booth in 1874. After graduating from St. John's College (later Fordham University) in 1900, Jamie begins a career as an actor, often in his father's company, but drinking undermines his aspirations.

1883   Birth of Edmund Burke O'Neill, brother of the playwright, in St. Louis, while his father is on tour. Left in the care of Ella's mother, the toddler contracts measles and dies in 1885. In 1883, James O'Neill begins performing in *The Count of Monte Cristo* and later buys the rights to the play he will perform more than four thousand times over the next three decades.

1888   Birth on October 16 of Eugene Gladstone O'Neill at the Barrett House, on Times Square in New York City. He is named after Eoghan mac Neill, a fifth-century Irish king of the land that later became County Tyrone. His middle name is after

William Gladstone, who was British prime minister four times in the late nineteenth century, as recently as 1886, and took a notably strong stand in support of Charles Parnell and Irish nationalism.

1889–1911   Early years are spent traveling with his parents on theatrical tours and at the family's summer house in New London, Connecticut. Attends boarding school beginning at the age of six. In summer 1903 discovers his mother's morphine addiction. Enters Princeton University in 1906 but is suspended before the end of his first year. Moves to New York, where he associates with artists and writers. Late in 1909, elopes with Kathleen Jenkins but soon abandons her, at his father's urging, to investigate a Honduran gold mine in which his mother has invested. A son, Eugene, is born to Kathleen in 1910. The boy is twelve before he first meets his father. In 1910–1911, he works on several sea voyages, eventually earning his papers as an able-bodied seaman. When in port, he drinks heavily.

1912   In the midst of a divorce from Kathleen Jenkins and feeling desperate, he attempts suicide by drug overdose in a room above a waterfront saloon in lower Manhattan. Taken into the care of his father, he assists in a touring production of *Monte Cristo* and later works as reporter and occasional poet for the New London newspaper. Diagnosed with tuberculosis in November, he enters a sanitarium on December 24, where while recovering he reads drama with the new aim of becoming a playwright.

1913–1928   Until 1919, writes mostly one-act plays, many concerning life at sea; his first production is in 1916 with the recently formed Provincetown Players. In 1918 he marries writer Agnes Boulton, who gives birth to a son, Shane, in 1919. James O'Neill dies of cancer in 1920, his mother of a stroke in 1922, and his brother of alcoholism in 1923. His one-act *Exorcism* (1919), which he later suppressed, dramatizes his suicide attempt of 1912. In 1920, *Beyond the Horizon,* his first full-length play to be produced on Broadway, wins the

Pulitzer Prize, as did *Anna Christie* in 1922 and *Strange Interlude* in 1928. Other important plays of this period include *The Emperor Jones* (1920), *The Hairy Ape* (1922), *Desire Under the Elms* (1924), and *The Great God Brown* (1926). Becomes recognized as the most important serious playwright in the United States and the first to draw widespread international attention. Overcomes his alcoholism in late 1925, with only a few brief relapses in later years. A daughter, Oona, is born in 1925, but his marriage to Boulton ends in 1928 during his scandalous affair with the actress Carlotta Monterey.

1929–1938 To escape public attention, he and Monterey live for three years in France, where they marry in 1929. *Mourning Becomes Electra* premieres in 1931, and *Ah! Wilderness,* a whimsical look at the time and place later explored in *Long Day's Journey Into Night,* opens in 1933. Is awarded the Nobel Prize for Literature in 1936 while living in Georgia. Moves to California in 1937.

1939–1944 Facing a decline in his health, including a worsening tremor in his hands, he interrupts his work on a huge "cycle" of plays tracing the progress of an American family over 150 years to take up more personal projects, beginning with *The Iceman Cometh* (written 1939, first produced 1946), then *Long Day's Journey Into Night,* work on which is halted temporarily by distress over the Nazi invasion of France. A first draft is finished in September 1940 and the final version in April 1941. In 1942–1943, he writes *A Moon for the Misbegotten,* the last play he will complete.

1944–1953 Moves to New York and, later, Marblehead, Massachusetts, increasingly afflicted by a neurological condition (cerebellar atrophy), which leads to a gradual decline in physical functioning, as well as deep unhappiness. Becomes estranged from each of his three children, as well as many of his old friends. His marriage to Carlotta also has periods of crisis, but she is with him at his death in Boston on November 27, 1953.

1956   Carlotta goes against the wish he had expressed when he deposited a copy of *Long Day's Journey Into Night* at Random House in 1945—that the play should not be staged and should only be published twenty-five years after his death—and allows publication by Yale University Press and production in Sweden and later on Broadway, where it wins the fourth Pulitzer Prize of his career.

Historical and Critical Perspectives

As early as 1927 Eugene O'Neill left evidence that he wanted to write a play like *Long Day's Journey Into Night* in notes for one or more plays about his mother, father, brother, and himself to be called "The Sea-Mother's Son." O'Neill's turn to intensely self-reflective work is a crucial moment in his career, indeed in theater, but it came as a consequence of a whole life story. At age thirty-eight he was acknowledged as America's foremost playwright, the first to achieve worldwide recognition. He had been writing plays for fourteen years and producing full-length plays since 1920. He was ranging widely and probing deeply in quest of an approach to drama that would put him among the defining figures of modern art.[1] He wished to leave far behind what he considered the triviality and commercialism of Broadway, which he called the "Show Shop" (a place to cobble together goods for quick sale).[2] Instead, he sought to follow the model of the Titan artist, creating for himself (and incidentally the audience) works of magnitude, deep meaning, power, and truth—all the terms associated with greatness in art since Aeschylus, Beethoven, Dostoyevsky, Strindberg, and many other immortals he admired.[3] A shop is also necessary for that sort of work—plays are built as well as envisioned—and O'Neill had assembled the proper tools and learned the skills. He had also paid attention to the question of what an audience would accept, but art—not profit—was his motive. As early as 1914, at age twenty-five, he declared, "I want to be an artist or nothing," and that remained his resolve even after the royalties began flooding in.[4] His vision was bold, his attitude uncompromising, and his ambition nothing less than epochal: to remake tragedy for the twentieth century. In a letter of 1928 he expressed this goal, saying that he was trying to

> dig at the roots of the sickness of Today as I feel it—the death
> of the old God and the failure of Science and Materialism to

give any satisfying new one for the surviving primitive religious instinct to find a meaning for life in, and to comfort its fears of death with. It seems to me anyone trying to do big work nowadays must have this big subject behind all the little subjects of his plays or novels, or he is simply scribbling around on the surface of things and has no more real status than a parlor entertainer.[5]

Just as he began to see the possibility of reaching his aspiration, O'Neill realized that his chief obstacle would be himself. A worsening tremor in his hands made it clear that his future as a writer had a limit, and even as he turned forty he understood his own mortality. One marriage was coming to an end, and another was taking shape. It seemed the proper time to take account of his life, and he found an image of himself as the son of a "sea-mother," an artist born out of early experience with the maternal and the nautical, mythically combined into one. Earlier in the 1920s, in three short years, O'Neill had lost all his immediate family members—first father, then mother, then brother—and shortly afterward had recognized that his drinking was setting him on a death course. He put alcohol aside in 1926 and rededicated himself to writing with confidence that he could, with his talent and determination, create a body of work, a legacy in drama, that would defy oblivion, if only he could rise above the fear of his own end.

A play to which O'Neill devoted much attention in the mid-1920s was *Lazarus Laughed,* about the biblical Lazarus whom Jesus brought back from the dead. O'Neill's Lazarus returns filled with laughter to announce, "There is no death!" The play gives a stunningly hopeful vision of the eternal, but the time-bound O'Neill discovered that the pragmatic world of 1920s Broadway wanted nothing to do with the play, in part because it required a cast of hundreds and more than a thousand masks and costumes. With this play, O'Neill overreached, but his desire to say something for all time and to celebrate his rebirth would come to fruition in other forms. A lesson he took from the experience was not to be distracted by the stunted vision, narrow concerns, and petty gratifications of Broadway. He instead wrote plays of epic scope, of three hours, four hours, plays of novelistic complexity, plays of world myth and metaphysics and the evils of materialism. To a remarkable degree, in a rather carefree era, the audience responded to his demanding art, though perhaps the reason had more to do with his willingness to reveal onstage the shocking limits of private experience, especially within family relations, and the human susceptibility to scandalous disaster. *Strange Interlude* (1928) took the audience into the inner recesses of the mind of an adulterous woman and the men clustered around her. The performance, much of it inner monologue, took four and a half hours. Nevertheless, it was the hottest ticket of the Broadway season.

By 1928, O'Neill had received three Pulitzer Prizes for his plays, and in 1936 he became the first (and to this day only) American playwright to receive the Nobel Prize in literature. But even those markers hardly gauge the impact of O'Neill in revolutionizing American drama. That seriousness might become a selling point for a play, that an evening at the theater might take an audience on a journey as profound as an epic poem, that an American play might be read and reread in an edition worthy of a first-rate novel, that books and essays might be written by first-rate intellectuals about an author of playscripts—all this can be largely attributed to O'Neill. Even then, as Tony Kushner has remarked, O'Neill was the rare case of a writer whose best work came *after* winning the Nobel Prize, and *Long Day's Journey,* written in 1939–1940 but not published or produced until 1956, has been considered by many the towering achievement of them all.[6] So, it awaited another generation to take the full measure of the man's work.

The more widely recognized O'Neill became, the more he withdrew into privacy, even isolation. The circumstances of his childhood and youth had not been happy, with many conflicts and agonizing episodes. But the loss of his parents and brother and the awareness of his own death wish led him to recognize himself as a man caught in tragic circumstances, not unlike a character in one of his own plays, such as the self-obliterating Edmund, who calls himself "a stranger who never feels at home, who does not really want and is not really wanted, who can never belong, who must always be a little in love with death!" (157).[7] O'Neill's height as an artist depended on the depths into which he was willing to go, but those depths could doom his ascent. The collateral facts of being, already, by the early 1920s, prosperous, admired, and settled in a decent marriage, blessed with children, and living in a series of beautiful homes did not stave off the overwhelming shame, guilt, self-hatred, and fear of death to which he was subject. Doris Alexander argues that O'Neill again became suicidal after the death of his brother, Jamie, and that he was "painfully alive to his tragic heritage from Jamie. He had actually experienced in himself Jamie's tragic rush toward death and the pangs of his corroded genius."[8] These feelings made O'Neill a difficult man to know and love at times, but they also constituted the raw material of his art. His plays became the machines to transform these disturbed emotions into works of permanent importance.

The idea of directly using some aspect of his own life story as the material of a play goes back further, at least as far as 1919, when he wrote the recently retrieved *Exorcism*.[9] This one-act play dramatizes the moment in 1912 when he attempted suicide by overdose in a rented room above a derelict bar in lower Manhattan. Other residents broke down the door to save him, and O'Neill's father came to the rescue by luring him to the family's summer house in New London and getting him a job as a reporter for the local newspaper. In *Exorcism,* the suicidal character is named Ned Malloy, and the comparison with Edmund Tyrone is hard to miss. Ned's reason for taking such a drastic measure as attempting suicide is his shame for having impulsively made a mess by marrying a young woman and then abandoning her. Deepening the shame, he had arranged to be witnessed with a prostitute in order to establish legal grounds for a decree of divorce. All this in fact took place in O'Neill's life early in 1912, the year in which *Long Day's Journey* is set. He wrote *Exorcism* a year and a half after his remarriage to the writer Agnes Boulton when she was pregnant with his second child as well as hers, counting one from a previous relationship. He and his new wife had been raised Catholic, and both had, on some level, corrupted the sanctity of marriage. Agnes seemed troubled only slightly by this reality, but O'Neill took it to heart, probably because he could not avoid confusing the terms of his relationships with wife, mother, and son with his unresolved feelings about his parents and brother, the material that would be developed into *Long Day's Journey*.

O'Neill gave *Exorcism* to the Provincetown Players, the company that did the most to launch his career as a playwright, for production in spring 1920. By sad coincidence, his father was diagnosed with terminal cancer during rehearsal. No record tells us whether James

O'Neill or even Eugene O'Neill saw the production, which lasted just two weeks, but some feeling of remorse or shame led the writer to wish to eradicate his play, which in an oddly joking way mocks his own youthful despair and his father's compassion on that occasion. O'Neill called for the return and destruction of all copies of the script, but his own typescript resurfaced in 2011. The description of *Exorcism* in the Provincetown Players' playbill, "A Play of Anti-Climax," ironically applies to how this play jumps the gun on the mature self-representation he would venture in *Long Day's Journey.*

Travis Bogard, in his important critical study of all of O'Neill's plays, *Contour in Time,* makes the case that most of O'Neill's plays can be read as more or less disguised efforts at autobiography or at least self-reflection through interpretable codes. Bogard's point of view is one that defies a precept of mid-twentieth-century literary criticism—namely, that a work of literary art should be read "in itself," solely as a work of art, without external justification or rationale. O'Neill critics, especially when they consider *Long Day's Journey,* face the question whether to read the work in terms of the life, just as biographers face the question whether to read the life in terms of the work. Many have addressed these questions with subtle arguments, but Bogard prefers to look directly at O'Neill's choice to explore how drama might do something like the work of autobiography.[10] Indeed, we can understand the autobiographical turn as yet another gesture in O'Neill's career toward challenging the conventions of the theater. In 1919, his effort was awkward and embarrassing, but he did not reject the premise that self-dramatization was a worthy experiment, so that, for example, in his 1925 play *All God's Chillun Got Wings* he gave the two main characters the names Jim and Ella, exactly the names of his mother and father.

Then, in 1927, as his marriage to Agnes was fracturing, he wrote in his *Work Diary:* "Worked doping out preliminary outline for 'The Sea-Mother's Son'—series of plays based on autobiographical material."[11] In 1928, he referred to this idea as the "grand opus of my life," adding that it had "been much in my dreams of late." A few months later, he sketched a play with that title, which would depict a man of forty (O'Neill turned forty that year) in a hospital room at the point of death. He finds in himself a strong death wish but also the will to fight against it, "and he begins to examine his old life from the beginnings of his childhood."[12] He is "participant and spectator—interpreter" in his troubled life story. At the end, by "accepting all the suffering he has been through, he is able to say yes to his life, to come back to the plane of wife and children, to conquer his death wish, give up the comfort of the return to Mother Death."[13] When he wrote these words, far from returning to his wife and children, he was onboard a ship to China with the actress Carlotta Monterey. This woman, who would become his third wife, was not a figure of death but, to him, maternal, one in whom he felt he could be reborn. In 1932 he inscribed a typescript of *Mourning Becomes Electra* to her as "mother and wife and mistress and friend!!— / And collaborator! Collaborator, I love you!"[14] Mother—or some abstraction with that name—was on his mind as he sailed in search of a new home, perhaps already anticipating the words he would later give to Edmund: "I was set free! I dissolved in the sea, became white sails and flying spray, became beauty and rhythm, became moonlight and the ship and the high dim-starred sky! I belonged, without past or future, within peace and unity and a wild joy, within something greater than my own life, or the life of Man, to Life itself!" (156).

He tinkered with this "sea-mother" idea for a play or series of plays several times over the next few years, at one point describing it as "a combination autobiographical novel in play form for publication in book, not production on stage," but his attention turned to other grandiose projects in the 1930s.[15] Finally, in June 1939, at a point when he was facing another series of crises—chronic health problems, alienation from his children, tension in his marriage, and news of the approach of World War II—he set aside the enormous and never-finished series of plays on which he had been working for several years and turned to two plays he says he had planned years earlier. The first, which he wrote later that year, was *The Iceman Cometh,* a four-hour exploration of tragic self-delusion set in the same derelict bar as *Exorcism.* The second was what he called the "N[ew]. L[ondon]. family one," which seems to have been a portion of "The Sea-Mother's Son."[16] Within a month, he had outlined a play he was calling "Long Day's Journey." On a rainy February 22, 1940, he got the idea for a "better title": *Long Day's Journey Into Night.*[17]

Two other documents written by O'Neill attest to his effort to interpret his life story, though both of these might have been generated as part of the psychoanalysis in which he briefly engaged in the 1920s. They help us understand why O'Neill's play, aside from its power as drama, has been studied by psychologists for what it reveals about self-analysis, about family dynamics and patterns of addiction and co-dependency, and about such psychoanalytic concepts as narcissism and the "dead mother."[18] Freud's emphasis on a patient delving into earliest memories, especially the child's relationship with its parents, had become widely accepted in American psychiatric practice at the time O'Neill sought treatment for his drinking in 1925–1926.[19] O'Neill might well have written these notes for his sessions with Dr. Gilbert V. T. Hamilton or some other professional, but the terms used correspond so well with the story developed in *Long Day's Journey* that they might have also been used as early notes on "The Sea-Mother's Son." One is an unheaded page that reads, in part:

> M[other]—Lonely life—spoiled before marriage (husband friend of father's—father his great admirer—drinking companions)—fashionable convent girl—religious & naïve—talent for music—physical beauty—ostracism after marriage due to husband's profession—lonely life after marriage—no contact with husband's friends—husband man's man—heavy drinker—out with men until small hours every night—slept late—little time with her—stingy about money due to his childhood experience with grinding poverty after his father deserted family to return to Ireland to spend last days. . . .
>
> E[ugene (or Edmund?)]. born—with difficulty—M sick but nurses child—starts treatment with Doc. which eventually winds up in start of nervousness, drinking & drug-addiction. No signs of these before.[20]

The other is a diagram, a developmental timeline, showing O'Neill's passage from birth ("Nirvana") to an adolescent awakening to "reality." Notes along the line show the points at which he confronted the "inadequacy" of mother and father as a source of love and a heroic model, respectively. He correlates the pathway of discovery with the awakening of his imagination as an escape from fearful reality through fantasy, literature, religion, and alcohol.[21]

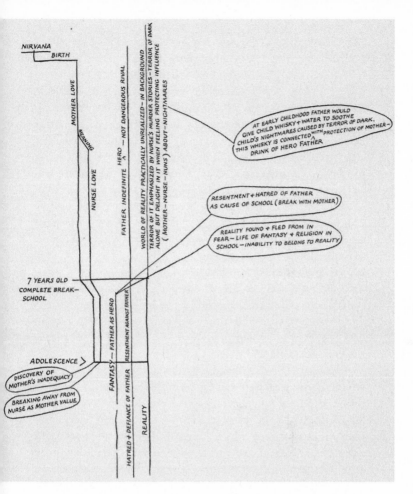

"O'Neill's Diagram," as transcribed by Louis Sheaffer, O'Neill's biographer, from a manuscript in the Eugene O'Neill Collection, Beinecke Rare Book and Manuscript Library, Yale University. O'Neill wrote the original in script so small it is nearly impossible to read. The transcript is in the Louis Sheaffer–Eugene O'Neill Collection, Linda Lear Center for Special Collections & Archives, Connecticut College. (Courtesy of the Estate of Louis Sheaffer)

Stephen A. Black has made the case, in his 2000 biography, *Eugene O'Neill: Beyond Mourning and Tragedy,* that O'Neill abandoned psychotherapy in the 1920s only to pursue his own ultimately successful self-analysis in his writing, a process he brought to a culmination in *Long Day's Journey.* That he generated two such deeply self-analytical documents as these from his brief experience of psychotherapy testifies either that the work advanced to an extraordinary degree or that he was supplying his own strengths as a creator and interpreter of character to himself. Ultimately, in order to build a better play, the art he employed in writing *Long Day's Journey* required him to manipulate the facts. So, for example, as Black points out, the autobiographical notes say that O'Neill's mother became a drinker as well as a drug addict after his birth. In the play, it works better to have the men use alcohol as an escape from the present, while Mary turns to morphine. O'Neill's mother could hardly have been encouraged by her father to marry James, since her father had been dead for three years when they wed, and most likely no elaborate wedding dress would have been stored in the attic because probably no such dress had been worn.[22] These and other details have been studied closely in Doris Alexander's important 2005 study, *Eugene O'Neill's Last Plays: Separating Art from Autobiography.*[23]

The story of O'Neill's family, as he limns it in the play, corresponds in most details with facts that can be established in other ways; yet there was no one day in 1912 when all these events occurred. The long August day of diagnosis and relapse, reminiscence and confession, was a lens through which a larger life history could be brought into focus. O'Neill's father rose from poverty as a promising young actor who then attached himself to a money-making romantic role. *The Count of Monte Cristo* was "that God-damned play I bought for a song." His performance as Edmond Dantès defined and delimited his career, as over thirty years he appeared more than four thousand times in the role. Alexandre Dumas's revenge story, set mainly in the post-Napoleonic years, addressed the fraudulent values and materialism of the era in which James O'Neill grew up. But it is also a story of broken families, especially fathers separated from sons, and there are ironies in the way Dumas's story, which was itself somewhat autobiographical, lurks in the background of *Long Day's Journey.* Around the time when O'Neill's play is set, August 1912, James O'Neill was playing Dantès in *Monte Cristo* yet again for the first and only movie he was ever in, a fifty-six-minute version, perhaps the longest movie ever made at that time, which can now be found easily on the Internet. The scenery and acting seem painfully artificial except for one scene, in which James O'Neill, at the age of sixty-six, playing a not-yet-forty Dantès, swims to shore from Long Island Sound, climbs onto a rock, and lifts his drenched arms so that we can imagine him speaking the famous line, "The world is mine!"

The world was no longer James O'Neill's in 1912; he had just lost a large investment in a failed tour of the play on the vaudeville circuit, and he would lose more from the movie version. It is difficult to calculate exact equivalencies in income, but the $35,000 to $45,000 per season that he recalled earning would equal around $1 million to $2 million today. Much of that money was invested in real estate, so the O'Neills continued to live in comfort in the last decade of their lives despite the financial losses. In 1931, O'Neill recalled his impression of his father's empty triumph in that role:

> I can still see my father, dripping with salt and sawdust, climbing on a stool behind the swinging profile of dashing waves. It was then that the calcium lights in the gallery played on his long beard and tattered clothes, as with arms outstretched he declared that the world was his.
>
> This was a signal for the house to burst into a deafening applause that overwhelmed the noise of the storm manufactured backstage. It was an artificial age, an age ashamed of its own feelings, and the theatre reflected its thoughts. Virtue always triumphed and vice always got its just deserts. It accepted nothing half-way; a man was either a hero or a villain, and a woman was either virtuous or vile.[24]

The aesthetic of *Long Day's Journey* stays as far from such artificiality as possible, but the foghorn reminds us of that same overwhelming sea, and virtue and vice seem to wrestle within each character, so that villainy and innocence stand at odds in a way that might seem, from moment to moment, melodramatic. It's the art of the actor or sensitive reader that keeps the characters realistic.[25] For Eugene O'Neill, the image of his actor father amid such artificial theatricality gave an

"The World is Mine"

"Saved ! . Mine the treasures of Monte Cristo!"

James O'Neill in *The Count of Monte Cristo,* from an 1880s souvenir program. (Louis Sheaffer–Eugene O'Neill Collection, Linda Lear Center for Special Collections & Archives, Connecticut College)

unfortunate perception of his all-too-real father. On the other hand, the image of James Tyrone on a stage is always the creation of some man who is an actor, yet an actor who aims to embody something authentic about James O'Neill, and not by "dripping with salt and sawdust." The realistic constantly bumps up against the real in this play, but both bear traces of the artificial or fake.

The other gauge of Tyrone's achievement is in the memory of having performed opposite Edwin Booth (1833–1893), the most esteemed American actor of his era, known for his naturalistic style of acting, especially in roles like Hamlet. By 1912, though, James O'Neill was at the end of his career, which was increasingly vested in the romantic and melodramatic at a time when the larger trends, even in the commercial theater, were toward the realistic. He was saddled with two sons who were given chances to work in the theater, but neither had relished the opportunity. Eugene was less than a year from his suicide attempt and showing signs of consumption (tuberculosis). James, Jr., at thirty-four, had played parts in his father's company over the years, but he was a chronic alcoholic, deeply embittered and self-hating. They might all have felt that 1912 was a moment when the family had outgrown the theater, which had been its way of life. As young Eugene watched his mother escape into her own artificial reality, he might well have come to a resolve about the dangers of theatricality. In that autobiographical diagram, he writes of his early years that the "world of reality [was] practically unrealized" until "discovery of mother's inadequacy."[26]

James, Sr., was a rapidly rising actor when he met Mary Ellen (Ella) Quinlan in 1872 and again in 1874, and he was near the acme of his career when they married three years later. Jamie was born in 1878. Life on the road with a child was difficult, and more so when a second child was born five years later, in 1883. They named the boy Edmund Burke O'Neill after the eighteenth-century Irish political theorist and advocate for Irish independence, though the Edmond of *Monte Cristo* may also have come to mind. Newspaper reports confirm the sad facts of the toddler contracting measles in 1885 while in the care of Ella's mother. Ella received this news when she was with James on tour in Denver and did not arrive back in New York before little Edmund died. In 1919 she told Eugene's pregnant wife, Agnes: "He might not have died if I hadn't left him; we had a good nurse, a very good nurse, and James wanted me to go on tour—he can't seem to manage without me."[27] Eugene was born three years later, on October 16, 1888, in a hotel room on Times Square. The morphine used to treat Ella's labor pains became an addiction that erupted periodically over the next quarter of a century until she finally overcame it in a Brooklyn convent in 1914.

By the time of Eugene's birth, the O'Neills had purchased for summer use the first of two houses they occupied in New London, and

Mary Ellen Quinlan, around the time she married James O'Neill in 1877. (Eugene O'Neill Collection, Beinecke Rare Book and Manuscript Library, Yale University)

no doubt an element of anguish and guilt was also formed into that *home,* such that the word might have seemed inappropriate, as Mary Tyrone expresses it: "Oh, I'm so sick and tired of pretending this is a home!" (69). They chose New London because Ella's mother had moved there to be near her sister, but many successful actors of the day established summer homes on the Connecticut shore.

The second of the two New London houses, into which they moved when Eugene was about twelve, still stands and is accessible to those interested in seeing the rooms described (accurately) by O'Neill in his stage directions. Most people find the house, known as Monte Cristo Cottage, with its broad front porch overlooking a double lot on the

Monte Cristo Cottage, New London, in 1937. (Louis Sheaffer–Eugene O'Neill Collection, Linda Lear Center for Special Collections & Archives, Connecticut College)

bank of the Thames River, near where it joins Long Island Sound, to be not what one would expect of a miser. Still, what constitutes a good home cannot be reduced to carpentry and a good view. It was in this house that Eugene discovered his mother's addiction in 1903, when he was nearly fifteen, at a point when she lacked a supply of the drug and nearly threw herself into the river in agony.[28]

Eugene and Jamie developed little affection for New London, which they saw as a backwater, but they lived in a beautiful area a long trolley ride from town. O'Neill biographers have tracked down

Eugene O'Neill, at about twelve, on the front porch of Monte Cristo Cottage, with his brother Jamie, about twenty-two, and his father, James, about fifty-six. (Louis Sheaffer–Eugene O'Neill Collection, Linda Lear Center for Special Collections & Archives, Connecticut College)

the New London bars and clubs frequented by the O'Neills, as well as the brothel here called Mamie Burns'.[29] In 1932, after his last visit to Monte Cristo Cottage, O'Neill wrote one of the few comedies he ever plotted out and the only one to be produced and published in his lifetime. *Ah! Wilderness* takes place in "a large small-town in Connecticut," just down the street, as it were, from *Long Day's Journey.* Far from an autobiography, the play is rather a fantasia on the adolescence he might have had in New London, making it clear that his cynical attitude about that environment was mixed with some nostalgia.

James O'Neill did indeed buy a lot of property in the area. Eugene inherited much of it in 1923, at which point he found that the investments were below average for that high-yielding era, though he managed to sell most of the "bum properties" before values plummeted in the Great Depression. One parcel was farmed by a man known as "Dirty" Dolan, who was the model for Shaughnessy, while the millionaire with the ice pond was a composite of two tycoons with estates in the vicinity, one of whom was an heir to Standard Oil money. By strange irony, that estate is now the Eugene O'Neill Theater Center, an institution created to nurture theater artists, especially playwrights.

Though in a sense the first draft of *Long Day's Journey* was life, in which a story was inscribed on the subject, the writing of the play needs to be separated out as a constructive act, and an amazing piece of construction it is. O'Neill worked on the play in several distinct periods over about two years. His third wife, Carlotta, described the difficult experience of his writing: "When he started *Long Day's Journey*, it was a most strange experience to watch that man being tortured every day by his own writing. He would come out of his study at the end of a day gaunt and sometimes weeping. His eyes would be all red and he looked ten years older than when he went in in the morning."[30] He began on June 25, 1939, taking a little over a week to write a scenario, then, six months later, spent two and a half months drafting the first act (February–April 1940). Illness and an obsession with the dire news of the Nazi occupation of France interrupted the work for about two months (May–June 1940). Over the summer, he wrote the rest of the play, finishing the first draft on September 20. He immediately began work on a revised draft, finishing on his fifty-second birthday, October 16, 1940. In mid-March 1941 he began cutting and revising what he called the first draft, which Carlotta had typed. On March 30 he finished "going over" the final draft, commenting in his diary, "[I] like this play better than any I have ever written—done most with the least—a quiet play!—and a great one, I believe." Then, two days later, he added "father's M[onte]. C[risto]. speech."[31] Carlotta typed the final manuscript over the next six weeks, and Gene (as she called him) gave her the original longhand manuscript of the play, with his inscription, on their twelfth wedding anniversary, July 22, 1941.[32]

As early as 1929, O'Neill wrote to his friend and sometime producer Kenneth Macgowan: "Hereafter I write plays primarily as literature to be read—and the more simply they read, the better they will act, no matter what technique is used."[33] From the time of his first (self-published) book in 1914, O'Neill had always taken care to see that his plays were published in well-designed and readable volumes, in editions signifying that these were works of literature, comparable to editions of Henrik Ibsen, G. B. Shaw, August Strindberg, and other modern masters. But his intention with *Long Day's Journey* was that it should be made available, twenty-five years after his death, as a published work only, and these stipulations were accepted in 1945 by Bennett Cerf, the head of Random House. O'Neill reaffirmed his intention in 1951. Carlotta, whom O'Neill designated executor of his estate, insisted that he changed his mind when he was near death, leaving her free to handle the play as she saw fit. Cerf and others who had known O'Neill expressed outrage that she was overriding her husband's wishes. O'Neill's close friend and editor Saxe Commins declared: "She's determined to exhume Gene's body and give him no peace—even in death."[34] Some have hypothesized that her motive was self-justification, giving evidence that her influence on O'Neill had been to the good, despite stories that had circulated concerning the sometimes violent conflicts she had with him in his later years. Furthermore, she had not been kind to many of O'Neill's friends over the years, and they took her handling of the release of *Long Day's Journey* as an occasion to make public their opposition to her. In reaction to their protests, in 1956, Carlotta revoked Random House's rights to the play and reassigned them to Yale University Press.

The Yale University library had long been the chosen archive for O'Neill's papers, and Carlotta was in close communication with the university, transferring materials and eventually literary and production rights to many of O'Neill's writings, so it seemed a good choice to select the nonprofit university press as publisher, if only because it would show that her aim was not to enrich herself. A letter she wrote on December 18, 1956, to Norman Donaldson, director of Yale University Press, makes clear how she understood her purpose:

> I was responsible for O'Neill's being brought back & appreciated by the American public—who had brushed him aside— none too gently—for the past ten years! God knows what would have happened if Dr. Gierow of the Swedish Royal Theatre had not produced "Long Day's Journey Into Night"—as Gene so wished. Destiny!

Then you—& your Press—made a beautiful book of it—&
it went on & on.[35]

The book jacket featured a black-and-white photograph of O'Neill
standing on the back porch of the château known as Le Plessis, outside Tours, France, where he and Carlotta had lived from 1929 to
1931. Wearing an elegant wool sweater, he poses casually, handsome,
unsmiling, not looking at the camera. The photo, taken by Carlotta,
has been somewhat obviously retouched to suggest that it is night, as
well as to provide a black background for the title. All in all, the image
reminds us more of the man with whom Carlotta fell in love than the
sickly man who wrote the play a dozen years later or the sickly man
who was the model for Edmund Tyrone in 1912. Yet it holds the eye
as the title holds the ear as an emblem of high seriousness in art. His
vision is into the distance.

The play does not follow the classic form of tragedy, though it
is "serious, complete, and of a certain magnitude," as Aristotle asks,
while evoking some combination of "pity and fear." The web of cir-
cumstance in which the characters are all caught seems akin to tragic
fate, but it consists of nothing more substantial than "the Past." No
gods have gone crazy, no war or plague or heresy has beset, no Iago
or Trigorin or Stanley Kowalski has worked his ill way. The more we
learn of the past of the characters, the more ordinary or less singular
they seem. A child died of measles; a man did not rise to his own expectations; a brother could not curb the hostility that underlay his
love; a poet's health broke down. Meanwhile, no downfall or reversal
is traced, no hero is wounded, and each character comes equally to
insight and blindness, anagnorisis and oblivion. But the upshot is that
they will bear on through other days, because that is what life is. They
are not mythic figures on whom story has been written in bold letters,
though they habitually fantasize about themselves as such—as the romantic actor, the blessed virgin, the Frankenstein, the seer beyond the
veil of illusion. But when their stories fully unfold, they present individuals who could not bear the not-uncommon difficulties to which
life has subjected them—deep-seated fear of poverty, physical addiction to escape physical and emotional pain, gnawing guilt over an ac-
cidental death, sadness at being slighted by a parent, diminution of
religious faith, disappointment at one's own weakness or inarticulacy,

and so on. The family has experienced these trials in a concentrated form through these sixteen hours, but still, this is not the material on which Sophocles or Shakespeare would stretch a plot.

Michael Hinden argues that O'Neill's characteristic approach to the tragic should be seen as a synthesis of the Aristotelian and the Nietzschean: "It pictures the hero as a moral agent who ignores life's underlying realities and who consequently must be held accountable for his own self-destruction." However, in *Long Day's Journey*, O'Neill has avoided structuring his plot around a central hero, so that the moral implication cannot be so easily extracted. Instead, as Hinden points out, "At the end of the play the question of who is at fault has lost most of its meaning." In its place, O'Neill has provided the occasion for what Hinden calls a "theater of forgiveness," which he sees as a profound redefinition of tragedy for the twentieth century.[36]

Long Day's Journey bears little trace of the well-made play, which was known for intricate plot development meant to bring forward a buried truth, restoring happiness out of confusion and, by coup de théâtre, surprising the audience into a recognition of the author's perspicacity, thus giving reassurance that the universe in which human drama occurs is ultimately benevolent. The well-made play established a pattern for producing the "feel-good" experience in an audience; the truth, once known, will reward you double with freedom and understanding. O'Neill despised manipulating dramatic action to create that effect, and his understanding of human destiny was far from optimistic. Yet buried truth does come forward in *Long Day's Journey*, and the genius of the author, who comes to seem a benevolent figure, capable of understanding, forgiveness, and love for these characters, becomes palpable.[37] O'Neill described the admixture of the fortunate and unfortunate in the play's ending in a letter to George Jean Nathan, written after he had drafted only the scenario and first act: "At the final curtain, there they still are, trapped within each other by the past, each guilty and at the same time innocent, scorning, loving, pitying each other, understanding, and yet not understanding at all, forgiving but still doomed never to be able to forget."[38] The past, a blend of pleasures and pains, reconstructed at full scale, suffuses the present, giving the audience the feeling of having lived through the long journey rather than seeing a story resolved, much less delivered to a happy ending, as in the well-made play.

Still less is the play a melodrama. O'Neill confines his drama to one ordinary setting, using only the passing of day into night as an effect, and his family of characters face no outside foe, no face of modern wickedness. If evil is to be found, it is alongside the good in each character. They all reflect a moral balance, so that no hero versus villain pattern emerges, though moment to moment they often polarize. Kurt Eisen, in *The Inner Strength of Opposites: O'Neill's Novelistic Drama and the Melodramatic Imagination,* quotes the literary theorist Peter Brooks's book on melodrama:

> The desire to express all seems a fundamental characteristic of the melodramatic mode. Nothing is spared because nothing is left unsaid; the characters stand on stage and utter the unspeakable, give voice to their deepest feelings, dramatize through their heightened and polarized words and gestures the whole lesson of their relationship. They assume primary psychic roles, father, mother, child, and express basic psychic conditions.

In these ways, O'Neill's play retraces melodramatic patterns, but Eisen then points out that "*Long Day's Journey* transforms the melodramatic self-other antithesis into a more complex intersubjectivity in which family is not merely a system of 'primary psychic roles' but the scene of a continual construction and dissolution of identity for each individual and for the family as a whole."[39] The family that had seemed unsteadily whole at the beginning of the play, all in good humor after breakfast, progressively loses its bonds through the day and night, until at the end each member is as far from the others as can be, and yet in their shared distance they have something in common, something that makes them one. The family is complete—completely fractured. The play is finished—endlessly. In a sense they have become transparent to one another, fully revealed to the degree that they see through one another and are seen through, as if they are, like the audience, witnesses to a drama in which they can take no action even though they are deeply implicated.

At the time O'Neill wrote the scenario for the play, he imagined Mary's final scene proceeding somewhat differently from the moment when Edmund attempts to speak directly with her about his diagnosis. At first, she converses with him more directly, following the family pattern of pity and resentment, guilt and blame, hatred and love, as the others have done, but then she pulls away, using some key terms not evident in the final script:

> But you might as well give up trying now—you can't touch me now—I'm safe beyond your reach. You can't make me remember, except from [the] outside, like a stranger—audience at a play—the real may make her cry but the events and tears [are] part of [the] play, too—she [is] not really hurt—and anyway I won't remember anything now tonight except what I want to remember.[40]

These notes move from first person ("me") to third ("her") suddenly, just at the moment when the involved noninvolvement is conceptualized in terms of an audience at a play. By the end (approaching midnight in evening performances of the play, to match the midnight of the fourth act), the strange "outside" condition of being an audience has become "real" for her and all the characters, even as the actual audience members might have come to feel part of the family. Everyone is a spectator at the end of the play, and the spectacle is all in the past, leaving only the night itself.

Then it begins again the next evening or at the next reading, with one production after another, audience upon audience. Generations of students by now have read the play, often connecting with Edmund's point of view, still reading Nietzsche, still in touch with that impulse to go to sea or "be always drunken" or write a play. Then, perhaps a year or a decade later, after a rereading, they might identify with Jamie's point of view—bitter, frustrated, angry. Some will look for ways to express that. And maybe, after many years, they will recognize a world peopled by James Tyrones, whose stories are of success that amounts to failure, bold quest that leads to loss of soul. In Tyrone is the parable of a child who had to grow up fast, only to become an adult who clings to youthful fantasy. Where is youthful hope, where is the wisdom of age in such a life? Similarly, a whole life's experience can be felt in Mary Tyrone, but on one reading the reader might connect with her naïveté, then again with her deceptiveness or compulsion or despair. In her, too, the child is in the adult, and the adult is in the child. There's a sonnet in all that, as well, or a cautionary tale or an essay for Psychology 101. Wherever you stand in life, at the end of the play, dark as it is, there is something to say the next day, maybe even a play to write.

Long Day's Journey is the accumulated sum-total of all those plays. It is a play a reader can grow through. Edmund at twenty-four is a product of Eugene at fifty-two, who, like Mary and Tyrone, understood his own failure to establish a real home to reflect on. He also had two disappointing sons, rueful reflections on great promise and past celebrity. One, like Edmund, seemed adrift and aimless, and the other, about a decade older, like Jamie, seemed poisonously abusive of his great promise. O'Neill also confused wife with mother, Virgin Mary with Fat Violet, except when all women seemed entirely alien. Yet he was able to come to a recognition, literally to know himself again and, as he says in the dedication, "to face [his] dead at last and write this play—write it with deep pity and understanding and forgiveness for *all* the four haunted Tyrones." For his family and himself he could bring some kind of closure, such as one needs to make a proper memorial. *Long Day's Journey* sits on O'Neill like the perfect tombstone, both expressing and honoring him.

All of that might seem as distant as a dusty biography, a mere footnote on bygone genius, but the family O'Neill depicts so precisely in 1912 is the sort of family we know even better a century later, when addiction tears at the domestic fabric, when adult children find themselves living at home with no prospect of independence, when religious faith seems for many like a hazy memory, when the fortunes so readily gained in the recent past fail to establish happiness in the present, when the longing to be at one with the natural world paradoxically coincides with a suicidal despair, and when great poetry, music, and plays no longer seem to offer transcendence, as they did once. O'Neill seems to have understood in 1912 that a different kind of art was going to become necessary for him to survive in a world without home. It took him twenty-eight years to see the problem as clearly as he does in this play, only by then the problems that had been personal in his youth had become widespread in the world. *Long Day's Journey Into Night* suggests the new kind of art that would be necessary, and it remains necessary today to complete the journey, as midnight again approaches. Who will become the Edmund of now?

Notes

1. As early as 1920 he wrote to the critic George Jean Nathan about the "faith" by which he was living: "That if I have the 'guts' to ignore the megaphone men and what goes with them, to follow the dream and live for that alone, then my real significant bit of truth and the ability to express it, will be conquered in time—not tomorrow nor the next day nor any near, easily-attained period but after the struggle has been long enough and hard enough to merit victory." O'Neill to Nathan, June 20, 1920, in *"As Ever, Gene": The Letters of Eugene O'Neill to George Jean Nathan,* ed. Nancy L. Roberts and Arthur W. Roberts (Rutherford, NJ: Associated University Presses, 1987), 41.

2. "I'm a bit weary and disillusioned with scenery and actors and the whole uninspired works of the Show Shop. . . . The ideas for the plays I am writing and going to write are too dear to me, too much travail of blood and spirit will go into their writing, for me to expose them to what I know is an unfair test. I would rather place them directly from my imagination to the imagination of the reader." O'Neill to M. Eleanor Fitzgerald, May 13, [1929], *Selected Letters of Eugene O'Neill,* ed. Travis Bogard and Jackson R. Bryer (New Haven: Yale University Press, 1988), 338–339.

3. In a 1925 letter to the historian of American drama Arthur Hobson Quinn, O'Neill repudiated those who would try to assign him to one or another of the contemporary "schools" (e.g., naturalist, romanticist), and then he declared: "But where I feel myself most neglected is just where I set most store by myself—as a bit of a poet who has labored with the spoken word to evolve original rhythms of beauty where beauty apparently isn't—*Jones, Ape, God's Chillun, Desire* etc.—and to see the transfiguring nobility of tragedy, in as near the Greek sense as one can grasp it, in seemingly the most ignoble, debased lives. And just here is where I am a most confirmed mystic, too, for I'm always, always trying to interpret Life in terms of lives, never just lives in terms of character. I'm always acutely conscious of the Force behind— (Fate, God, our biological past creating our present, whatever one calls it— Mystery, certainly)—and of the one eternal tragedy of Man in his glorious, self-destructive struggle to make the Force express him instead of being, as an animal is, an infinitesimal incident in its expression. And my profound conviction is that this is the only subject worth writing about and that it is possible— or can be!—to develop a tragic expression in terms of transfigured modern values and symbols in the theatre which may to some degree bring home to members of a modern audience their ennobling identity with the tragic figures on the stage. Of course, this is very much of a dream, but where the theatre is concerned, one must have a dream, and the Greek dream in tragedy is the noblest ever!" O'Neill to Quinn, April 3, 1925, *Selected Letters,* 195.

4. O'Neill to George Pierce Baker, July 16, 1914, ibid., 26.

5. O'Neill to Nathan, August 26, [1928], *"As Ever, Gene,"* 84.

6. Tony Kushner, "The Genius of O'Neill," *Eugene O'Neill Review* 24 (2004): 248–256. Kushner's essay was originally published in the *Times Literary Supplement* in 2003.

7. Dr. Gilbert V. T. Hamilton, a psychoanalyst whom O'Neill saw in 1925–1926, said, "There's a death wish in O'Neill." Arthur and Barbara Gelb, *O'Neill* (New York: Harper and Brothers, 1962), 597.

8. Doris Alexander, *Eugene O'Neill's Creative Struggle: The Decisive Decade, 1924–1933* (University Park: Pennsylvania State University Press, 1992), 64.

9. Volume 34, no. 1 (2013) of the *Eugene O'Neill Review* is filled with critical and historical discussions of *Exorcism,* including its implications for *Long Day's Journey.*

10. Travis Bogard, *Contour in Time: The Plays of Eugene O'Neill,* rev. ed. (New York: Oxford University Press, 1988). Bruce J. Mann connects the play to the tradition of "creative autobiography," as identified by M. H. Abrams, including works like Augustine's *Confessions* and William Wordsworth's *Prelude,* in order to address what he calls the "presence" of O'Neill as a sort of fifth character in the play. "O'Neill's 'Presence' in *Long Day's Journey into Night,*" in *Eugene O'Neill's* Long Day's Journey into Night: *Modern Critical Interpretations,* ed. Harold Bloom, 2nd ed. (New York: Chelsea House, 2009), 7–18.

11. Virginia Floyd, ed., *Eugene O'Neill at Work: Newly Released Ideas for Plays* (New York: Frederick Ungar, 1981), 181.

12. Ibid., 180.

13. Ibid.

14. Quoted in William Davies King, *Another Part of a Long Story: Literary Traces of Eugene O'Neill and Agnes Boulton* (Ann Arbor: University of Michigan Press, 2010), 14.

15. Floyd, *O'Neill at Work,* 181.

16. Eugene O'Neill, *Work Diary, 1924–1943,* 2 vols., ed. Donald C. Gallup (New Haven: Yale University Library, 1981), 2:351.

17. Ibid., 2:372.

18. The "dead mother" is a concept introduced by André Green in *On Private Madness* (London: Karnac, 1986), 142–173; a recent use of the term in reference to *Long Day's Journey* can be found in Harriet Thistlethwaite's "The Replacement Child as Writer," in *Sibling Relationships,* ed. Prophecy Coles (London: Karnac, 2006), 123–151. For a more general psychoanalytic discussion of *Long Day's Journey,* see Walter A. Davis, *Get the Guests: Psychoanalysis, Modern American Drama, and the Audience* (Madison: University of Wisconsin Press, 1994); and Philip Weissman, *Creativity in the Theater: A Psychoanalytic Study* (New York: Delta, 1965).

19. An interesting discussion of O'Neill in relation to the emergence in America of "depth psychology" can be found in Joel Pfister, *Staging Depth: Eugene O'Neill and the Politics of Psychological Discourse* (Chapel Hill: University of North Carolina Press, 1995).

20. This document is in the O'Neill collection of Dr. Harley Hammerman and can be found on his website: eOneill.com.

21. Louis Sheaffer, *O'Neill: Son and Playwright* (Boston: Little, Brown, 1968), 506.

22. The words used in the play to describe Mary's wedding dress seem to have been written by Carlotta, who may have had the wedding dress from her first marriage in mind. Floyd, *O'Neill at Work,* 296.

23. Doris Alexander, *Eugene O'Neill's Last Plays: Separating Art from Autobiography* (Athens: University of Georgia Press, 2005). Many others have paid close attention to the discrepancies, notably the biographers Arthur and Barbara Gelb, Louis Sheaffer, and Stephen A. Black.

24. S. J. Woolf, "O'Neill Plots a Course for the Drama," *New York Times,* October 4, 1931, reprinted in *Conversations with Eugene O'Neill,* ed. Mark W. Estrin (Jackson: University of Mississippi Press, 1990), 117. A drama professor at Ohio University wrote to O'Neill in the spring of 1940 to inquire about two different versions of the *Monte Cristo* scripts, which he was comparing in preparation for a production of the play. O'Neill, who a few years earlier had donated his father's copy of the script to the new Museum of the City of New York, was at that time finding himself unable to resume work on *Long Day's Journey* because he was obsessed with the war news, but he took time to respond to Robert G. Dawes: "The deliberate kidding approach to old melodramas is pretty stale stuff now. It belongs to the radio comedian. *Monte Cristo,* produced as seriously as it used to be, will be amusing enough to a modern audience without any pointing for laughs. And, played seriously, it should also have an historic interest for the student of Americana, as the most successful romantic melodrama of its time, and one of the most successful plays of all time in America. For over twenty years my father took it all over this country, to big cities and small towns, in a period when nearly every place on the map had a theatre. The same people came to see it again and again, year after year. This is hard to believe, when you read the script now, even considering the period. The answer, of course, was my father. He had a genuine romantic Irish personality—looks, voice, and stage presence—and he loved the part. It was the picturesque vitality of his acting which carried the play. Audiences came to see James O'Neill in *Monte Cristo,* not *Monte Cristo.* The proof is, *Monte Cristo* never had much success as a play at any time, either here or abroad, except for the one dramatization done in this country by him. He bought that outright for very little, because no one believed there

was any money in it. / I'm afraid you'll find in producing it that *Monte Cristo* without a James O'Neill is just another old melodrama, better than most of them, but with little to explain how it could ever have had such an astonishing appeal for the American public." O'Neill to Dawes, June 3, 1940, in *Selected Letters,* 505.

25. O'Neill did not have faith in the theater artists of his day to realize his artistic intentions. As early as 1924, he told an interviewer: "I hardly ever go to the theater, although I read all the plays I can get. I don't go to the theater because I can always do a better production in my mind than the one on the stage.... Nor do I ever go to see one of my own plays—have seen only three of them since they started coming out. My real reason for this is that I was practically brought up in the theater—in the wings—and I know all the technique of acting. I know everything that every one is doing from the electrician to the stage hands. So I see the machinery going round all the time unless the play is wonderfully acted and produced. Then, too, in my own plays all the time I watch them I am acting all the parts and living them so intensely that by the time the performance is over I am exhausted—as if I had gone through a clothes wringer." "Eugene O'Neill Talks of His Own and the Plays of Others," *New York Herald Tribune,* November 16, 1924, reprinted in Estrin, *Conversations with O'Neill,* 62–63.

26. "O'Neill's Diagram," reproduced in Sheaffer, *O'Neill,* 505.

27. Agnes Boulton, *Part of a Long Story: "Eugene O'Neill as a Young Man in Love,"* ed. William Davies King (Jefferson, NC: McFarland, 2011), 192. Ella added: "I think Eugene is going to be the same about you."

28. Sheaffer, *O'Neill,* 89; see also Louis Sheaffer, "Correcting Some Errors in Annals of O'Neill (Part 1)," *Eugene O'Neill Newsletter* 7:1 (1983): 17–18.

29. See Robert A. Richter's article on New London and Brian Rogers's on Monte Cristo Cottage in Robert M. Dowling's *Critical Companion to Eugene O'Neill,* 2 vols. (New York: Facts on File, 2009), 2:673–677, 662–666.

30. Dowling, *Critical Companion,* 1:270.

31. O'Neill, *Work Diary,* 2:403–404.

32. Carlotta wrote in a November 6, 1955, letter to Dudley Nichols: "Gene insisted that if I published 'Long Day's Journey Into Night' I must *insist* that the 'inscription' be published also,—& no other 'foreword' or 'introduction' be used *in place of it* or *with it.* I did just that. He claimed that the 'inscription' showed what his mood was when writing it—& what hell he went through!" Quoted in Judith E. Barlow, *Final Acts: The Creation of Three Late O'Neill Plays* (Athens: University of Georgia Press, 1985), 180 n. 60.

33. O'Neill to Kenneth Macgowan, June 14, 1929, in *"The Theatre We Worked For": The Letters of Eugene O'Neill to Kenneth Macgowan,* ed. Jackson Bryer (New Haven: Yale University Press, 1982), 191.

34. Sheaffer, *O'Neill,* 635.

35. Carlotta Monterey O'Neill to Norman Donaldson, December 18, 1956. I own this manuscript. Again, some would dispute her version of how and why the play came to light in 1956.

36. Michael Hinden, Long Day's Journey into Night: *Native Eloquence* (Boston: Twayne, 1990), 84, 87, 89.

37. There are dissenters to this point of view on *Long Day's Journey,* notably Matthew Wikander, who views O'Neill's late plays as "acts of aggression and revenge rather than of forgiveness and understanding." Wikander, "O'Neill and the Cult of Sincerity," in *Cambridge Companion to Eugene O'Neill,* ed. Michael Manheim (Cambridge: Cambridge University Press, 1998), 232.

38. *Selected Letters,* 506–507.

39. Kurt Eisen, *The Inner Strength of Opposites: O'Neill's Novelistic Drama and the Melodramatic Imagination* (Athens: University of Georgia Press, 1994), 126.

40. Floyd, *O'Neill at Work,* 291.

The Play in Production

The stage history of *Long Day's Journey Into Night* might not have been. O'Neill made it clear that the play must never be produced and that it should be published only in the distant future. Thus, the history of so many unforgettable productions and films of this masterpiece must begin with Carlotta O'Neill, who decided to override her late husband's wishes and grant performance rights to the Royal Dramatic Theatre in Stockholm.[1] The world premiere was February 10, 1956, less than three years after O'Neill's death. Carlotta explained that her unusual decision was made in gratitude to the Swedes for how they had consistently honored O'Neill's work. Some suspected that she had, by turning to a European theater company, eluded a potential legal challenge in the United States courts to her apparent defiance of O'Neill's expressed wish. She asserted that he had changed his mind near the end of his life and, in any case, that he had unmistakably given her the authority to manage his estate, so the rights to *Long Day's Journey* were now in play.

A Broadway production followed within months, though not before the play was again staged in Germany and Italy. It was notably strange that an American masterpiece would speak first to audiences in foreign translations. Further vexing the New York theatrical and literary establishment, for the American premiere Carlotta O'Neill chose José Quintero, a young off-Broadway director. Earlier that year Quintero had directed an eye-opening revival of *The Iceman Cometh*. The "Hickey" in that production, a relative newcomer named Jason Robards, was cast as Jamie in *Long Day's Journey,* and a complete unknown, Bradford Dillman, was cast as Edmund, with Carlotta's approval (she said he reminded her of Gene). Many Broadway veterans coveted the roles of Tyrone and Mary, but there was no question in Quintero's mind that they would go to anyone but the Broadway legends "the Marches," Fredric March and Florence Eldridge, who had

Florence Eldridge as Mary Tyrone with Jason Robards as Jamie, Bradford Dillman as Edmund, and Fredric March as James Tyrone in the final scene of the Broadway premiere production of *Long Day's Journey Into Night,* which opened November 7, 1956. (Photograph by G. Mili; Eugene O'Neill Collection, Yale Collection of American Literature, Beinecke Rare Book and Manuscript Library, Yale University)

been married since 1927 and often appeared onstage together. The financing also came from Broadway stalwarts, including Roger L. Stevens. The production, which opened in New York on November 7, 1956, proved to critics and audiences that the play not only deserved but needed to be seen as well as read, and generations of theater artists have found ways of creating the play anew each time the curtain opens on act 1.

Before the first production, when the play was available only in published form, the critic and director Harold Clurman predicted that some would call the play impractical, but he reminded his readers that O'Neill's plays worked better on the stage than on the page. He declared *Long Day's Journey* "the testament of the most serious playwright our country has produced," adding, "For in a time and place where life is experienced either as a series of mechanistic jerks or sipped in polite doses of borrowed sophistication . . . O'Neill not only lived intensely but attempted with perilous honesty to contemplate, absorb and digest the meaning of his life and ours. He possessed an uncompromising devotion to the task he set himself: to present and interpret in stage terms what he had lived through and thought about." Directors who undertake this play have had to discern those "stage terms" within a script crafted for a reader. Clurman articulated the particular challenge the work would pose for actors: "Every character speaks in two voices, two moods—one of rage, the other of apology. This produces a kind of moral schizophrenia which in some of O'Neill's other plays has necessitated an interior monologue and a speech for social use . . . or . . . two sets of masks. In this everlasting duality with its equal pressures in several directions lies the brooding power, the emotional grip of O'Neill's work."[2] Another critic commented that O'Neill had created not four but eight principal characters in this play because each family member has a doppelgänger, an alter ego, as defined by the dualities of love and hate, innocence and guilt, and past and present.[3]

Several New York critics traveled to Stockholm to see the world premiere, performed in Swedish. The power of the play, especially in the performance of Inga Tidblad as Mary, such that one critic identified its climax as the end of the third act, shone when the power of the addiction opposes the love expressed by Tyrone in a battle for Mary's soul.[4] After the New York opening, Henry Hewes wrote:

> *Long Day's Journey Into Night* is not so much a "play" as a continuously absorbing exegesis of Mary Tyrone's line, "The past is the present, isn't it? It's the future, too. We all try to lie out of that but life won't let us." O'Neill steers as far from conscious plots and phony resolutions as he can. In their place he offers character development. Each of the quartet advances from morning's surface jocularity into evening's soul-shaking revelations of self-truth. . . .

For those who are familiar with some of the details of O'Neill's tragic life and with the twenty-five full-length plays that gained him his reputation as America's greatest playwright, this merciless autobiography is enormously interesting. But even for those who are not, there is a breadth to *Long Day's Journey Into Night* that may make it the most universal piece of stage realism ever turned out by an American playwright. For doesn't it expose the forces that work both to unite and tear asunder all human groups? What family does not have its private disgraces, its nasty recriminations, its unforgotten grievances? What family is not obliged to put up with some sort of unreasonable behavior from its breadwinner, some self-centeredness from its dominant figure? What brothers or sisters do not possess a pinch of jealousy that pollutes their love of each other? . . . All these things O'Neill has put into this play, baldly and directly. The terror it inspires comes not from the day's events, but from the gradual intensification of its torment and violence as night moves in.[5]

Even among those who had reservations about the play (length and repetition were often mentioned), praise for the actors and for Quintero's subtle directing was unanimous. Quintero has left in his memoir an invaluable account of the work he did in bringing this play to the stage. He records an inner dialogue, as it were, of the actors finding their characters in conversation with him. He knew that the play was a masterpiece when he first read it, and he knew that his opportunity as its first American director could not be exceeded in importance.[6] Theodore Mann, who was one of the producers, wrote that at the New York opening there was total silence when the actors stood for the curtain call. He recalled that it took a minute or two before the audience began "applauding wildly. And then they started approaching the stage, en masse, applauding and vociferously shouting 'Bravo!' Audiences did not stand up in theatres in the fifties. I think this might have been the start of the standing ovation on Broadway."[7] The Pulitzer Prize, two Tony Awards (best play and best actor for March), the Drama Critics' Circle Award, and countless glowing reviews certified that this opening was a momentous event in American theater. Quintero went on to direct numerous other O'Neill plays over the next three decades in a still-unclosed era that has been called "the O'Neill revival."

Brenda Murphy's book in the *Plays in Production* series encapsulates much of the history of how this play was staged in New York and elsewhere worldwide in its first four decades. The book's appendixes catalog some ninety professional productions through 2000 and six versions on film or video, and the pace has continued unabated since then. Countless regional and community theaters have produced the play at least once. The bibliography of critical discussions of the production history would fill an entire volume.[8]

Long Day's Journey has largely resisted boldly conceptual interpretations and adaptations, owing to restrictions by the guardians of O'Neill's rights. Stage directors have been hindered from much cutting or manipulation of the script, and film and television directors have been blocked from redeveloping the script as a screenplay. Sidney Lumet's 1962 film included one short scene between Tyrone and Jamie in the garage on the property, and several productions have made a little use of the front porch, but mostly the work remains in the four walls of the living room and the four acts of the play. Even so, small changes can make for significant differences in emphasis and thus interpretation. At issue are the casting and blocking, the costumes, setting, and props, but above all the work done to build distinct characters who combine to create that subtle structure, the Tyrone family at home.

Internal references seem to demand that the play be set in 1912 in New England. Some productions have supplied scenic details based on the O'Neill house in New London, as well as costume and makeup details from O'Neill family photographs. Others have steered away from treating the play as a documentary of sorts, but the story still seems to require a realistic mise-en-scène.[9] Some productions emphasize the climactic development of the play to underscore the tragic insight uniquely revealed at the end of this particular long day, while others emphasize the continuum, the existential bind in which the characters, like all human beings, are locked: the difficulty of going on being oneself in spite of life's cruel effects.

The play offers four exceptionally rich characters for actors to interpret, and it seems designed to give equal depth and focus to each. Most productions, however, suggest greater centrality for one or another of the characters, and significant differences in interpretation result.[10] A discussion of each character in turn highlights issues that arise in performing the play.

When the role of Tyrone is taken by a well-known actor (such as Fredric March or Laurence Olivier), he often seems to be the dominant member of the family and is revealed by the end as the key causal factor in the family's trials. The very same theatricality that made Tyrone a romantic figure for the young Mary, simultaneously winning him popular acclaim and bloating his self-esteem, might also be taken for the inauthentic, even deceitful tendency of an American society insistent on selling the illusion of maximum happiness for a tidy profit. A commanding actor, especially one who brings an element of celebrity to the production, will inevitably highlight the way showmanship has worked for and against the happiness of the Tyrone family. Social theorists have long debated the degree to which self-interest, even selfishness, is required for success within free-enterprise capitalism. Tyrone wants to believe that his self-advancement has been pursued for the good of his whole family, but Jamie especially hears a hollow idealism in his father's success, since it has come at a direct cost to his mother, himself, and now Edmund.

In 1906, at the time O'Neill was beginning to think seriously about the role of the modern writer, he absorbed George Bernard Shaw's critique of how ideals—belief systems enlisted in the name of morality, progress, beauty, civility, and so on—might stand in the way of an accurate perception of reality or something still deeper. In a 1924 tribute to August Strindberg, whom he revered above all other modern dramatists, O'Neill wrote:

Yet it is only by means of some form of "super-naturalism" that we may express in the theater what we comprehend intuitively of that self-defeating self-obsession which is the discount we moderns have to pay for the loan of life. The old "naturalism"—or "realism" if you prefer . . . no longer applies. It represents our Fathers' daring aspirations toward self-recognition by holding the family kodak up to ill-nature. But to us their old audacity is blague; we have taken too many snap-shots of each other in every graceless position; we have endured too much from the banality of surfaces. We are ashamed of having peeked through so many keyholes, squinting always at heavy, uninspired bodies— the fat facts—with not a nude spirit among them; we have been sick with appearances and are convalescing; we "wipe out and pass on" to some as yet unrealized region where our souls, maddened by loneliness and the ignoble inarticulateness of flesh, are slowly evolving their new language of kinship.[11]

The fine phrases and artful poses of his father's theater would never touch those depths, but as he suggests here, neither would the gratuitously sordid displays of the naturalistic theater. One might argue that *Long Day's Journey* itself operates according to that "super-naturalism," perhaps especially in the long journey taken by Tyrone.

The romantic values of Tyrone's theater, in which the battle between good and evil is often conceived as a conflict of hero and villain, with the villain always losing, present a myth aligned with idealism. His sons adopt instead the pessimistic outlook of the decadent writers, and Mary has her own form of idealism in the remnants of her Catholic faith, which aims at separation from the fallen world. At the start, Tyrone believes he is the realization of an American success story, an embodiment of national ideals. He has freed himself from poverty by adapting to his American environment, refashioning himself as a hero, and fulfilling the promise by getting rich. In the process, he flatters himself for having married a woman who upholds idealism in her religious and cultural values, establishing a home sweet home, and earning friends and respect as a successful artist.

Of course, his sons radically disagree, seeing him instead as a figure of greed, materialism, self-indulgence, egotism, and fakery—an embodiment of the sordid reality behind capitalistic enterprise. Mary, too, has lost her romantic belief in her husband, adopting a sometimes harshly realist view of his behavior. Productions that concentrate on Tyrone often seem to explore the possibility that the seed of tragedy in this family can be found in his success story, a version of the American Dream that the play might be construed to criticize—even in the rueful words of Tyrone himself ("What the hell was it that I wanted to buy . . ." [153]). The way Edmund hears his father's saga, with amused pity at the cruel joke that life plays on us, seems to promote this Tyrone-centered perspective on the play. What Tyrone has "never admitted . . . to anyone before" (152), the recognition that he sold his soul by misusing his talent for profit, begins a sequence of revelations that all members of the family have lost their souls because of conditions in the modern world (materialistic values; chemical substitutes for vitality; abandonment of spirituality for sensuality, pride for self-hatred, beauty for decadence, and family for ego). These revelations might be the "secret" Edmund sees and enables us to see in his play. Perhaps by the end of the play, having witnessed the disconnect between the heroic and the pathetic in his family, Tyrone himself sees the need for that "new language of kinship" called for by O'Neill.

Jamie is insistently contemptuous of Tyrone, and Mary and Edmund also voice bitterness toward him, so it becomes a challenge for the actor to keep Tyrone likeable for the audience. Fredric March, who created the first Tyrone for an English-speaking audience, marked his script with many handwritten notes, including the following: "For all his bluster (& he *should* bluster in a fine, *Irish* way) he is something of a gentleman—he is self-made, surely—but so is Gene Tunney [a famous boxer] & so is Jim Cagney [a hard-nosed Hollywood actor]." The *New York Times* review nicely captures the complexity of the character March devised: "Petty, mean, bullying, impulsive and sharp-tongued, he also has magnificence—a man of strong passions, deep loyalties and basic humility." For a generation, all other performances of Tyrone were compared to March's, with Laurence Olivier "more domestic, perhaps more human," Jack Lemmon more likeable ("a decent man with some indecent traits, a faded dandy aware of his self-delusions, a man as much victim as victimizer"), Jason Robards more ferocious, Anthony Quayle weaker, William Hutt more sympathetic, and so on.[12]

Productions that center on Mary seem to view her downfall as the most extreme and poignant of the four characters, thus conceiving the play more as a tragedy than a critique. Over the course of the play we assemble an image of Mary in the past as a victim—at least, that is how she perceives herself. Formerly a figure of innocence and purity, faith in the church, love of music, and family unity, she then descended into a lonely, godless, inauthentic, and degraded world in which drug addiction barely masks the pain of alienation from her sense of self. Try as she may, she is unable to escape this overwhelming condition of downfall. A crucial question, to which different performers have given different answers, is how active she is in this descent. Is she weak, a liar, helpless in the face of circumstances that doom her? Or is she someone who uses a facade of innocence to mask her angry rejection of the demanding world and her preference for release into chemical solitude? Florence Eldridge, who played Mary at the Broadway premiere, left notes stating that Mary was a "victim, not only of her life but of her own inadequacies, and must be played as an immature person." In Eldridge's portrayal, Mary's presentation of herself was given a deliberately practiced, rhetorical quality, as if she were delivering a performance of her own innocence and victimhood. In the 1958 London premiere, Gwen Ffrangcon-Davies took Mary's behavior into the realm of culpability, making her relapse into addiction, in the words of one critic, "seem a negation of all honesty, the final murder of truth," and Jessica Lange, in 2000, took this interpretation even further, creating a Mary whom one critic described as "an emotional sniper . . . a clinging woman with a killer emotional backhand." Geraldine Fitzgerald, in contrast, found a way to construct Mary's actions as an aggressive assertion of the maternal. Her Mary was "not trying to escape *from* something so much as going *toward* something—a place where her son could not be in danger—in other words, a reality of her own creating."[13]

O'Neill does not specify when Mary takes the first dose of morphine in this particular relapse. From the very beginning of the play, Mary is an object of scrutiny who is herself obsessively concerned about her appearance, but she might already have something to conceal. Did she use the drug the previous night in the spare room or that morning before breakfast in order to keep up an illusion of calmness in the face of stressful circumstances? Has she been discreetly and unobtrusively using the drug for days or even weeks to help her cope with Edmund's gradually worsening health? Or is the first act of the play the occasion when relapse becomes unavoidable? Each performer must develop a sense of the emotional logic leading to her break with the family's wishes, and the effect of a mind-altering substance must be factored into every moment of the performance.[14] The same is true of the men, who drink an astonishing amount of whiskey over these eighteen hours. But we must remember that O'Neill could write from his own experience about the effect of heavy drinking (though he had been sober, with only a few relapses, for about fifteen years when he wrote the play), whereas he understood the effect of morphine addiction only from observation and distant memory of his mother. Different performances suggest varying ways the drug might affect Mary.[15] Similarly, different productions suggest varying degrees of alcoholic influence affecting the men.[16] But Mary is usually more extremely in her own world.

Her isolation as a woman, which is only heightened by her scene with Cathleen, suggests a feminist angle on the play to some directors and performers.[17] Several productions over the past decade have looked at the condition of Mary as a woman in a male-dominated world, notably the Tony Award–winning performance by Vanessa Redgrave in 2003, which created the most accessible and pitiable Mary Tyrone to date. Others, however, have felt that O'Neill effectively locks Mary into the "spare room" of this drama by displacing her, mentally and physically, from the stage. The premiere production in Sweden heightened the sense that O'Neill's depiction of Mary might be hostile. One critic wrote: "This might almost be called the Strindbergian interpretation of O'Neill: compulsively insisting with all the Swedish playwright's demonic power that, where there is a vortex of destruction and self-destruction, a woman must be near the center."[18]

In contrast, feminist critic Geraldine Meaney reads the play as illustrative of a modern and postmodern "crisis in figurability," specifically a loss of maternal reality, leaving a world in which representation itself is destabilized. She interprets Mary as an effective expression of the tension between modernism and postmodernism in O'Neill's writing and the literature of his era: "As lost origin, the loss of which denies the possibility of the original or truthful, [Mary] symbolises what modernism mourned, sought and feared. In *Long Day's Journey Into Night*, the pain of loss, the understanding that the loss is necessary and the struggle to articulate from the other side of the unknown do battle. Only in the closing speech does it succumb to the nostalgia which besets modernism. In this respect O'Neill's conclusion is reminiscent of Joyce's conclusion to *Ulysses*. Both finally fake the voice of the (M)Other."[19] Judith Barlow also reads Mary's character as much in terms of her absence as her presence within the play. Considering that O'Neill in his plays habitually equates the feminine with the maternal and often characterizes his women as either Madonnas or whores, she writes, "In part, Mary Tyrone's dilemma is that she has found herself in an O'Neill play." Nevertheless, she identifies Mary as O'Neill's "most fully realized female character," and argues: "Mary Tyrone is finally neither mother nor virgin, and in this lies much of the tragedy of the Tyrone family. The men demand that she be a mother in all senses of the word, but she cannot and will not fulfill that role. Yet even in her drugged stupor she cannot regain the virginal innocence for which she so desperately yearns."[20]

In some productions, the character of Jamie seems surprisingly to stand out, though reasons might be found in how O'Neill constructs the family. Each of the others has some happy memory, a little fire by which to warm themselves in memory. Mary has the peace and acceptance of the convent, Tyrone the thrill of acting with Booth, Edmund the ecstatic experience of oneness with the sea, but Jamie has only a corrupted remembrance of being united with his mother before the births of Eugene and Edmund, and he draws little comfort from that insubstantial memory.[21] Having so little of the light in his soul, he plunges further than anyone into the dark, even the demonic. Jamie twice quotes Iago, the infamous antagonist in Shakespeare's *Othello,* twice provokes a physical attack, and usually prefers to play the role of antagonist or even villain. Near the end of a typical melodrama, the hero comes face to face with the villain, whose challenge the hero must overcome to reach a happy ending. *Long Day's Journey* is no melodrama, but O'Neill plays with this structural feature in Jamie's revealing of himself as one who deeply hates as well as loves his brother—a backstabber as well as a pal. Productions that give prominence to Jamie might seem to imply that he is the heart of darkness, a glimpse of the satanic or death itself, and yet, for all that, the most loveless and woeful of the characters, most in need of "deep pity and understanding and forgiveness," but perhaps beyond reach. To some degree, O'Neill must demonize Jamie to provide a climactic moment to the fourth act. O'Neill still also carried anger toward his brother for things that happened in the final year of Jamie's life, when alcoholism was literally poisoning his mind.[22] It has been suggested that O'Neill compensated for using Jamie as a villain in *Long Day's Journey* by next writing *A Moon for the Misbegotten,* which centers more sympathetically on the story of Jim Tyrone, as he is named in that play.

Jason Robards, who played Jamie in the Broadway premiere and later in the Sidney Lumet film, set the standard for all-out passion in the fourth act confrontation with Edmund. On opening night, he brought the show to a standstill with his "think of me as dead" speech, with the audience audibly expressing its disturbed feelings. Later he said, "It's easy to do—if you're an actor who knows his craft."[23] This anecdote expresses one of the paradoxes of Jamie's part since he makes such a point of rejecting every aspect of his father's art. Robards's own father was a famous actor of Irish heritage, so he inevitably brought some family associations to the part, though he was not a Method actor and in general disparaged those who brought personal material to the art of acting. But it is notable that Jamie, seemingly against his will, is the character most prone to play on the theatricality of his scenes in the play—to parody his father's acting style or quote poetry or highlight dramatic ironies, as in his hostile interjection, "The Mad Scene. Enter Ophelia!" (174). Kevin Spacey took Jamie to the other extreme, portraying him as a weak man, sunk in depression, who backs away from involvement and is, by the final line, asleep—dead to the world. Philip Seymour Hoffman similarly gave Jamie an untheatrical yet compelling quality. In the first act, the audience could see evidence of Jamie's deep, loving bond with his mother, making the rapidly growing alienation all the more painful. The dulling effect of chronic drinking, intensified during this long day, could barely still the pain in his tortured depths. Other Jamies, such as Ulf Palme in the Swedish premiere and Dennis Quilley, who played opposite Olivier, found "cruelty" in the character, the violence of a creature so lacking in resources.

Rarely does Edmund come across as the key character, which might seem odd since virtually every production reminds the audience in the program and publicity that the play is autobiographical.[22] Yet even Edmund declares that his outspoken moments, when he might define for us his point of view, represent little more than "stammering." He is the listener who learns more than anyone else during this day and night about his implication in the family's tragic history, but his actions, like his diseased body and corrupted will, are weak. Travis Bogard writes that Edmund "remains a participating observer, a little apart, an eavesdropping creature of the imagination," and yet his passivity might be said to stand in ironically for the chief action of the play.[25] At a key moment during act 1 he is absent from his duty to watch his mother, and he's not there for dinner or for his father. More generally, he has not lived up to the expectation that his life would make up for the lost baby, and recently he has not been present at all, indeed has made an effort not to *be* at all. Yet he is a transformative character, perhaps the only one capable of metamorphosis. In 1975, Jason Robards, who was directing a production for the Kennedy Center in Washington, DC, told an interviewer: "It's about the growth of Edmund—of O'Neill—of his finally cutting the cord away from his mother." In 1988, Campbell Scott, playing Edmund in a production in which his mother, Colleen Dewhurst, took the part of Mary, managed to put the focus of the last act "more on the encounter between Edmund and his father than on the confrontation between the brothers."[26] Nevertheless, remarkably often reviews of *Long Day's Journey* point to the performance of the Edmund character as the weak part of the performance. Is that assessment an inevitability, a flaw, a mistake, or is it a deferral to the moment when Edmund, transformed into the author of this "play of old sorrow," would reenter the scene as the only one of "the four haunted Tyrones" who could complete the "Journey into Light—into love"? The great Swedish film and stage director Ingmar Bergman's 1988 production drew attention to this completed journey by having the family all exit the stage at the end, going in different directions, with Edmund last to leave. Edmund picked up a notebook, which had been present throughout the play and from which he had read to his father about his experiences at sea, to suggest that he had more writing to do. As he left the stage, an image of a brightly illuminated tree was projected to suggest the new life that would come of this night.[27]

Curiously, the actress playing Cathleen almost always receives praise for bringing a welcome note of humor and normality in the otherwise pain-ridden world opened by O'Neill. That said, most productions surprise the audience with how much laughter and, yes, good humor can be generated by each of the characters. From the opening anecdote about Shaughnessy to Tyrone lamenting that he had never known Mary "to drown herself in it as deep as this" and then adding, "Pass me that bottle, Jamie," O'Neill plays on the proximity of the abyss and the absurd in a way that echoes Shakespeare (*Hamlet, King Lear*), Strindberg (*The Dance of Death*), even Anton Chekhov (everything he wrote), and anticipates Samuel Beckett (*Waiting for Godot, Happy Days*) and Edward Albee (*Who's Afraid of Virginia Woolf?*).

Of course, a production demands that extraordinary melding of all into a unity, an ensemble that can show, by the responsive art of acting, how these individuals form a family. As in any family, there are shared codes, interlaced memories, patterns of conditioned response and subconscious reaction, as well as distinctive marks of trauma borne unequally by all but by all reconstituted into separate strategies for survival.[28] The rehearsal room, in which all this has to be found, must be a place of profound group exploration so that the play can open itself to similar exploration by the audience. For enabling that exploration to take place, we should all thank Carlotta Monterey O'Neill.

A Note on Scenic Design

Home and the lack of such a place is a theme on which—or in which—Mary Tyrone dwells. She has blissful memories of places where formerly she felt at home and traumatic memories of moving into places that, despite her husband's efforts, she could not recognize as home (hotels, theaters, the spare room). James Tyrone has lived through a different experience of home and its disruptions, but he prefers to recognize this summer house as an adequate home. The fourth act especially reflects the difficulties the four family members face in finding themselves at home in this space. Each has an entrance (or an exit) that could be taken as a cameo portrait. For this reason, scenic design plays a central role in telling the story.

While writing the play, O'Neill drew a floor plan of the house as he remembered it from 1912 (part of the porch was removed in a later renovation). The drawing is remarkably accurate in its proportions and general layout. The front door, up a broad set of stairs at one end of the long front porch, leads to an entryway from which stairs ascend to the second floor. To the left is a front parlor through which one passes to get to the living room on the opposite side of the house, where most of the play takes place. This room has windows on three sides and a door to the front porch. In it he shows a center table, a small writing table to the side, two other chairs, and a couple of bookcases. O'Neill drew a separate sketch of the room in which he

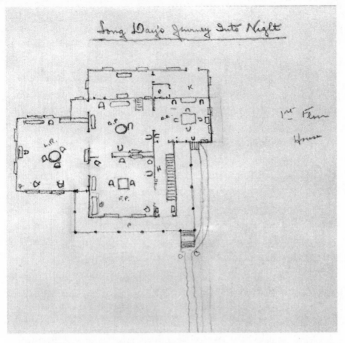

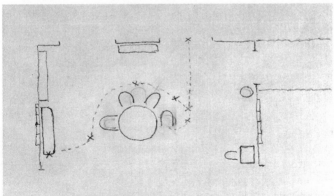

O'Neill's two diagrams of the setting of *Long Day's Journey Into Night*. The first is a floor plan of Monte Cristo Cottage. The second is more of a stage setting of the living room in which the play takes place. (Eugene O'Neill Papers, Yale Collection of American Literature, Beinecke Rare Book and Manuscript Library, Yale University)

rearranged the furniture and windows, suggesting a rethinking of the space as a stage set. (Here is a piece of evidence that he was mindful of a possible performance.) He positions the chairs around the center table in a way that orients the scene toward the front wall, which he does not draw in. He seems to indicate a door at the rear of that room, which, according to his stage directions, would lead to the back parlor, where Mary's piano is located. In the actual house, that parlor is through the side door, and the dining room is beyond that, in the room behind the front stairs.

It is difficult to discern the floor plan of the set for the original Broadway production from production photographs. The designer, David Hays, made no use of the actual floor plan of the house or O'Neill's diagrams, as he later explained: "I went up to New London to see the types of houses up there and someone showed me photographs of the actual house, but when I drove up there, no one from the management pointed out to me which house it was. I didn't particularly care. The only thing from the house that came out in the set was a little bit of porch detail, a very small bit of it, quatrefoil, which was outside the windows anyway and was seen by no one but a few people and me."[29]

Quintero told Hays to put the stairs upstage right and the door to the garden stage left; also, the room was not to face the street and was to have as little furniture as possible. In other words, he paid little heed to either the actual room or O'Neill's scene description. Hays mentions that he and Quintero even discussed the idea of setting the play in an entirely different space, such as a screened-in porch.[30] Production photographs show partially colored windows in the background, which were used to reveal the sunlight moving from morning to noon to evening to dark night, but little else of the house is apparent. It's almost an abstract space, with minimal details and an enfolding darkness. The New York critics uniformly praised the set, which Brooks Atkinson described as "a cheerless living-room with dingy furniture and hideous little touches of unimaginative décor." He added that the "shabby, shapeless costumes by Motley and the sepulchral lighting by Tharon Musser perfectly capture the lugubrious mood of the play."[31]

Many directors and designers since then have adhered more closely to O'Neill's description of Monte Cristo Cottage and studied the actual floor plan for ideas about creating the play's environment, while others have used little more than furniture—a round table with mismatched wicker chairs, for instance—to encapsulate the domestic environment, with the house itself barely indicated. An exploration of one especially successful design suggests how aspects of the house can articulate the problem of home.

Santo Loquasto was the scenic designer of the 2002 Goodman Theatre production of *Long Day's Journey*, directed by Robert Falls, with Brian Dennehy and Pamela Payton-Wright.[32] Falls and Dennehy had worked together on the 1999 Goodman production of *Death of a Salesman,* which later moved to Broadway for a Tony Award–winning run. Dennehy, who is of Irish ancestry and was raised Catholic in Connecticut, wished to resume his "unrequited romance" with O'Neill by playing the role of James Tyrone, and the aim was to take this production in a similar way from Chicago to Broadway.[33] Falls's directing of the play took on new meaning when his mother died during rehearsals of the Goodman production. Loquasto, whose work on Broadway goes back to the Drama Desk Award–winning *Sticks and Bones* in 1972, had worked with Falls only once before, on Chekhov's *Three Sisters* at the Goodman. He had extensive experience with classic and new plays, operas, and dance, as well as two dozen Woody Allen films. He had previously designed sets and costumes for the Hartford Stage Company *Long Day's Journey* in 1971, working with an excellent cast (Bob Pastene, Teresa Wright, Tom Atkins, and John Glover), but the design possibilities for that production were limited by the use of a three-quarters staging, so he was delighted to return to the play at the Goodman.[34] The production moved to Broadway, opening May 6, 2003, with Vanessa Redgrave taking over as Mary, Philip Seymour Hoffman as Jamie, and Robert Sean Leonard as Edmund. Dennehy continued in the role of Tyrone. It won the 2003 Tony Award for Best Revival, as well as many other awards, and is remembered by many as the production that redefined the play for a new century.

The Albert Theatre at the Goodman was rebuilt in the 1990s from a much older theater and currently seats 856. It features a large and lofty proscenium stage on which Loquasto sought to suggest a modest seaside cottage, impressive from the outside but plain in the interior. A visit to the Monte Cristo Cottage in New London many years earlier gave him a sense of the weather-beaten wraparound porch, the generic doors and windows, the dark paneling and wallpaper done in a

Two images of the stage set for the 2002–2003 Goodman Theatre and Broadway production of *Long Day's Journey Into Night,* designed by Santo Loquasto. (Photographs courtesy of Goodman Theatre)

way that would confirm Mary's attitude about the house's "cheapness," as well as its gloominess. In his design, he portrayed the home as "an uninsulated wooden world," with scrubbed wooden floors, few rugs, and "dark, warm gray walls that would recede in the dark of the evening" to leave the family ultimately in a more abstract, obscure space. He aimed to suggest "an ache about the house." In this era when production costs run so high that many designers aim for a more minimalist or conceptual design, what is lost is a sense of the specificity, the physicality, the materiality of the structure in which this family lives, all of which is inscribed precisely in Loquasto's setting. This house is a presence, dismally real yet also expressive of a longing to reach higher, like each of the characters trapped within it.

Loquasto wanted to have a strong suggestion of the physical structure of the house on stage, because the house is effectively a character in the scene. We do not see the events upstairs, but the sound and sight of the dark wooden staircase help us imagine that high. Loquasto

knew O'Neill's description and diagrams, but he altered several details to tell the story better and to suit the large stages on which the production would be played.

The living room occupied almost the entire downstage area—literally downstage, as the characters had to step from the foyer through one wide passageway down into the room from the front hall (right) and step up through another passageway into the back parlor (left). The formal front parlor, which O'Neill describes as intervening between the living room and the front hall, instead lay in deep shadow beyond the stairway, barely visible. This allowed the front door to be seen within the unlit front hall. As in Monte Cristo Cottage, the staircase stood opposite the front door. O'Neill calls for a screen door to the porch on the right wall; this is used, for example, by Tyrone in the fourth act when he goes onto the porch to avoid confronting Jamie. Loquasto instead put a door on the back wall at the left. Only a little of the back parlor could be seen; characters crossed through this room to the dining room and kitchen. The two rugs in the living room seemed inadequate—too cheap—to bring warmth to the space, and the strong vertical lines in the set emphasized its stark qualities.

Mary's sense that there is "something wrong" about the house seemed palpable in Loquasto's design.

The room was set at an angle, showing the window-seated side wall along the front and only a corner of the downstage wall, which gave a glimpse of the weathered clapboard exterior of this seaside house. A strip of the front porch could also be seen on the right. The first three acts showed the passage of the sun on its long day's journey, with the morning sun coming from the right and the sunset from the left. As in the Sidney Lumet film version of *Long Day's Journey*, a rotating lighthouse beam played through the structure at regular intervals in the night scene.

The furniture had a mismatched, inelegant, but not shoddy quality. Tyrone's chair was the sturdy wooden one at the center table. Along with the center table, the chair had to be strongly reinforced with metal braces to allow Brian Dennehy to step on them to turn out the lights in the overhead fixture in the fourth act. The rest of the furniture was of inexpensive wicker, to show the more insubstantial relation of the other characters to this house. Edmund's desk, on the left, held some of his books, but the room had only one bookcase, beneath the portrait of Shakespeare, with sets of books and other memorabilia associated with Tyrone. The isolated divan on the right was where Mary sat at the end, looking directly at the audience as she remembered being "happy, for a time."

Broadway's Plymouth Theatre, to which the production moved for its 2003 opening, is, like the Albert Theatre, a reconstructed old theater (built in 1917) with a large proscenium stage. These big stages allowed Loquasto to extend the walls of the set to a height of twenty-four feet, creating what Frank Galati described as "a cathedral of sorrow." Some critics disliked this looming quality, but the expanse of wood paneling enabled Loquasto to suggest in a poetic-realist way many of the sensual and emotional aspects of this oppressive house. The scrubbed grayness of driftwood spoke of the sad passage of time through this space, a simple and natural beauty that had lost luster through wear, as in an Andrew Wyeth painting. Loquasto's set opened up a shadowy, uninviting interior, one we could well believe was haunted by ghosts among whom you could not help but live—fraught memories of failed aspirations of the harrowing sort that O'Neill and his family knew so well.

Notes

1. The artistic director of that theater, Karl Ragnar Gierow, having heard that an unproduced play by O'Neill might be available, took the step of asking Dag Hammarskjöld, the Swedish secretary-general of the United Nations, in December 1954, to inquire whether rights unavailable to American producers might be open to the Swedes. In June 1955, Carlotta told Hammarskjöld she would offer Sweden the play, with no royalties, adding that she would not allow production in the United States. See Brenda Murphy's *O'Neill: Long Day's Journey into Night,* a key resource for this entire discussion of the play in production (New York: Cambridge University Press, 2001), 5. Ample evidence exists to show that on many occasions Carlotta adapted facts to suit her version of reality, so any story of her involvement in the history of *Long Day's Journey* or O'Neill more generally should be approached with caution.

2. Harold Clurman, review of *Long Day's Journey, Nation,* March 3, 1956, reprinted in *O'Neill and His Plays: Four Decades of Criticism,* ed. Oscar Cargill, N. Bryllion Fagin, and William J. Fisher (New York: New York University Press, 1961), 214, 216.

3. Gilbert Seldes, review of *Long Day's Journey, Saturday Review of Literature,* February 25, 1956, 16.

4. Frederic Fleisher, review of *Long Day's Journey, Saturday Review of Literature,* February 25, 1956, 16.

5. Henry Hewes, review of *Long Day's Journey, Saturday Review of Literature,* November 24, 1956, reprinted in Cargill, Fagin, and Fisher, *O'Neill and His Plays,* 217–218.

6. José Quintero, *If You Don't Dance They Beat You* (New York: St. Martin's, 1988), 203–264.

7. Theodore Mann, *Journeys in the Night: Creating a New American Theatre with Circle in the Square: A Memoir* (New York: Applause, 2007), 149.

8. Jordan Y. Miller's *Eugene O'Neill and the American Critic* (New York: Archon, 1973) records major productions from the premiere through 1972. Madeline C. Smith and Richard Eaton do a similar listing for the years 1973–1999 in *Eugene O'Neill: An Annotated International Bibliography* (Jefferson, NC: MacFarland, 2001). Also useful is Jackson R. Bryer and Robert M. Dowling, eds., *Eugene O'Neill: The Contemporary Reviews* (New York: Cambridge University Press, 2014), which reprints opening-night reviews of many O'Neill plays.

9. Among the few who have "departed from naturalism" in the staging of the play, the great Swedish director Ingmar Bergman is notable; as one actor in the cast put it, in his 1988 production Bergman aimed "to do it more like a dream that becomes a revelation in the night" (Murphy, *O'Neill,* 101).

10. One critic saw a rare perfect balance in the 1986 Jonathan Miller production, which was later filmed for television. Although it featured the film

star Jack Lemmon as Tyrone, the critic commented: "Never before has the bickering, savaging Tyrone family seemed so much like one flesh, one nervous system" (ibid., 81).

11. "Strindberg and Our Theatre," program note for a 1924 production of Strindberg's *The Spook Sonata* (now usually translated as *The Ghost Sonata*), in *Eugene O'Neill: Comments on the Drama and the Theater: A Source Book,* ed. Ulrich Halfmann (Tübingen: Gunter Narr, 1987), 31–32.

12. Murphy, *O'Neill,* 32, 55, 81.

13. Ibid., 36, 53, 65. Carla Power, review of *Long Day's Journey, Newsweek,* December 6, 2000.

14. Geraldine Fitzgerald, who played the part in 1971, noted: "Mary gets what's called the 'cat reaction' to the drug. She gets more and more excited, not depressed, and I use that. And I thought about how easily she uses the needle, another key to her toughness." Quoted in Murphy, *O'Neill,* 66.

15. Geraldine Fitzgerald commented: "If Mary Tyrone had never had a drug in her life, she would have been more or less the same! She is what she is because of her sense of guilt. She feels deeply guilty about her relationship with her mother, whom she didn't like, and about her father, whom she adored but who died young. Many of O'Neill's characters are based on ancient prototypes, and Mary Tyrone was a kind of Electra. Her behavior is based on the fact that she was a person who felt she was going to be given the worst of punishments for her own crime of cutting out her mother with her father." Quoted in Virginia Floyd, *The Plays of Eugene O'Neill: A New Assessment* (New York: Frederick Ungar, 1987), 539–540.

16. The dynamic of a family with addiction at its core, as well as other psychological aspects, is analyzed by Walter A. Davis in *Get the Guests: Psychoanalysis, Modern American Drama, and the Audience* (Madison: University of Wisconsin Press, 1994), with a chapter devoted to *Long Day's Journey* and another to *The Iceman Cometh*. See also Gloria Dibble Pond, "A Family Disease," *Eugene O'Neill Newsletter* 9:1 (1985). For a discussion of O'Neill as alcoholic, see Tom Dardis, *The Thirsty Muse: Alcohol and the American Writer* (New York: Houghton Mifflin, 1989), 211–256. Steven F. Bloom applies the discourse of alcoholism and codependency to *Long Day's Journey* in "Empty Bottles, Empty Dreams: O'Neill's Use of Drinking and Alcoholism in *Long Day's Journey Into Night,*" *Critical Essays on Eugene O'Neill,* ed. James J. Martine (Boston: Hall, 1984), 159–177.

17. See Laurin Porter, "'Why Do I Feel so Lonely?': Literary Allusions and Gendered Space in *Long Day's Journey into Night,*" *Eugene O'Neill Review* 30 (2008): 37–47.

18. Murphy, *O'Neill,* 97.

19. Geraldine Meaney, "*Long Day's Journey into Night:* Modernism, Post-Modernism, and Maternal Loss," *Irish University Review* 21 (1991): 218,

reprinted in *Eugene O'Neill's* Long Day's Journey into Night: *Modern Critical Interpretations,* ed. Harold Bloom, 2nd ed. (New York: Chelsea House, 2009). Meaney uses Alice A. Jardine's *Gynesis: Configurations of Woman and Modernity,* which in turn uses Luce Irigaray's *Speculum of the Other Woman* to argue that Mary transgresses a limit imposed on women in patriarchy, namely (quoting Irigaray) "that prohibition that enjoins women ... from ever imagining, fancying, re-presenting, symbolizing, etc. . . . her own relation of *beginning.* The 'fact of castration' has to be understood as a definitive prohibition against establishing one's own economy of the desire for origin. Hence the hole, the lack, the fault, the 'castration' that greets the little girl as she enters as a subject into representative systems" (212). Meaney comments: "In establishing her own 'mad' relation to origin, Mary Tyrone denies her men the possibility of any sense of home. . . . They seek from her the consolatory denial of the fictionality of their identities. She punishes them with the truth" (ibid.).

20. Judith E. Barlow, "O'Neill's Female Characters," in *The Cambridge Companion to Eugene O'Neill,* ed. Michael Manheim (Cambridge: Cambridge University Press, 1998), 164, 172, 173. A literal recuperation of Mary's character can be found in Ann Harson's play *Miles to Babylon,* which depicts Ella O'Neill's final recovery from addiction in a convent in 1913. Harson, *Miles to Babylon: A Play in Two Acts* (Jefferson, NC: McFarland, 2010).

21. A recent discussion of this way of looking at Jamie can be found in Robert M. Dowling, "Eugene O'Neill's *Exorcism:* The Lost Prequel to *Long Day's Journey Into Night,*" *Eugene O'Neill Review* 34 (2013): 9–10.

22. Jamie died in 1923, at the age of forty-five. After the death of his father in 1920, he lived a more stable and sober life with his mother, Ella. They were together in California in 1922 when she unexpectedly died. Jamie made the train journey back east, with Ella's body in the baggage car, in the company of a prostitute and drinking heavily. O'Neill relates this story in *A Moon for the Misbegotten,* but the play omits the details of how Jamie, cynical about his brother's growing fame and angry over efforts to manage the estate, publicly insulted Eugene's wife as a prostitute. See the Gelb or Sheaffer biography for more details on these episodes.

23. Murphy, *O'Neill,* 39.

24. Virginia Floyd comments: "As a self-portrait, Edmund wears no mask, presumably because the author sees himself as a fully integrated person, more acted upon than acting. He provides precious few insights into his own nature. He alone is not stripped naked to the core of his soul." *Plays of Eugene O'Neill,* 536.

25. Travis Bogard, *Contour in Time: The Plays of Eugene O'Neill* (New York: Oxford University Press, 1972), 435.

26. Murphy, *O'Neill,* 71, 86.

27. Ibid., 103.

28. To his son Eugene, Jr., O'Neill wrote in 1945: "My family's quarrels and tragedy were within. To the outer world we maintained an indomitably united front and lied and lied for each other. A typical pure Irish family. The same loyalty occurs, of course, in all kinds of families, but there is, I think, among Irish still close to, or born in Ireland, a strange mixture of fight and hate and forgive, a clannish pride before the world, that is peculiarly its own." Travis Bogard and Jackson R. Bryer, ed., *Selected Letters of Eugene O'Neill* (New Haven: Yale University Press, 1988), 569.

29. Quoted in Edwin J. McDonough, *Quintero Directs O'Neill* (Chicago: A Cappella, 1991), 50–51. O'Neill's diagrams were not published until 1981 in Virginia Floyd's *Eugene O'Neill at Work: Newly Released Ideas for Plays* (New York: Frederick Ungar, 1981).

30. Quintero includes a valuable account of his discussions with David Hays and the other designers in *If You Don't Dance They Beat You,* including his idea that there must be a rocking chair among the furniture: "A rocker is a woman, it's a mother, rocking back and forth until you have fallen peacefully and completely asleep against her belly, your little arm gently resting on her breast. How deeply Florence [Eldridge] will have to suffer in that rocking chair. They will turn it into a witness box and lock her in it every once in a while. They will watch her, first out of the corner of their eyes, and then the trial will begin. First, it will be covered up with jokes and compliments and light conversation which ought to tremble in the air. They don't want to believe she's guilty. They are praying that she is not guilty, but they have to make sure she is not found guilty again. Give her time and she herself will give herself away. She knows that they know. She knows that by making the tiniest incorrect movement, they will know that she's been driven to sinning again." Hearing this, Eldridge spoke: "Yes, David, I must have a rocking chair" (220).

31. "Tragic Journey," *New York Times,* November 9, 1956.

32. I interviewed Santo Loquasto on the telephone on January 13, 2013. I am grateful to him for giving perspective on his design process and for sharing pictures of his work.

33. Brian Dennehy recounts some of his long history with O'Neill's plays in the online journal *Drunken Boat* in an issue (no. 12) devoted to O'Neill's relation to Irishness. Dennehy speaks of the need to return again and again to the project of realizing O'Neill's characters in a video clip on that website: www.drunkenboat.com/db12/04one/dennehy/dennehy3.php.

34. Teresa Wright fondly remembered Loquasto's Hartford set and other aspects of the production in Yvonne Shafer, *Performing O'Neill: Conversations with Actors and Directors* (New York: St. Martin's, 2000), 201–203.

Annotated Bibliography

Primary Sources

Complete Plays, 1913–1920; Complete Plays, 1920–1931; Complete Plays, 1932–1943. Edited by Travis Bogard. New York: Library of America, 1988. This has become the standard edition of fifty of O'Neill's finished plays. For *Long Day's Journey,* Bogard follows the text of the fifth printing of the Yale University Press edition, which corrected several small omissions from what O'Neill wrote. However, the year after Bogard's edition was published, Yale issued a "corrected edition," which made several other small corrections. The text used in this volume is that edition.

The one finished O'Neill play not included in Bogard's edition is the recently rediscovered *Exorcism* (1919), which was published by Yale University Press in 2012. A multi-authored investigation of that play, including the story of why it was lost and its relevance to our understanding of *Long Day's Journey,* can be found in the *Eugene O'Neill Review* 34:1 (2013).

Eugene O'Neill at Work: Newly Released Ideas for Plays. Edited by Virginia Floyd. New York: Frederick Ungar, 1981. Contains excerpts from and a minute report on O'Neill's notes and scenarios for *Long Day's Journey,* as well as many other plays, including "The Sea-Mother's Son."

Work Diary, 1924–1943. Two vols. Transcribed by Donald C. Gallup. New Haven: Yale University Library, 1981. Transcript of O'Neill's daily record of his work, including the years of writing *Long Day's Journey.* Only at a few points does he express his ideas or feelings about the play, but it is interesting to consider the extent of time he put into the writing (he notes a total of some 147 days of work on the play in several discrete bursts of effort over about two years), as well as the coincident health problems, family visits, and the outbreak of World War II.

Selected Letters of Eugene O'Neill. Edited by Travis Bogard and Jackson R. Bryer. New Haven: Yale University Press, 1988. Includes important letters written by O'Neill about *Long Day's Journey*—the key sources of information on what O'Neill thought about his play, since the play was not made public until after his death.

Conversations with Eugene O'Neill. Edited by Mark W. Estrin. Jackson: University Press of Mississippi, 1990. Includes numerous interviews and profiles of O'Neill; a great source of his opinions about his art and his moment in history.

There are important archival collections of O'Neill material at many universities, including Connecticut College, Harvard University, Princeton University, and the University of Virginia, as well as at the New York Public Library and in the collection of Dr. Harley Hammerman, but the main repository of O'Neill papers and the site of the *Long Day's Journey* manuscripts and the correspondence concerning its publication and productions is the Yale Collection of American Literature at the Beinecke Rare Book and Manuscript Library, Yale University.

FILMED VERSIONS OF THE PLAY

1962.   Directed by Sidney Lumet. With Ralph Richardson, Katherine Hepburn, Jason Robards, and Dean Stockwell. Versions of this film can be found at 136 minutes and 174 minutes, with the latter including more extended scenes from the first act. The combined brilliant work of director and cast make this still an indispensable realization of the play. It is the only version to date conceived from the beginning as a film.

1973.   Directed by Peter Wood, based on the staging by Michael Blakemore. With Laurence Olivier, Constance Cummings, Dennis Quilley, and Ronald Pickup. Developed for British and American television from the 1971 National Theatre production, which earned much praise for Olivier's performance.

1982.   Directed by William Woodman, based on the staging by Geraldine Fitzgerald. With Thommie Blackwell, Ruby Dee, Earle Hyman, and Peter Francis James. This version, developed from a 1981 stage production, was made for television, featuring an all-black cast.

1987.   Directed by Jonathan Miller, based on the staging by Miller. With Jack Lemmon, Bethel Leslie, Kevin Spacey, and Peter Gallagher. This fascinating and moving version, at 170 minutes, is notable for the overlapping and remarkably fast pace of the dialogue in the first act, as well as the fine performances.

1996.   Directed by David Wellington, based on a staging by Diana Leblanc. With William Hutt, Martha Henry, Peter Donaldson, and Tom McCamus. Developed from a 1994 production at Canada's Stratford Festival, this televised version presents nearly the entire script, with moving performances.

Secondary Sources

REFERENCE BOOKS

Bloom, Steven F. *Student Companion to Eugene O'Neill.* Westport, CT: Greenwood, 2007. An introduction to O'Neill's life and writing, geared to high school and college students.

Bloom, Steven F., ed. *Critical Insights: Eugene O'Neill.* Pasadena, CA: Salem, 2012. Critical and biographical essays on O'Neill by multiple authors, reflecting the most recent scholarship, geared to high school and college students.

Bryer, Jackson R., and Robert M. Dowling, eds. *Eugene O'Neill: The Contemporary Reviews.* American Critical Archives series. New York: Cambridge University Press, 2014. A compendium of reviews of O'Neill premieres.

Cargill, Oscar, N. Bryllion Fagin, and William J. Fisher, eds. *O'Neill and His Plays: Four Decades of Criticism.* New York: New York University Press, 1961. A fine sourcebook of statements and interviews of O'Neill, as well as reviews and other critical discussions.

Dowling, Robert M. *Critical Companion to Eugene O'Neill: A Literary Reference to His Life and Work.* 2 vols. New York: Facts on File, 2009. A comprehensive reference book, with articles about O'Neill, his family, his collaborators, and other topics, along with synopses and discussions of each play.

Halfmann, Ulrich, ed. *Eugene O'Neill: Comments on the Drama and the Theater: A Source Book.* Tübingen: Gunter Narr, 1987. A compendium of documents intended to give insight into O'Neill's thoughts about his art.

Ranald, Margaret Loftus. *The Eugene O'Neill Companion.* Westport, CT: Greenwood, 1984. An older but still valuable reference book on O'Neill, including synopses, historical and critical notes, and biographical articles about the O'Neill family.

BIBLIOGRAPHICAL SOURCES

An excellent source for bibliography, information, documents, media, and many other sources on O'Neill is the website privately maintained by Dr. Harley Hammerman, eOneill.com.

Atkinson, Jennifer. *Eugene O'Neill: A Descriptive Bibliography.* Pittsburgh: University of Pittsburgh Press, 1974. A valuable listing of primary and secondary sources through the early 1970s, following on the first comprehensive O'Neill bibliography, by Ralph Sanborn and Barrett H. Clark, published in 1931.

Miller, Jordan Y. *Playwright's Progress: O'Neill and the Critics: A Bibliographical Checklist.* Hamden, CT: Archon, 1973. Annotated bibliography of critical sources.

Smith, Madeline, and Richard Eaton. *Eugene O'Neill: An Annotated International Bibliography, 1973 through 1999.* Jefferson, NC: McFarland, 2001. Brings the work of Atkinson and Miller forward a quarter of a century.

DOCUMENTARY FILMS ABOUT O'NEILL

Adato, Perry Miller, and Paul Shyre. *Eugene O'Neill: A Gathering of Ghosts.* PBS: *American Masters,* 1986. 150 mins. Biographical documentary, featuring readings by many fine actors, including Jason Robards and Colleen Dewhurst. Jeffrey DeMunn speaks as O'Neill, and Zoe Caldwell plays Carlotta Monterey O'Neill.

Burns, Ric, Arthur Gelb, and Barbara Gelb. *Eugene O'Neill: A Documentary Film.* PBS: *American Experience,* 2006. 120 mins. Biographical documentary with strong emphasis on the *Long Day's Journey* story; includes readings of scenes from the play

with Zoe Caldwell and Vanessa Redgrave as Mary, Christopher
Plummer as Tyrone, Liam Neeson as Jamie, and Robert Sean
Leonard as Edmund.

CRITICAL AND BIOGRAPHICAL STUDIES

Many writings on *Long Day's Journey* can be found in the official journal of the Eugene O'Neill Society (eugeneoneillsociety.org),
which between 1977 and 1988 was published as the *Eugene
O'Neill Newsletter* (those issues are accessible at eOneill.com),
at which point it was renamed the *Eugene O'Neill Review* (accessible through JSTOR). The journal is currently published by
Pennsylvania State University Press as a biannual. Noteworthy
essays published since 2000 include Vivian Casper, "The 'Veil':
Neoplatonism and Genre in *Long Day's Journey Into Night*"
(2007); Laurin Porter, "'Why Do I Feel so Lonely?': Literary Allusions and Gendered Space in *Long Day's Journey Into
Night*" (2008); and Robert Combs, "Bohemians on the Bookcase: Quotations in *Long Day's Journey Into Night* and *Ah! Wilderness*" (2012).

Alexander, Doris. *Eugene O'Neill's Last Plays: Separating Art from
Autobiography*. Athens: University of Georgia Press, 2005. A
cautionary look at efforts to read *Long Day's Journey* as autobiography: "If there was anything O'Neill himself was clear on,
it is that a literal following of the historical facts in a case will
never add up to a tragic revelation of the meaning of human life
or a moving reliving of another person's emotional experience.
No one can achieve emotional truth, much less philosophical
truth, by reporting everything irrelevant or contradictory that
falls within a particular set of facts" (3).

Barlow, Judith E. *Final Acts: The Creation of Three Late O'Neill Plays*.
Athens: University of Georgia Press, 1985. Close examination
of the manuscript and other documents to uncover O'Neill's
process of writing *Long Day's Journey*: "Examining the manuscript and scenario confirms that O'Neill gradually worked toward making the play's closing minutes climactic. The concluding act in the early drafts suggests that this is a familiar pattern
to the Tyrones: they have seen Mary like this before and they

will see her like this again. The published text's last act, in contrast, implies that this is a final and tragic situation, a moment beyond which no future can be seen" (80).

Berlin, Normand. *O'Neill's Shakespeare.* Ann Arbor: University of Michigan Press, 1993. An exploration of the "essential, basic, even natural" (2) connection of O'Neill and Shakespeare: "When we think of Shakespeare in the work of O'Neill, the past *is* the present, once again" (188).

Bigsby, C. W. E. *A Critical Introduction to Twentieth-Century American Drama,* Vol. 1: *1900–1940.* Cambridge: Cambridge University Press, 1982. The foremost British historian of American drama devotes a long chapter of his four-volume study of American playwrights to Eugene O'Neill. He traces the author's engagement with major philosophical and aesthetic interpretations of the tragic in modern life. Ultimately, he argues, O'Neill finds his way beyond that inherited discourse: "[The truth] lies, his final plays seem to assert, in the power of the individual to create or destroy the lives of others; in the absolute necessity to renew even the love which is itself the source of irony. For where else can opposites be reconciled but in the human heart; how else can meaning be generated but in the relationships, bitter and loving, between individuals who meet not as embodiments of abstractions, but as expressions of conflicting but real emotions, and as evidence of the losing struggle to imprint order, and at least a provisional purpose, on a life defined by the absoluteness of its ultimate end?" (94–95).

Black, Stephen A. *Eugene O'Neill: Beyond Mourning and Tragedy.* New Haven: Yale University Press, 1999. A biography of O'Neill, informed by psychoanalytic perspectives: "O'Neill found a way to use the writing of plays as a form of self-psychoanalysis. The analysis was successful to the extent that it allowed him to mourn his dead and to create in his last plays work that must have come very close to fulfilling even so large a talent as his" (xviii).

Bloom, Harold, ed. *Eugene O'Neill's* Long Day's Journey into Night: *Modern Critical Interpretations.* New York: Chelsea House, 1987. An anthology of critical essays on *Long Day's Journey,* ranging from 1958 to 1982, reflecting the first generation of critical studies of the play. A second edition of this book, issued in 2009, includes excerpts from several books in this bibliography, also some newer essays on the play.

Bogard, Travis. *Contour in Time: The Plays of Eugene O'Neill.* Rev. ed. New York: Oxford University Press, 1988; orig. publ. 1972. Still the most important comprehensive study of O'Neill's writings, with particular attention to O'Neill's sources and his involvement in the autobiographical: "[*Long Day's Journey*] is O'Neill's last mirror, the last time he would look to see if he was 'there.' In itself, the image of the young, gentle, unhappy man he saw proved nothing, but having gone through the door in the mind to the fogbound room in the past, he perhaps understood himself as his figure was illuminated by the pain and concern of those about him. In the agony of the others, it is possible, the playwright's identity was at last to be found" (450–451).

Boulton, Agnes. *Part of a Long Story.* Edited by William Davies King. Jefferson, NC: McFarland, 2011. Boulton was O'Neill's second wife (1918–1929), and in 1958 she published this memoir of the first two years of their marriage. It contains vivid scenes showing O'Neill with his parents and brother. As a literary version of distant memory, her book poses its own questions about the truth value of autobiography, but it remains a crucial document in O'Neill studies. Indeed, the editor argues that her memoir could be seen as an epilogue of sorts to his play (3).

Brietzke, Zander. *The Aesthetics of Failure: Dynamic Structure in the Plays of Eugene O'Neill.* Jefferson, NC: McFarland, 2001. Discussion of the importance of O'Neill paradoxically in light of his many experimental failures, thus highlighting the peculiar motivations and ambitious goals of his writing: "There's great humor in the melodrama of youthful angst, to be sure, but the theme of belonging is one of O'Neill's principal concerns. The here and there model suggests that an O'Neill character is never at home on stage, that he or she always fights to be somewhere else, somewhere beyond the scope of representation. The desire to be elsewhere and the corporeal reality of the visual scene creates dynamic tension" (104–105).

Chothia, Jean. *Forging a Language: A Study of the Plays of Eugene O'Neill.* Cambridge: Cambridge University Press, 1979. A study of all of O'Neill's plays in terms of the patterns of language: "The overwhelming effect of the last four lines of [*Long Day's Journey*] comes, I think, because, just when it appears that the play has drawn to its conclusion and has reached some kind of resting place, however dismal, the sentence, '*That was* in the winter of senior year,' pushes the interview back into the distant past and returns Mary to the present and the family, from which there can be, after all, no escape for any of the four Tyrones. The quiet ending of the play is not a conclusion but another relentless beginning" (183–184).

Davis, Walter A. *Get the Guests: Psychoanalysis, Modern American Drama, and the Audience.* Madison: University of Wisconsin Press, 1994. An extensive investigation of systems of defense, displacement, and projection in *Long Day's Journey:* "The family is a system of interlocking chains with no single point of origin or agent of control. Reciprocity inhabits it from every point in time. If our children never get free of our psychic wounds, it is also the case that we are never free from what they may do to return the favor. The only summing up that does justice to any of the agents in a family must formulate the way in which each individual disorder contributes to the development of the system as a whole" (200).

Diggins, John Patrick. *Eugene O'Neill's America: Desire under Democracy.* Chicago: University of Chicago Press, 2007. The author brings an historian's perspective to O'Neill's background and his developing thoughts about the United States: "O'Neill saw the same sins of self-deceit in America as he tended to see within himself and his own family.... A study of O'Neill's wrestling with the deceits of desire and power may also help us understand why our country allowed itself to believe it could bring democracy to the rest of the world even by means of military conquest. To be blind to our own follies is one definition of tragedy" (8–9).

Dubost, Thierry. *Struggle, Defeat or Rebirth: Eugene O'Neill's Vision of Humanity.* Jefferson, NC: McFarland, 1997. A search for underlying patterns in all of O'Neill's plays: "Through writing, O'Neill may have been striving to attain a degree of plenitude he failed to reach otherwise. The freedom he achieved enabled him to live with his ghosts, and gave birth to works which, at times, produce effects identical to those described by Mary. In the rapture of an evening, the author and the audience enter into communion, through the medium of a text interpreted by actors" (230).

Eisen, Kurt. *The Inner Strength of Opposites: O'Neill's Novelistic Drama and the Melodramatic Imagination.* Athens: University of Georgia Press, 1994. An incisive critical study emphasizing O'Neill's bold reshaping of dramatic form for his purposes and locating his place as a modernist: "Identity typically remains unproblematic in melodrama, but in the modern novel—especially in Conrad, Joyce, and Proust—it forms a basic interest of the exposition, as a character struggles to know and express himself and his place in the world. The apparent emphasis on a discrete self in *Long Day's Journey* proves illusory on close examination, for each Tyrone is constructed dialogically as an other within the various personal melodramas enacted by all four family members. As the play progresses and the fog outside grows denser, the distinction between heroes, villains, and victims becomes increasingly vague" (135).

Falk, Doris V. *Eugene O'Neill and the Tragic Tension: An Interpretive Study of the Plays.* New Brunswick, NJ: Rutgers University Press, 1958. Looks at how four character types from O'Neill's earlier plays are exemplified by the characters in *Long Day's Journey,* in whom the "tragic conception of life as an endless struggle between opposite images of the self" is most comprehensively realized: "So ends the lifelong day that dawned with O'Neill's searchers in the fog, children of his mother, Mary Tyrone, proceeded with the mad extremists led by his father, James, soared to ecstatic noon with the young Edmund and the finders—before the afternoon fog settled upon the trapped victims of the family fate" (194).

Fleche, Anne. *Mimetic Disillusion: Eugene O'Neill, Tennessee Williams, and U.S. Dramatic Realism.* Tuscaloosa: University of Alabama Press, 1997. A deconstructive reading of the realism in *Long Day's Journey:* "In *Long Day's Journey* the lines of connection are tenuous: language doesn't seem to connect truth with experience, or to connect character with character, or to connect character with the material world. As the play wears

on, the characters seem less 'motivated,' the 'dialogue' more dif-
fuse, and material reality more dense, opaque, threatening, an
obstacle course by act 4" (26).

Floyd, Virginia. *The Plays of Eugene O'Neill: A New Assessment.* New
York: Frederick Ungar, 1987. A comprehensive reading of all
of O'Neill's plays, making strong use of her study of O'Neill's
notes: "Originally the drama was set in 1907 on the parents'
'30th Wedding Anniversary.' One of the early titles, 'Anniversary,' suggests that he intended to make the parents the play's
central characters. Perhaps the emphasis on the small but precise autobiographical details is the most startling point about
the notes, for it reinforces the idea that O'Neill and his family
actually endured and survived the torturous, soul-shattering
events depicted" (553).

Gelb, Arthur, and Barbara Gelb. *O'Neill.* New York: Harper and
Brothers, 1962 (enlarged ed., 1973). Still the most readable
of the biographies, rich with anecdotes and information from
numerous interviews of people close to the subject, including
Carlotta O'Neill: "Carlotta's explanation for disregarding her
husband's recorded wishes was that O'Neill had agreed to with-
hold publication of the play only because his son, Eugene Jr.,
had asked him to, and that Eugene's subsequent death had removed the restriction. O'Neill himself had changed his mind
frequently and radically about how he wanted his plays handled, and he had, in a sense, bequeathed to Carlotta the right to
be inconsistent for him" (862).

Hinden, Michael. Long Day's Journey into Night: *Native Eloquence.*
Boston: Twayne, 1990. Insightful close analysis of *Long Day's
Journey* from many points of view: "That the word 'forget'
appears twice as many times in the play as the word 'forgive'
graphically describes the family dynamic. A similar word count
discloses that 'love' is mentioned on more than sixty occasions
and 'hate' on fewer than thirty. . . . These numbers only confirm what any responsive audience intuitively knows about the
Tyrones. . . . The dynamic tension between love and hate is the
binding force that keeps the Tyrone family together" (36).

Manheim, Michael, ed. *The Cambridge Companion to Eugene O'Neill.*
Cambridge: Cambridge University Press, 1998. Anthology of

essays on O'Neill from the 1980s and 1990s, including Matthew Wikander's provocative "O'Neill and the Cult of Sincerity": "O'Neill's failure to recognize his last works as acts of aggression and revenge rather than of forgiveness and understanding is less disturbing than the endorsement by the majority of his critics of his own self-delusion about these works. . . . O'Neill's work is not a testimonial to self-knowledge and forgiveness. It is a testament of rage" (232–233).

Manheim, Michael. *Eugene O'Neill's New Language of Kinship.* Syracuse, NY: Syracuse University Press, 1982. Reads all of O'Neill's work as variations on the autobiographical themes, even obsessions, which would become explicit—and resolved—in *Long Day's Journey:* "The play does not end with Jamie's great paraphrase of the line from the Mass, probably because O'Neill was determined to the end to eschew Messianic conclusions. The concluding statement of the play is instead a scenic image: a tableau of family disintegration and family unity in one—the men assembled in awe around the unhearing Mary, with Jamie reciting Swinburne and Mary delving ever deeper into the 'little Temple' of her memories. No easy conclusions, positive or negative, are to be drawn from this tableau, but Jamie has already said what is to be said. The larger vision of the play frees man to live in that it frees him to love and reciprocate love—in the way men and women do those things, by attacking and defending, appealing and succoring. Only the fears associated with the past destroy kinship—and those fears are what father and son, brother and brother, clear away briefly in their deep encounters late in this play" (190).

Murphy, Brenda. *O'Neill: Long Day's Journey into Night.* Plays in Production. New York: Cambridge University Press, 2001. A survey of the stage and screen versions of *Long Day's Journey,* from premiere through 2000. See "Notes on Performance," elsewhere in this volume.

Porter, Laurin. *The Banished Prince: Time, Memory, and Ritual in the Late Plays of Eugene O'Neill.* Ann Arbor: UMI Research Press, 1988. A study of the structural and thematic patterns, especially the function and image of time, in O'Neill's late plays: "Unlike the other Tyrones, whose ideals all include both individual and familial components, Edmund's ideal is exclusively individual. His transcendental moments can only be experienced when he is alone with nature. In fact, insofar as they require an abdication of individuality, they actually represent a kind of death wish. He describes the experience to James as becoming 'the sun, the hot sand, green seaweed anchored to a rock, swaying in the tide.' . . . The seaweed, anchored firmly yet swaying in the tide, replicates the condition of the fetus in amniotic fluid. Whether a death wish or a desire to return to the womb (which come to much the same thing), Edmund's ideal disqualifies him as priest-confessor" (89).

Quintero, José. *If You Don't Dance They Beat You.* New York: St. Martin's, 1988. Memoir written by the director of the Broadway premiere of *Long Day's Journey,* with anecdotes about the production and about how Carlotta O'Neill handled the decision to override O'Neill's intentions. He quotes Carlotta: "Poor Gene. He would come down the stairs from his study. His eyes were so red that I knew he had been crying. Day after day, walking down those stairs crying. It got to be agony. I tried not to look at his eyes. Then when the play was finished, he put it on my lap and said, 'Read the first page.' I not only read it [the wedding anniversary inscription], but I memorized it so well that it will probably be the only thing I'll remember when I die" (214).

Raleigh, John Henry. *The Plays of Eugene O'Neill.* Carbondale: Southern Illinois University Press, 1965. Important early critical interpretation of O'Neill's writings, especially valuable for its extended development of the following argument: "It should be emphasized first how powerfully, how inescapably, *The Count of Monte Cristo* was stamped into Eugene O'Neill's consciousness and memory. As he could never forget his family, he could never forget what can only be called the family play. That as a serious playwright O'Neill was in conscious rebellion against this old play and all it stood for: melodrama, sentiment, easy popularity, stage tricks, cardboard characters, stale rhetoric; this is all too obvious. He once said, 'I suppose if one accepts the song and dance complete of the psychoanalysts, it is perfectly natural that having been brought up around the old conventional theatre, and having identified it with my father, I should rebel and go in a new direction.' . . . But underneath 'the song and dance' of the psychoanalysts is the deeper insight of classical psycho-analysis that there *is* no escape finally from the earliest years, or at least no easy and immediate one" (179–180).

Richter, Robert A. *Eugene O'Neill and Dat Ole Davil Sea: Maritime Influences in the Life and Works of Eugene O'Neill.* Mystic, CT: Mystic Seaport, 2004. Takes a careful look at O'Neill's experience of the sea, including the experiences that inspired Edmund's nostalgic speech about "the Squarehead square rigger" and the "old hooker driving fourteen knots" (the imagery comes from O'Neill's voyage to Buenos Aires in 1910 on a ship called the *Charles Racine,* a sailing vessel first launched in 1892, which transported lumber, wool, and hides). Richter's book also includes many wonderful photographs.

Robinson, James A. *Eugene O'Neill and Oriental Thought: A Divided Vision.* Carbondale: Southern Illinois University Press, 1982. A study of O'Neill's adoption of Eastern religious ideas in several of his plays, including, though problematically, *Long Day's Journey:* "The play's central symbol, the fog, thickens during the play, pointing to the inescapable confusion and loneliness that were O'Neill's heritage as both a 'haunted Tyrone' and a Western man. And the steady march of Mary and the other Tyrones into the past demonstrates—as does the very act of writing the play—O'Neill's inability to effect escape from history, despite his momentary mystical withdrawals from time" (177).

Shaughnessy, Edward L. *Down the Nights and Down the Days: Eugene O'Neill's Catholic Sensibility.* Notre Dame, IN: University of Notre Dame Press, 1996. An analysis of O'Neill's writings in light of his (lapsed) Catholic beliefs: "[Mary] is the vessel of honor: in the beginning the virgin lover and lifelong partner to husband; later the nonpareil feminine model to her sons. For these men, the sacrament of matrimony has sealed the conjugal union in holiness. . . . In the Irish-Catholic family all characteristics of this beatification were intensified. The culture had nearly deified the wife-mother and equated her station with that of the Blessed Virgin Mary" (161).

Sheaffer, Louis. *O'Neill: Son and Artist.* Boston: Little, Brown, 1973.

———. *O'Neill: Son and Playwright.* Boston: Little, Brown and Company, 1968. The most thorough and well-documented biography, in two volumes (. . . *Playwright* is up through 1920, . . . *Artist* is beyond), based on exhaustive research and numerous interviews. Of the unheaded page of autobiographical notes, Sheaffer writes: "The summary of early family history contains several surprises, the chief one being that devout, convent-bred Ella O'Neill had, after her second child's death, a 'series of brought-on abortions.' (It is interesting to recall that Carlotta's mother also induced a series of miscarriages before she gave birth, unwillingly, to her first and only child.) The paper is still more fascinating, however, when juxtaposed with *Long Day's Journey*, for a comparison of the two—the literal account and the selective, dramatized family portrait—yields revealing glimpses of the way O'Neill's creative mind functioned" (*O'Neill: Son and Artist*, 510).

Törnqvist, Egil. *Eugene O'Neill: A Playwright's Theatre.* Jefferson, NC: McFarland, 2004. Following on his earlier volume of critical analysis, *A Drama of Souls: Studies in O'Neill's Super-Naturalistic Technique,* Törnqvist gives close attention to the stylistic and structural features of O'Neill plays, including *Long Day's Journey:* "When Mary in one of the play's key lines states that 'The past is the present, isn't it? It's the future, too. We all try to lie out of that but life won't let us,' she formulates the ideological basis for the analytical drama structure. By providing us with a uniquely comprehensive prescenic action focusing on the past of the parents, O'Neill creates a deterministic counterpart of Mary's fatalism. When the play has come to an end, we can see how the characters are determined by their own past as well as by that of their parents" (177).

Voglino, Barbara. *"Perverse Mind": Eugene O'Neill's Struggle with Closure.* Madison, NJ: Fairleigh Dickinson University Press, 1999. A study of how O'Neill closes his plays, looking at eight plays, including *Long Day's Journey:* "Images of existential man alone in a dark world and stumbling to find his way pervade the play. The picture of Tyrone alone and drunk, playing solitaire in the spotlighted darkness, wasting the talent once praised by Edwin Booth on the various domestic problems that beset him, seems to fit Albert Camus's description of the absurd condition: neither man nor the universe is the singular cause of the absurd, but 'it is born of their confrontation'" (110–111).

Weissman, Philip. *Creativity in the Theater: A Psychoanalytic Study.* New York: Delta, 1965. Contains extensive discussion of "O'Neill's Conscious and Unconscious Autobiographical Dramas": "[O'Neill's] aggressive rebellion included his unconscious wish to outdo and remove his father and have his mother as a sexual object. The passive submission included a surrender of his masculinity and becoming a passive feminine love object like his mother as a punishment for his aggressive strivings" (132).